TANZANIA

Local Politics and the Structure of Power

TANZANIA

Local Politics
and the Structure of Power

JOEL SAMOFF

The University of Wisconsin Press

Published 1974
The University of Wisconsin Press
Box 1379, Madison, Wisconsin 53701

The University of Wisconsin Press, Ltd.
70 Great Russell Street, London

First printing

Printed in the United States of America

For LC CIP information see the colophon

ISBN 0-299-06410-7

Publication of this book was made possible in part by a grant
from the Andrew W. Mellon Foundation

Contents

Maps

Tables

List of Tables

Preface

The major debt of gratitude of this study is, of course, to the people of Tanzania. It was their willingness to open to outside scrutiny and criticism their experiments in developing political institutions that made it possible in the first place. It was their assistance in securing access to the relevant materials that permitted the fieldwork to be carried out successfully. And the analysis presented here has benefited immeasurably from their willingness to share with me their keen insights into what their problems were and what they were trying to do about them.

With an apology for the long delay in getting it to them, then, this book is dedicated to the people of Tanzania.

The size of the task, together with my promises of anonymity, precludes my mentioning individually the many Tanzanians who assisted me in the gathering of the data and the formulation of the ideas presented here. The assistance of the residents of Moshi and Kilimanjaro, and of the TANU office, government offices, and other individuals and groups in Moshi was of course invaluable. I am especially indebted to Mzee Yusufu Ngozi, who with patience and kindness led me through the back streets of Moshi town and Moshi politics. I am also grateful to the University of Dar es Salaam (then University College, Dar es Salaam), Kivukoni College, and the Tanzania National Archives for their hospitality, for their assistance in obtaining materials, and for their probing queries and stimulating comments on my inquiry.

Professor Crawford Young of the University of Wisconsin, whose careful comments lie at the root of many of the thoughts presented here, provided a brilliant mix of intellectual challenge, friendly support, and freedom to explore. This study has benefited also from the comments of Henry Bienen, E. A. Brett, and Fred M. Hayward.

Support for fieldwork and writing was provided by a grant from the Foreign Area Fellowship Program, which of course bears no responsibility for the opinions and conclusions presented here.

The insights of my wife Rachel appear on each and every page of this study. It was her ingenuity and persistence, as she tramped through the alleys of Moshi to the various cell leaders' homes, that made it possible to include the Moshi cell leaders in the study. A perceptive, and patient, critic, she shared with me the excitements and the frustrations of every phase of the fieldwork and writing.

What I have to say here, of course, is my responsibility, and mine alone. My hope is that the enthusiasm, the commitment, and the hard work of the people of Tanzania can be seen clearly through the academic overlay.

Ann Arbor, Michigan   *Joel Samoff*
May 1973

TANZANIA

Local Politics and the Structure of Power

Abbreviations

ASPR   *American Political Science Review*

EAJ   *East Africa Journal*

EAPH   East African Publishing House

JMAS   *Journal of Modern African Studies*

KNCU   Kilimanjaro Native Cooperative Union

NUTA   National Union of Tanganyika Workers

TANU   Tanganyika African National Union

TAPA   Tanganyika African Parents Association

TNR   *Tanganyika Notes and Records;* and its successor, *Tanzania Notes and Records*

TYL   TANU Youth League

UWT   Union of Tanganyika Women (Umoja wa Wanawake wa Tanganyika)

Introduction

"To plan is to choose. [Planning] involves making decisions about the allocation of scarce resources; it means choosing between many desirable activities,
because not everything can be done at once."[1] Tanzania's President, introducing the Second Five-Year Plan, told party delegates that in working toward the
goals they had established, in fashioning the Tanzania they desired, the nation's leaders and its people were required to choose among alternative strategies. Directly and explicitly involved were considerations of who would benefit from the choices made, in what order, and to what extent.

This study of local politics in Tanzania is concerned with choosing. It is
an attempt to explore the nature of politics—and thus the choices possible and
those actually made—in one up-country urban area in Tanzania.[2]

The study of African politics, and of the politics of development and
modernization, by social scientists, though a relatively recent undertaking, has
by now produced an extensive literature.[3] Much of the work done thus far has
been macroanalytic in its approach, concerned with behavior (or institutions
and ideologies) at the national level. While this concern with politics at the national level in the study of recently independent states is certainly understand-
able and perhaps inevitable, the danger is, as Zolberg has argued, that "The situation in most of tropical Africa is so extreme that studies focused primarily on
incipient central institutions almost necessarily exaggerate their importance in
relation to the society as a whole."[4] Although these macroanalytic works have
made substantial contributions to the understanding of politics in Africa and

1. President Julius K. Nyerere of Tanzania entitled his address, which introduced
Tanzania's Second Five-Year Plan to the National Conference of the Tanganyika African
National Union (TANU) in 1969, "To Plan is To Choose." The address is reprinted in
Tanzania, *Tanzania Second Five-Year Plan for Economic and Social Development, 1st Ju-
ly–30th June, 1974,* 2 vols. (Dar es Salaam: Government Printer, 1969), 1: vii–xxii; the
quotation is from p. ix.

2. For the fuller report of this study, see Joel Samoff, "Politics, Politicians, and
Party: Moshi, Tanzania 1968–69" (Ph.D. diss., University of Wisconsin, 1972).

3. It is not the purpose here to review once again for readers who are already familiar with them the state-of-the-art in the study of African politics or the intellectual history of such studies. These introductory comments are intended simply to set the intellectual framework for this essay. For brief, and pungent, critiques of approaches to the
study of comparative politics, see the Introduction to Jean Blondel, ed., *Comparative
Government* (Garden City, N.Y.: Anchor, 1969), and the papers by Colin Leys and J. P.
Nettl in *Politics and Change in Developing Countries,* ed. Colin Leys (Cambridge: Cambridge University Press, 1969). For a comprehensive study of the intellectual origins and
the societal implications of the current study of comparative politics (and of social science in general), see Alvin W. Gouldner, *The Coming Crisis of Western Sociology* (New
York: Avon, 1970).

4. Aristide R. Zolberg, "The structure of Political Conflict in the New States of

3

offered perceptive insights into the nature of political change, the theoretical frameworks they provide have proved dissatisfyingly incomplete for the purposes of this study. Scholars have been least successful in focusing attention on and understanding the rapid change and flux that is perhaps the most salient characteristic of African politics. They have focused largely on the exercise of authority in situations where the absence of effective authority is key. Although concerned with problems of national integration, they have been insufficiently sensitive to the lack of agreement on the nature and form of the political community and only rarely interested in the why, rather than the what, of greater national unity. And in directing their attention primarily to politics at the national level, they have taken inadequate account of the lack of governmental penetration into the countryside and the inability of governments to initiate and control developments in the various localities throughout the country.[5] More recently, political scientists have paid greater attention to local settings and have attempted to incorporate an understanding of up-country politics into a national analysis. It is toward that sort of micropolitical analysis that this study is directed.

In very simple terms, then, this study represents an attempt to move out of the national capital and to explore the nature of politics in a single local setting. It is an attempt to provide some of the basic source data at the micropolitical level on which more comprehensive models must rest.

From its microanalytic perspective—a setting where government and populace can experience face-to-face communication and direct interaction—the study is directed toward an examination of the form, the content, and the outcomes of politics in a major up-country urban area of Tanzania. But phenomenology and typology, though important and essential to a broader understanding, are insufficient.

In describing local politics in Moshi, Tanzania, therefore, this study will be largely concerned with the relationship of structures of local power to social and political change. It will explore the implementation of developmental objectives in the local setting. And it will examine the role of local politics in providing a base for democratic participation. In the ideology and orientation of Tanzania's national leaders, the single political party, the Tanganyika African National Union (TANU), is key to all of these elements of local politics. It is the institution charged with promoting and managing political change. To a large extent, then, this book is a study of TANU in Moshi.

Tropical Africa," *APSR* 62, no. 1 (March 1968): 86. Zolberg stresses the need for a greater microanalytic perspective in his *Creating Political Order* (Chicago: Rand McNally, 1966), p. 153.

5. An outstanding exception among the macroanalytic studies is, of course, Zolberg, *Creating Political Order.*

Introduction

Politics: A Process

One impact of the behavioral revolution in the study of politics has been a search for precision in terminology. Unfortunately, one of the outcomes of that search has been a welter of common terms defined differently by different authors, with little agreement among students of politics on what is meant by politics, by the political process, by power, and the like. This is not an essay on methodology, and it would serve little purpose, therefore, to add one more voice to the orchestrated but cacophonous terminological debate. It is appropriate, however, to discuss very briefly the major conceptual understandings employed.

It seems to me that it is useful to consider politics as a process, a series of events, concerned with the distribution of resources, with the allocation of scarce goods, with the selection of one set of values or objectives over another, or with the implementation of one or another of a set of goals.[6] To define politics in that way is a recognition of, and an attempt to overcome, the limitations implicit in a focus on specific structures and functions.[7] I am less concerned with the question of why a series of events is political than with exploring the impact of that series of events on fundamental societal allocations and choices. In fact, my research suggests to me that we have much to lose, and little to gain, by attempting to establish well-defined and fixed boundaries between what is political and what is, say, religious, or economic. Political structures are only one, and often only a modest, determinant of the distribution of power. This is especially so in Tanzania, where the leadership has proved ready to make fundamental structural rearrangements as goals have been defined and as understandings of obstacles to change have developed.

To view politics as a process, then, is an attempt to develop a more encompassing approach. It is basically concerned with who benefits from particular political arrangements and why, and with who is pressing for change, why, and with what resources. That in no way excludes attention to ideas and institutions, but rather, by not taking them to be the sum total of politics, seeks to set them in the broader context of the relationship of ideas, institutions, and behavior to outcomes. I do not wish to belabor this point, but simply to stress

6. The danger of a process approach is, of course, that, in its attention to interactions, to coalitions, to factions, to contests, to exchanges, and the like, it tends to lose sight of outcomes. A thorough understanding of who benefits from particular arrangements, and why, is sacrificed to the explication of the rules of the game. A provocative, but nonetheless ultimately disappointing, example of this dilemma is F. G. Bailey, *Stratagems and Spoils: A Social Anthropology of Politics* (New York: Schocken, 1969).

7. My thinking on this point and on the following point about relevant political actors has much in common with the approach of Marc J. Swartz and his colleagues. See especially, Marc J. Swartz, ed., *Local-Level Politics* (Chicago: Aldine, 1968), Introduction; and Marc J. Swartz, Victor W. Turner, and Arthur Tuden, ed., *Political Anthropology* (Chicago: Aldine, 1966), Introduction.

that local politics in Moshi refers to a series of events related to conflicts over the allocation of resources and the implementation of goals.

If politics refers to a series of events, clearly the actors—the individuals, groups, and institutions—involved in one specific event may not be involved in another, however much the observer might see the two events as closely related. For example, an individual who plays a key role in the granting of remissions of primary school fees may participate very little in the consideration of the location of new primary schools. Moreover, the actors concerned with a specific issue may vary over time, as the issue becomes more or less salient to different individuals and groups. Therefore, for the purposes of this study, the relevant political strata in Moshi are those directly and indirectly involved in the events being studied. The importance of this is that the set of individuals and groups concerned with a specific issue may not be defined by any convenient geographic, administrative, or temporal space. Just as it is essential that we not presume that a given structure has a key and relatively constant role in the evolution of a specific series of events, so too it is essential that we recognize that the set of individuals and groups concerned with a specific event or series of events is continuously changing in its composition. Finally, I suggest that in order to situate a series of events and the actors concerned with them, it is important to examine the wider setting that encompasses them, itself continuously changing.

One approach developed for the study of politics in micropolitical settings involves the identification of the set of key local political notables, the collection of data on their backgrounds, attitudes, and behavior, and the analysis of politics through the combination and comparison of that data. But such an approach involves several a priori assumptions about the stratification of the community, the concentration and/or dispersion of power, and the congruence of influence patterns that seem unwarranted.

An alternative approach directs attention toward a set of specific, governmental decisions and outcomes and describes local politics in terms of those decisions and the individuals and groups participating in the decision-making process.[8] That approach also has severe limitations for the purposes of this study. It seems to me useful to consider specific decisions, however critical they may be in determining patterns of allocation, stratification, and deprivation in a community, as only one of several key points in the policy-making process that must be examined.[9] To develop a more complete understanding of the allocation of resources in a given setting, it is important to look first at

8. These approaches are examined in more detail as they are employed in the study of local politics in Moshi, below in Parts II and III.

9. This point draws heavily on the work of Peter Bachrach and Morton S. Baratz. See especially, *Power and Poverty: Theory and Practice* (New York: Oxford University Press, 1970), which elucidates, clarifies, and expands some of the notions originally presented in "Two Faces of Power," *APSR* 56, no. 4 (December 1962): 947–52; and "Decisions and Nondecisions: An Analytical Framework," *APSR* 57 (1963): 632–42.

Introduction

the prevailing values and mores of the community, which themselves may prevent certain issues from ever being formulated formally or from ever reaching
a decision point. Second, the community's procedures and institutions, which
by their nature and operation may exclude particular issues and certain types
of issues from consideration, must be examined. Third, of course it is essential
to examine carefully the formal decision-making points, both governmental and
nongovernmental, where proposals may be rejected, altered, and approved.
And, fourth, it is also essential to explore the process of implementation, which
often, if not always, operates to permit new proposals to be offered for consideration and approved proposals to be altered or even rejected. Again, not to
belabor the point, what I am suggesting is that to be concerned primarily with
formal, governmental decisions, like concentrating on formal structures or a
presumed elite, would cause us to overlook much of the essence of politics in
Moshi. This suggests that the appropriate research strategy is to synthesize
what is useful from these alternative approaches, all the while remaining cog-
nizant of their limitations.

An Eclectic Methodology

The theoretical basis and the methodology of this study are, therefore,
self-consciously eclectic. While I presume that there is conflict over the allocation of scarce resources in the area studied, a presumption for which there
is ample supporting evidence, I have attempted to draw on those approaches
that seem able to assist me in understanding and explaining the phenomena I
have observed.[10] An eclectic methodology poses two important problems.
First, where a particular paradigm suggests that certain events are more important than others, or supports one interpretation over alternative views, it is essential that the major assumptions underlying that paradigm not be accepted
uncritically. For example, I think it is both possible and useful to consider
particular structures in terms of functions without asserting that the political
system is characterized by a fundamental orientation toward harmony and
equilibrium, an assertion that would be at odds with the conflict orientation
of this study. Second, eclecticism in methodology must not be a substitute
for coming squarely to grips with major problems of analysis and interpretation. Although this eclectic approach makes excursions into theory-building
in widely scattered areas very tempting, I have tried to avoid those excursions,
however tempting, where they would detract from the major goal—the study
of local politics in Moshi. For that reason, and also because this study is not
primarily concerned with problems of approach and methodology, I have

10. An eclectic approach is essential not only to a comprehensive understanding of
the complexities of African politics but also to an evaluation of competing major paradigms. An eclectic approach is of course not new to social science. Arthur L. Stinchcombe stresses the utility of such a point of view: "If one approach does not work for explaining a particular phenomenon, the theorist should try another"; see *Constructing Social Theories* (New York: Harcourt, Brace & World, 1968), p. 4.

found it most useful to discuss the specific methodology employed where appropriate through the course of the study.

Reported as a case study, this examination of local politics in Moshi has, I think, a wider utility in the understanding of African politics. In an important sense, some situations are of interest precisely because they are unique. To deal with its problems (which are common to much of the Third World) Tanzania has fashioned a set of institutions that have few parallels in the rest of the world. The increasing number of publications on Tanzania attests not only to the excitement with which many observers regard that country but also to the importance of examining patterns there for an understanding of fundamental problems of social change. Within Tanzania conflicts among alternative strategies of development are manifest as those who are most committed to basic structural change struggle against those who have, thus far, been the major beneficiaries of existing patterns of allocation. As will shortly be detailed, Moshi has been, and will continue to be, an important locus for that struggle. Hence, the importance of understanding its politics more fully.

The Setting: Tanzania and Moshi

Tanzania, which has been independent for barely a decade, is the setting for this study.[11] It is one of the few African states with a functioning single-party system, a system entrenched in Tanzania's constitution. Although Tanzania's regime has been subjected to various stresses and strains throughout its brief existence, it has remained quite stable. The mass popular support developed during the struggle for independence seems not to have dissipated substantially since then. The set of structures and relationships defined as the single party has been modified many times and continues to be the key political institution in Tanzania. The national leadership has made a concerted, albeit at times unsuccessful, effort to manage and direct the nature of social change. And, committed to understanding change in order to manage it, Tanzania's leaders have been receptive, relatively more so than the leaders of most other African states, to the study of its peoples, its institutions, and its goals.

This study concerns an up-country urban area in Tanzania. Of the several urban centers of similar size in Tanzania in 1968–69, Moshi seemed to have especially well-developed patterns of interaction between the town and its rural hinterland and seemed readily accessible and hospitable to the sort of research envisioned. The peoples of Kilimanjaro District, in which Moshi town is locat-

---

11. The United Nations Trust Territory of Tanganyika, administered by Great Britain, became independent in 1961. After the union of Tanganyika and Zanzibar in 1964, the resultant Republic was named Tanzania. In this essay, Tanganyika will be used exclusively to refer to what is now mainland Tanzania prior to its union with Zanzibar, and Tanzania will be used to refer to the country as a whole. Since the perspective on national government will largely be that of one local area, in references to the national government no attempt will be made to differentiate the constituent mainland and island elements of the government of the United Republic of Tanzania.

ed, are relatively educated, modern, and prosperous in comparison with the rest of Tanzania. Kilimanjaro peoples are proportionately overrepresented in the Tanzania government and civil service. Yet the rapid growth of the competing neighboring town (Arusha) after the location there of the headquarters of the East African Community and the commitment of national leaders to divert allocations from the most to the least developed areas of the country are seen in much of Kilimanjaro as threats to the rapid development and key leadership role of the district. Kilimanjaro residents, therefore, might be expected to be among the most hostile of Tanzania's citizens to the national socialist goals and the most resistant to central direction. Thus, while Moshi may be somewhat unique among Tanzania's towns (in fact, none could be satisfactorily described as representative of the others), a study of its politics contributes not only to an understanding of the functioning of the single party in an up-country setting but also to an assessment of the ability of national leaders to direct and manage social change.

This study, then, is concerned with the nature of politics in Moshi, Tanzania. But Moshi is not simply a convenient locale for the study of politics, a laboratory for the examination of alternative theories and hypotheses. It is a living, vibrant community, intensely active, where European buyers fly in each week to taste and purchase the coffee harvest, where children crowd the schools, where street vendors, cloth merchants, hardware salesmen, tailors, shoemakers, and other artisans mingle with the shoppers and the government officials and the rural cowherders on the sidewalks, and where the backdrop consists of the luxuriant growth of Kilimanjaro's lowlands, joined to its snow-capped peaks by thick clouds. It is situated in a district whose populace is often characterized, both by Tanzanians and by foreign visitors, as the enterprising and industrious go-getters of Tanzania. And it is a town whose residents, like people elsewhere, attempt to devise institutions that meet their needs, not as an academic exercise, but because they have a vision of the good life and they are willing to work hard for it.

To convey something of the activity and vibrancy that make Moshi a town, not merely a subject for study, I have attempted to organize this work to share with readers the process of discovery in the exploration of local politics there. What seems important to people in Moshi? And then, what lies behind that? While this pattern of organization may mean that at times the impact of particular structures becomes clear before their form is distinctly visible, that is how most local residents see their polity. Equally important, that encourages us not to confuse structures with behavior.

The study begins with a brief historical overview to set modern developments into their broader context. It then proceeds to draw on the insights of studies of community power in examining the nature of local politics: first by exploring conflict over the allocation of resources through detailed studies of three key issue-areas, and then by studying the local political elite, focusing especially on members of the town council and party cell

leaders.[12] What issues are local people concerned about? Who prevails in those conflicts? Who are the local leaders? What are their origins, who comes to see them, how do they picture the local political system? The book then proceeds to a detailed look at the local party organization and its ability to initiate and manage change in Moshi and concludes with a brief comment on the politics of self-reliance.

Readers primarily interested in the comments on party and government in Moshi might prefer, after reading the historical survey and structural overview in Chapter 1, to turn directly to the concluding chapters. The basic questionnaires used in the survey of local elites, along with brief explanatory notes, are found in the Appendices.

Publications on Tanzania have proliferated in recent years; the Bibliography includes those works cited in this book, as well as a selection of other publications deemed useful.

---

12. For a summary of findings and a bibliography of studies of community power in Africa, see William J. Hanna and Judith L. Hanna, *Urban Dynamics in Black Africa* (Chicago: Aldine, 1970).

PART I / *The Background*

1

Politics in Kilimanjaro:
A Historical Survey

Introduction

Kilimanjaro District is located in northwestern Tanzania, extending from a semicircle girdling the west, south, and east of the snow-capped mountain from which the district draws its name down into the dry, dusty plain south of the mountain. The district borders Kenya, and has direct road and rail transport to Nairobi, Mombasa, and Dar es Salaam (good road connection with the latter has been established only recently, and rail connection is still subject to the vagaries of the annual rains). Moshi town, located to facilitate construction of the railway by the German colonial administration, sits just below the most fertile areas of the mountain, at 2,900 feet. In 1967 there were almost one-half million inhabitants in the district and some 27,000 in the town.

Situated on a major trading route and attractive because of the allure of its snow-capped peaks and pleasant hillside climate, Kilimanjaro has been visited and studied by outsiders for more than a century. There are accounts of its scenery, its people, and its politics written by explorers, by naturalists, by colonial administrators, by professional historians, as well as by some prominent Chagga themselves.[1] As is the case with much of the history of Africa written during the colonial period, most of the commentary on Kilimanjaro relies heavily on impressionistic accounts by early visitors and on the reports of selected informants from those peoples receptive to the early travelers. It is infused with the explorer's ardor for making new conquests or the missionary's zeal for bringing the light to the heathens, and only rarely does it attempt a comprehensive, systematic analysis of the history of this area. Even the most recent efforts are sorely lacking in this regard.[2]

1. See especially Charles Dundas, *Kilimanjaro and Its People* (1924; reprint ed., London: Frank Cass, 1968), which includes references to the observers who preceded Dundas to Kilimanjaro, and Kathleen M. Stahl, *History of the Chagga People of Kilimanjaro* (The Hague: Mouton, 1964), a study commissioned and financed by the Chagga themselves. For a listing of the major works on Kilimanjaro, see the Bibliography in the special issue of *TNR* on Kilimanjaro, 64 (March 1965):153–62. See also the Bibliography, below, in this book.

2. For a critical review of the problems in Stahl's approach, essentially a diplomatic

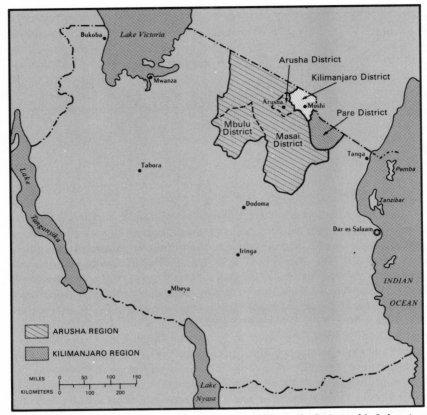

University of Wisconsin Cartographic Laboratory

Tanzania, showing Kilimanjaro Region and District with surrounding region

history of the major Chagga chiefs, see the reviews of her work by J. M. Ostheimer and J. M. Lonsdale, *TNR* 64 (March 1965): 150–52. Several local accounts, though claiming to deal with the Chagga in general, in fact refer to specific areas of the district. See, for example, P. Marealle, *The Life of a Mchagga on Earth and After Death* (Nairobi: English Press Ltd., 1947), and S. J. Ntiro, *Desturi za Wachagga* (Nairobi: The Eagle Press, 1953). Others offer the perspective of particular participants in Kilimanjaro life. See Anza Amen Lema, "The Lutheran Church's Contribution to Education in Kilimanjaro 1893–1933," *TNR* 68 (February 1968): 87–94; Alex O. Lema, "The Role of the Machame Chiefdom in the Politics of the Wachagga since 1930's," J. E. S. Makundi, "Pre-colonial Forces Against the Creation of One Chagga Nation," and Oliver J. Maruma, "Chagga Politics: 1930–1952" (all senior dissertations, Department of Political Science, University College, Dar es Salaam, March 1969). An exception is the work of Basil P. Mramba, "Kilimanjaro: Chagga Readjustment to Nationalism," *East African Institute of Social Research,* Conference

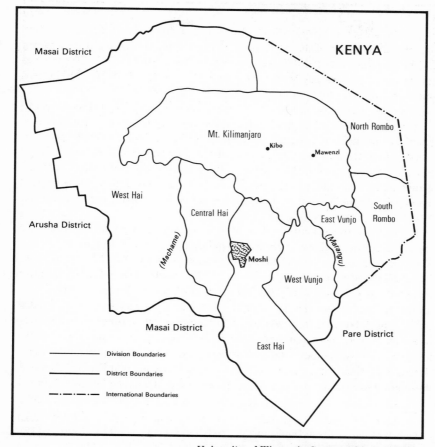

Masai District

KENYA

North Rombo

Mt. Kilimanjaro
• Kibo
• Mawenzi

West Hai

Central Hai

East Vunjo

South Rombo

Arusha District

(Machame)

• Moshi

(Marangu)

West Vunjo

Masai District

Pare District

East Hai

Division Boundaries

District Boundaries

International Boundaries

University of Wisconsin Cartographic Laboratory

Kilimanjaro District

It is not the purpose here, nor is it possible, to attempt to offer a detailed history of Kilimanjaro or of the Chagga-speaking peoples. Rather, the attempt will be to highlight the events, the interactions, and the recurring patterns of the history of this area to set in context the analysis of modern politics that follows. It should be stressed, then, that the historical survey presented here rests largely on my own reconstruction of salient events.[3]

Papers, Part E. no. 35 (January 1966), and "Some Notes on the Political Development of the Chagga of Kilimanjaro" (unpublished paper, Makerere University College, Kampala, 1967).

3. I am indebted to Susan Rogers for sharing with me her insights into recent Chagga

The Background

Background to Modern Politics

Kilimanjaro was peopled by a succession of migrations.[4] Peoples of Taita, Kamba, Masai, Pare, Kahe, and Shambaa origins, that is, people from all sides of the mountain, settled in its fertile belt, between 3,000 and 7,000 feet. Settlement was gradual, and small communities developed, separated by the numerous ravines on the mountain.

As the population increased, these communities grew into chiefdoms of varying sizes.[5] The very name Kilimanjaro was not used locally, but was applied by outsiders, and the tribal appellation Chagga in fact refers to peoples speaking related but often mutually unintelligible languages.[6] Thus, by the time of the major colonial intrusion in the nineteenth century the people of Kilimanjaro were divided into several small, more-or-less independent, states, among which the pattern of interaction was one of recurring conflict and coalition.[7]

The trend toward enlargement of scale and amalgamation was accelerated by colonial rule, and especially by the policy of indirect rule instituted by Great Britain after it replaced Germany following World War I.[8] As the British sought local administrators they looked to the chiefs they and their informants could identify. Frequently the impact of this process was to fix very fluid power relationships. That is, some chiefs whose reign was tenuous were assisted in consolidating their power by British support, while other relatively prominent chiefs were rendered more open to challenge by their opponents because of lack of British support. Of course, this process was not one-sided. Chief Marealle of Marangu managed to convince the Germans that his kingdom had hegemony over most of Kilimanjaro, when in fact it was one of the minor

---

politics, on which she is completing a doctoral dissertation. I am also grateful to several members of the faculty at University College, Dar es Salaam (now the University of Dar es Salaam), for their assistance in understanding the intricacies of Chagga politics.

4. See Dundas, *Kilimanjaro and Its People,* Chapter 2.

5. Every European traveler remarked on these chiefdoms. Dundas reported twenty-eight small states, of which the population varied from 1,000 to 20,000, in 1924 (ibid., p. 50).

6. See J. A. Hutchinson, "The Meaning of Kilimanjaro," and W. H. Whiteley, "Chagga Languages," *TNR* 64 (March 1965): 65–67, 68.

7. Stahl, *History of the Chagga People of Kilimanjaro,* details the relationships both within and among these states.

8. What was later called Tanganyika became German East Africa in 1885–86, was occupied by the British during World War I, and became a British Mandated Territory under the League of Nations in 1920 (and subsequently a Trust Territory under the United Nations). For a penetrating analysis of a portion of the German period, see John Iliffe, *Tanganyika under German Rule 1905–1912* (Cambridge: Cambridge University Press, 1969). For detailed descriptions of Tanganyika under British rule see B. T. U. Chidzero, *Tanganyika and International Trusteeship* (London: Oxford University Press, 1961), and J. Clagett Taylor, *The Political Development of Tanganyika* (Stanford, Cal.: Stanford University Press, 1963).

kingdoms, and he was even able to manipulate German administrators into eliminating most of his enemies.[9]

The introduction of coffee by Catholic missionaries at the end of the nineteenth century and its development as a small-holder crop after World War I[10] furthered the trend toward amalgamation, as the organization of the collection and transportation of the cash export crop assumed greater importance. In recent years the development of more advanced agricultural techniques and substantial population growth have made land shortage a serious problem in Kilimanjaro,[11] and in 1969, after several less successful attempts, many Kilimanjaro residents were persuaded to move to other areas of Tanzania. The pressure on the land, however, remains severe.

Moshi town itself was a manifestation of the centralizing impact of colonial rule. Moshi was one of the major Chagga chiefdoms, defeated by the Germans only after fierce resistance in 1892. But the German government, taken in by the wily Marealle, located its capital in Marealle's Marangu. Moshi town, on its present site, did not develop until the German Tanga railway line was extended from Mombo to Kilimanjaro in 1911; apparently engineering considerations dictated the location of the railway terminus, some distance down the hillside from the capital of the traditional Moshi chiefdom. The railway terminus quickly became the central collecting point for the transport of coffee, and Moshi town became the administrative headquarters of the district for both the German and the British colonial administrations.

By 1931 Moshi's[12] African population had reached only 2,561. The town population did not begin to grow rapidly until the 1950s, a period of high coffee prices: in 1948 the town population was 8,048, in 1952, 9,079, and in 1957, 13,716. Moshi town has grown much more rapidly than Kilimanjaro District (see Table 1.1) and has a more heterogeneous population than Kilimanjaro District (see Tables 1.2 and 1.3). The relationship of Moshi to its rural hinterland is perhaps much closer than is the case for other towns of similar size in Tanzania. The major cash crop is grown on the hillsides and eventually collected in the town. It is common for people to come to town to work, to shop, to transact business, and then return to the hillsides each evening. Prosperous Kilimanjaro residents build substantial homes on the hillsides and take

9. See Stahl, *History of the Chagga People of Kilimanjaro,* Chapter 14.

10. See J. Kieran, "The Origins of Commercial Arabica Coffee Production in East Africa," *African Historical Studies* 2, no. 1 (1969): 51–67.

11. Predictions that the land shortage would lead to serious political problems were common in the annual reports of British administrators. See, for example, the Annual Report of the District Commissioner, 1944.

12. Both in the historical literature and even today Moshi is used to refer to the town and to the district. In this book, unless otherwise noted, Moshi will refer exclusively to the town, Kilimanjaro District to the administrative district as currently defined by the Tanzanian government, and Kilimanjaro (without qualifier) to refer to the mountain, its surrounding land, and the peoples living there.

The Background

Table 1.1. Kilimanjaro District and Moshi Town: Population

	Population			Annual growth rate	
	1948	1957	1967	1948–57	1957–67
Kilimanjaro District (excluding Moshi town)	259,600	351,300	473,800	3.4%	3.0%
Moshi town	8,048	13,726	26,969	3.0%	7.0%

Source: Tanzania, *Recorded Population Changes 1948–1967, Tanzania* (Dar es Salaam: Government Printer, 1968), Tables 3 and 5.

Table 1.2. Kilimanjaro District and Moshi Town: Ethnic Origin

	1957		1967[a]	
	Kilimanjaro	Moshi	Kilimanjaro	Moshi
African	98.4%	68.4%	98.1%	89.1%
Asian[b]	1.1	26.6	0.1	7.6
Arab	0.0	0.5	0.0	0.3
European[c]	0.3	3.2	0.3	0.9
Other, NS[d]	0.1	1.2	1.4	2.1
Total	99.9%	99.9%	99.9%	100.0%

Source: East Africa High Commission, *Tanganyika Population Census, 1957. Analysis of Total Population,* mimeographed (Nairobi, 1958), Tables 2 and 3; Tanzania, *1967 Population Census,* 4 vols. (Dar es Salaam, 1969–71), 2, Table 115; and 3, Table 215.

[a] Data refer to heads of private households. Because there are no data available on the incidence of multi-ethnic households, due caution must be exercised in extrapolating these figures for the population as a whole.

[b] Includes those listed as Indian, Goan, and Pakistani in the 1957 census.

[c] Includes all white peoples.

[d] Includes all others in the 1957 census and those listed as Not Stated in the 1967 census.

Table 1.3. Moshi Town: Religion (1967)

	Number[a]	Percent
Christian	4,151	53.8
Muslim	2,930	37.9
Other world religion[b]	278	3.7
Local belief[c]	107	1.4
Other	19	0.2
Not stated	241	3.1
Total	7,726	100.1

Source: Tanzania, *1967 Population Census,* vol. 2, Table 113.

[a] Refers to heads of private households. Because there are no data available on the incidence of miltireligious households, due caution must be exercised in extrapolating these figures to the urban population as a whole.

[b] For example, Hindus.

[c] Independent, though nonsystematic, observation indicates this figure may be understated, suggesting a tendency to report to census enumerators an affiliation with Christianity or Islam, regardless of actual belief or practice.

pride in returning to them each evening. Most leading urban political figures consider themselves Chagga, and the Chagga peoples consider Moshi their town.

Development of Modern Politics

Since the arrival of the colonial powers, politics in Kilimanjaro has revolved around attempts to exercise control over local development and to minimize government interference. The continuing struggle for advantage among the small Chagga states, as well, defined differently over time, has been a major framework for political conflict. That is, conflicts have been rooted in disputes over the control of land, the control of coffee, and the control of the Chagga states, but the specific manifestation of the conflict depended on the nature of the colonial political system, only partially under local control.

Antigovernment agitation developed in the late 1920s and 1930s, centered in the coffee growers' associations.[13] The Kilimanjaro Native Planters' Association and later the Kilimanjaro Native Cooperative Union provided the first and for a time the only mountain-wide forum for the discussion of Chagga problems and interests. Both associations were led by men who were at the

13. In other areas of Tanganyika as well, growers' associations became the centers of opposition to the chiefs. See John Iliffe, "The Age of Improvement and Differentiation (1907–45)," in *A History of Tanzania,* ed. I. N. Kimambo and A. J. Temu (Nairobi: EAPH, 1969), p. 137.

time the most highly educated and articulate farmers from throughout the district and who placed themselves firmly in opposition to the chiefs. Reforms in local government introduced by the British Tanganyika administration after World War II increased the authority of the divisional chiefs.[14] At the same time those reforms began to undercut the chiefs' position by introducing commoners into the various councils established and by making the chiefs more and more responsible for the implementation of government policy. This superstructure of chiefs-as-native-authorities, nurtured by the British administration, soon came to bear the brunt of the discontent of the Chagga, a discontent largely engendered by the vagaries of coffee prices and the increasing land shortage and reinforced by the realization that local people were less and less able to control the behavior of their own leaders. Elders and clan leaders looked back to a more democratic past when chiefs were more subject to their influence, while young modernizers chafed under chiefly rule and looked forward to a more democratic future.

In the late 1940s opposition to the divisional chiefs began to coalesce. The coalition that emerged included some of the leaders of the antigovernment agitation of the 1930s, some traditional leaders (lesser chiefs, clan heads) disturbed and threatened by the increased power of the divisional chiefs, and some younger, educated individuals determined to seek more rapid modernization for their people. This coalition, organized in the form of a Chagga political party, was able to boycott some local elections in Kilimanjaro and prevail in others.[15]

14. The more than thirty Chagga states were organized into three divisions; a hierarchy of chiefs was thus established, with the divisional chief superior to the area chiefs within his division. While this structure had traditional precedents in some areas, in others it forced chiefs to subordinate themselves to other chiefs they had previously taken to be their coequals.

15. The intricacies of party politics in Kilimanjaro in the 1940s and 1950s have yet to be adequately sorted out. Parties, plagued by leadership conflicts and often attempting to battle on two levels (the local and the national), appeared, disappeared, and reappeared with astounding rapidity. The party that led the struggle against the divisional chiefs was called the Kilimanjaro Union (KU), but apparently the KU was reorganized as a proto-national body, and its leaders considered the Arusha and Meru political organizations to be branches of the KU. The Kilimanjaro Chagga Citizens Union (KCCU), nominally the Kilimanjaro branch of the KU but hardly distinct from it, carried on the struggle for the paramount chief. An early political leader, Joseph Kimalando, who had been active in the Kilimanjaro branches of the African Association and the Tanganyika African Association (TAA) formed the Chagga Congress (CC) to oppose the KU-KCCU; the CC had the support of the chiefs, at least to the extent that it opposed KCCU attempts to reduce their power. After the election of the paramount chief, the CC was absorbed into the KCCU. As the antiparamountcy campaign developed, the KCCU, formerly the militant organization promoting radical change, became a conservative organization oriented toward preserving the status quo. The Chagga Democratic Party (CDP) was formed in the late 1950s to oppose the paramount chief, and the Chagga Progressive Party, in membership a rebirth of the by then defunct KCCU, was created to counter the CDP. The CDP was successful and was ultimately absorbed into the Kilimanjaro branch of the Tanganyika African National Union (TANU). Kimalando, who was ousted from TANU in 1956,

Politics in Kilimanjaro

By the early 1950s it was successful in securing the selection of a paramount chief as a means of reducing the power of the divisional chiefs and as an attempt to assert the Chagga interest in Tanganyikan politics. The paramount chief who was elected, a colonial civil servant, combined royal blood, modern education, and a westernized life-style. He seemed ideally suited to provide the image for and lead a wave of Chagga nationalism that would bring together the disparate elements of Kilimanjaro and at the same time secure a substantial role for the Chagga peoples in Tanganyikan politics.[16]

Thus, from the 1920s to the 1950s basic conflicts over fundamental allocations in Kilimanjaro—who would benefit from the new cash crop and the modernization, including education, that went along with it—focused on the chiefs. As the young political activists probed to determine where authority actually lay, some correctly recognized that it lay in Dar es Salaam, but British policy forced political contests inward among the leadership battles and profusion of parties in Kilimanjaro. Chagga political parties, of which there were many, were a secondary variable. That is, there were several sets of leaders and supporting networks, each vying for advantage, and each ready to form a party, to join a party, or to disband a party, as the strategy might dictate.

In the politicized atmosphere of the terminal period of British rule there developed a substantial Chagga nationalism, manifested in the pomp and ceremony of the paramount chief, and in the institution of a Chagga flag, a Chagga anthem, and an annual Chagga holiday. This is not to say that the numerous Chagga states, and the recurring conflicts among them, had disappeared. Rather it is to suggest that as it became clear that the relevant political arena was to be all of Tanganyika, a sense of cultural, and political, unity emerged among the Chagga-speaking peoples, and that the battles over the paramount chiefship fostered that emergent unity. At the same time branches of a Chagga tribal association were established in other areas of Tanganyika, and, encouraged by the paramount chief, they celebrated the Chagga holiday and venerated Chagga symbols, as well as provided welfare services for the numerous Chagga peoples living outside Kilimanjaro.[17]

---

attempted to start another TAA branch in Moshi. During this process there was also a Chagga Association, a vehicle for the chiefs and at the same time, with branches in other areas of Tanganyika, an organizational form for Chagga nationalism and welfare activities outside Kilimanjaro. (This very brief summary, which owes much to the work of Susan Rogers, does of course not do justice to the richness and fullness of Kilimanjaro party politics during this period.)

16. On this point see Kathleen M. Stahl, "The Chagga," in *Tradition and Transition in East Africa,* ed. P. H. Gulliver (Berkeley: University of California Press, 1969), pp. 211–12, 216–20.

17. The development of tribal welfare associations was, of course, common throughout Africa at this period. For an overview of the situation, see Immanuel Wallerstein, "Voluntary Associations," in *Political Parties and National Integration in Tropical Africa,* ed. James S. Coleman and Carl Rosberg, Jr. (Berkeley: University of California Press, 1964). Henry Bienen stresses the role of tribal organizations in the development of

The Background

Before long, however, important elements of the coalition that had secured the selection of a paramount chief began to realize that their grievances against the divisional chiefs, especially their dissatisfaction with decisions essentially made in Dar es Salaam and their complaints of abuses of authority, applied as well to the paramount chief. That he relied heavily on the divisional chiefs in order to govern contributed to the discontent. An antiparamount coalition then began to develop, again including some people with long backgrounds of antigovernment agitation, some traditional leaders unhappy with the loss of autonomy by the small Chagga states, and some younger, better-educated individuals. A new realignment of Chagga political parties took place, now organized to support and oppose the replacement of the paramount chief with an elected president. By the late 1950s the antiparamount coalition was successful in eliminating the paramountcy.[18] Much of this coalition, which had formed the nucleus of the Tanganyika African National Union[19] organization in Kilimanjaro since the middle 1950s, was absorbed into TANU after Independence. Because the paramountcy was a local issue, and because only a party and leaders with clearly a local base could oppose it, the local TANU organization was not utilized as the major vehicle of the antiparamountcy coalition.[20]

One major theme of politics in Kilimanjaro in the period immediately before independence was the focus on local issues and problems. Although Kilimanjaro leaders clearly recognized the links between national and local politics, and although they repeatedly attempted to join the two in their own struggles, the thrust of British policy and the fierce competition over allocations within Kilimanjaro combined to restrict the scope of Chagga politics to Kilimanjaro district. Even as TANU began to establish firm footholds throughout Tanganyika in the late 1950s, what was to become TANU in Kilimanjaro was still

modern politics in Tanganyika; see *Tanzania: Party Transformation and Economic Development,* rev. ed. (Princeton, N.J.: Princeton University Press, 1970), p. 25.

18. There is no single comprehensive summary of this conflict, and most sources focus on the parties, rather than the issues, involved. An exception is Basil P. Mramba, "Some Notes on the Political Development of the Chagga of Kilimanjaro." For the government's view of the election of the paramount, see the article by a Tanganyika District Officer, P. H. Johnston, "Chagga Constitutional Development," *Journal of African Administration* 5, no. 3 (July 1953): 134–40.

19. For the history of TANU, see Bienen, *Tanzania: Party Transformation;* Kimambo and Temu, eds., *A History of Tanzania;* and Lionel Cliffe, ed., *One Party Democracy* (Nairobi: EAPH, 1967).

20. The leader of the successful antiparamountcy effort, who had previously served in the Legislative Council and subsequently became a Minister in the independent Tanganyika government, told me that this strategy had the full support of the TANU leadership. He indicated that TANU's President, Julius K. Nyerere, did not want TANU to dissipate its energies at that point by involving itself formally in the Kilimanjaro paramountcy struggle, and at the same time Nyerere wanted a successful example of the rejection of chiefship by the local people concerned.

concerned with a local issue—paramountcy—which it fought as a Chagga party and not as a local TANU branch.

A second theme was the progressive reduction in the authority and autonomy of the chiefs during the colonial period. The local autonomous chiefships had not long replaced clan organization when the colonial powers arrived. Colonial policy, even indirect rule, undercut the chiefs' ability to establish a strong traditional legitimacy. As the British made the chiefs powerful by vesting them with the authority of the government, they removed their claims to traditional legitimacy (chiefs were appointed, and the spiritual role of the chiefs was discouraged) and imposed on them the antoganism to government programs. By the time of Independence in 1961, although some chiefs continued to retain power in their local areas, the commoners had prevailed and chiefship as an institution was clearly on the decline. In fact, chiefship developed and was eliminated in a very short period in Kilimanjaro, and it may be that the institution of chiefship never really became firmly established. Chiefs were little able to consolidate their reigns during the period of conquest and coalition. Those who did remain suffered the burden of serving as governmental agents during the colonial period, and they could not withstand the popular tide of the post World War II period. The former chiefs played little discernible role in Kilimanjaro politics after Independence.[21]

A third theme was the proliferation of informal alliances and formal party organizations. Individuals allied, competed, reallied, then competed again. At one point the Kilimanjaro District Commissioner, whose reports indicated that the colonial government often had difficulty distinguishing among the major Kilimanjaro parties, was unable to resolve an acrid dispute among three parties, one an offshoot of another, over which was the legitimate successor to an earlier party and thus entitled to its bank account. Change was so rapid that only if party labels were clearly dated were they useful in sorting out the major participants.

A fourth theme was the enduring nature of the conflict among the small Chagga states. Much of the preindependence conflict was expressed in terms of one part of the mountain against another. The victory of the antiparamountcy coalition in 1960 marked another shift from Marangu to Machame dominance in Kilimanjaro politics. (Marangu's preeminence was established when Marealle convinced the Germans he was the most powerful of the Chagga

21. The relative ease with which the chiefs were defeated in Kilimanjaro is perhaps atypical in Tanzanian history. Norman M. Miller details the ways in which traditional leaders among the Nyamwezi were able to redefine their roles and thus retain power after Independence; see "The Political Survival of Traditional Leadership," *JMAS* 6, no. 2 (August 1968): 183–201. Goran Hyden discusses the persistence of the traditional *nyaru-banja* land-holding system and of traditional leaders in Buhaya after Independence; see *Political Development in Rural Tanzania* (1968; reprint ed., Nairobi: EAPH, 1969).

chiefs. It was subsequently lost to British support for Chief Abdiel of Machame and then returned with the election of a paramount chief from Marangu.) This pattern of conflict among the former Chagga states, now reinforced by religious cleavages since missionary penetration in each of the Chagga states was limited to one of the two major religious groups, manifests itself even today in local contests for allocation of resources.

Leadership Changes

The indifference and antagonism of the chiefly leadership, coupled with the local orientation of the fight to reduce the power of the Kilimanjaro chiefs, impeded TANU's penetration into rural Kilimanjaro in the 1950s. As a result, TANU concentrated at first on establishing itself in Moshi town, where it could secure support from urbanized Chagga and the urban Muslim population.[22]

This is not to suggest that TANU was not active in the rural areas. The first TANU branch in rural Kilimanjaro was established in West Hai (Machame) by three brothers, of whom one was the first chairman of the rural branch, one is current chairman of the rural district, and one served as a Member of the Legislative Council, as President of the Chagga, and as a Member of Parliament and a Minister in independent Tanzania. This Machame origin for TANU in Kilimanjaro was a natural outgrowth of local hostility to Marangu and the paramount chief. The combination of the TANU activists with Machame's Chief Abdiel proved to be a powerful opposition to the paramount chief.[23] TANU's strength in Kilimanjaro was demonstrated in its sweep of the 1958 Legislative Council elections, when all three TANU candidates, even the Asian and European candidates who were not actually members of TANU, received more than twice as many votes as their closest opponents (see Table 1.4). But at least until the elimination of the paramountcy in 1960, and even beyond, the primary focus of Kilimanjaro politics was local and not directly nationalist in orientation.[24]

TANU developed strong support in town, but during the late 1950s and early 1960s the party urban leadership was charged with complicity in anti-TANU activity during the 1958 Legislative Council elections,[25] with mis-

22. Mramba, "Some Notes on the Political Development of the Chagga of Kilimanjaro," p. 15, stresses the Muslim support, but it is important to note that many of the urban Muslim TANU leaders, including the first town chairman, were Chagga. That is, from the beginning TANU was led by local people, not by recent immigrants to Kilimanjaro.

23. On this point see Stahl, "The Chagga," p. 219.

24. This point is made by A. J. Temu, "The Rise and Triumph of Nationalism," p. 197, in Kimambo and Temu, eds., *A History of Tanzania,* and by Basil P. Mramba, "Kilimanjaro: Localism and Nationalism," in Cliffe, *One Party Democracy.*

25. The European and Asian candidates selected by TANU headquarters to run in the Northern Province were largely unknown in Kilimanjaro; spurious posters appeared, picturing individuals rejected by the party as the TANU candidates. For a very personal account by one of the candidates, see Sophia Mustafa, *The Tanganyika Way* (Dar es Salaam: East African Literature Bureau, 1961).

Politics in Kilimanjaro

Table 1.4. Legislative Council Election Results, September 1958, Northern Province[a]

Candidates[b]	Affiliation	Votes
Africans		
S. N. Eliufoo	TANU	3,348
S. K. George	Independent	1,275
Asians		
S. Mustafa	TANU	2,248
H. K. Virani	Independent	864
M. Sharif	Independent	682
N. M. Mehta	Independent	660
D. Behal	Independent	169
Europeans		
D. N. M. Bryceson	TANU	3,300
J. M. Hunter	Independent	1,323

Source: E. B. M. Barongo, *Mkiki Mkiki wa Siasa Tanganyika* (Nairobi: East African Literature Bureau, 1966), p. 104.

[a] Northern Province included present-day Arusha Region and Kilimanjaro District.

[b] According to the "multiracial" electoral system, voters were required to vote for one candidate in each of the three racial groups.

management of party affairs, and with peculation of party funds. By 1964 the town branch had had four different chairmen, and when the town was constituted as a separate district (for TANU purposes) in 1965, a non-Chagga former civil servant was elected chairman.

Since government and party organization in Tanzania cannot be reduced to a neat and clear schematic chart, a brief word about political structures is in order here.[26] Both government and party maintain nominally legislative and executive institutions that parallel each other at each effective level of organization.

At the national level, there is a National TANU Conference, convened at least every two years, with broad representation from throughout the country, responsible for basic party policy. The party executive consists of a National Executive Committee that includes all Regional Chairmen, all Regional Commissioners (who are party Regional Secretaries), delegates from each region elected by the National Conference, representatives from party auxiliaries, and

26. The structures outlined here are discussed in more detail where appropriate throughout the course of this study. See also Bienen, *Tanzania: Party Transformation,* Part II; Cliffe, *One Party Democracy,* Part I; and William Tordoff, *Government and Politics in Tanzania* (Nairobi: EAPH, 1967), Chapters 3 and 4 and Appendices, Part B (the Interim Constitution of Tanzania, which includes the TANU Constitution).

the presidential appointees to the Central Committee. The Central Committee includes the major party officers, presidential appointees, and, as of 1969, individuals elected by the National Conference. The President of the party, nominated as the only candidate, serves as President of the country. There is a National Assembly, of which approximately one-half the membership is elected from mainland constituencies with the remainder directly or indirectly selected by the President, the President of Zanzibar, the party, and/or party auxiliaries. Though they are functionally distinct, the overlaps between the party and the government at the national level are substantial—for example, elected MP's are delegates to the party National Conference, while Regional Commissioners sit in both the Parliament and the National Executive Committee.

The party structure at the regional level is similar to that at the national level (regional conference, regional executive committee, regional working committee). Its chairman is the locally elected Regional Chairman, and its executive consists of Regional Secretary (a post filled automatically by the Regional Commissioner) and a Regional Executive Secretary appointed by party headquarters. The Regional Commissioner, a presidential political appointee,[27] is responsible for all governmental activity at the regional level, serves as the proper officer for district councils within the region, and presides at meetings of the regional development committee. There is no governmental council at the regional level.

The party structure at the district level (for party purposes, urban areas are considered separate districts) parallels that at the regional level, including the tripartite leadership (locally elected chairman, Area [District] Commissioner as District Secretary, and party-appointed District Executive Secretary). The Area (District) Commissioner, a presidential political appointee, is in charge of government business in the district (note that an administrative district that includes a town has in fact two TANU districts), and is chairman of the District Development and Planning Committee. The TANU District Chairman automatically serves as Chairman of the District (or Town) Council.

In urban areas the smallest governmental unit is the ward, while the party district is divided into branches, which are in turn divided into cells.

Thus, while there are distinct party and governmental structures at each level, there are substantial overlaps of personnel and responsibilities.

In the drive for independence TANU led a broad national movement willing to welcome anyone prepared to fight the colonial government.[28] After the sweeping TANU victories in the Legislative Council elections of 1958–59 it was clear that only TANU could govern in Tanganyika, and many lukewarm party supporters, even some opponents, began to take out party cards. As TANU's leaders began to redefine the party's goals after independence had been secured,

27. On the commissioners, see Bienen, *Tanzania: Party Transformation*, Chapter 4.
28. On this point see George Bennett, "An Outline History of TANU," *Makerere Journal* 7 (1963): 26.

as they began to develop specific content to party policy, it became clear that the alliance of mutual antagonisms and of contradictory utopias in Kilimanjaro (and throughout the country) could not endure. A growing discontent with the self-aggrandizing behavior of some of TANU's early leaders made the leadership alliance even more tenuous. Opponents of the leadership coalition in Kilimanjaro were far from silent.

A third major change in the Kilimanjaro political leadership (now fought within the TANU framework) took place from 1962 to 1965.[29] In hindsight it seems clear that the local middle class (including, and especially, the TANU activists), successful in eliminating the paramountcy, was attempting to establish its dominance. Its opponent was the alliance of prosperous farmers, traditional leaders, and some civil servants. Both groups claimed the TANU mantle. This struggle for local power reflected the continuing strain between local and national orientations.

Almost simultaneously the former District Commissioner was replaced by the new Area Commissioner (a political appointee who also served as party secretary), and a new chairman, of both the local council and the district party, was elected. Tension developed between them over the importance and authority of their respective roles and culminated in a request by the Kilimanjaro District Council for a meeting with the Minister for Local Government to criticize the Area Commissioner. The Council was rebuked by the Minister for not having made its complaints to its proper officer, the Regional Commissioner, and many of its key Chagga officials were replaced, among them its Executive Officer, who was succeeded by a non-Chagga.[30]

Shortly thereafter, the tension among the leaders manifested itself in conflicts between party and government officials and members of the newly elected Council. In July 1963, while in much of the country TANU candidates for local council seats had been returned unopposed, in Kilimanjaro almost a quarter of the councillors elected were independents, with the result that the TANU councillors formed an Elected Members Organization to caucus before Council meetings.[31]

In 1965 the Regional Chairman, a leader of the Old Guard who had also served as party District Chairman and as Chairman of the Moshi Town Council and who was then the president of the Kilimanjaro Native Cooperative Union (KNCU), was defeated in his bid for reelection by a primary school teacher. These party elections, together with the parliamentary elections in the same

29. The first major leadership change of this period took place during the battle to create a paramount chief and the second during the successful struggle to eliminate the paramountcy.

30. For a discussion of this conflict, see Mramba, "Some Notes on the Political Development of the Chagga of Kilimanjaro," pp. 15–17. See also William Tordoff, "Regional Administration in Tanganyika," Conference Papers of the *East African Institute for Social Research* (Kampala, 1964).

31. See Tordoff, *Government and Politics in Tanzania,* p. 115.

year,[32] provided another opportunity for realignment among the political leadership, with the result that several of the most prominent early party leaders no longer held party office. The TANU activists had finally won clear control of the local party.

The elections of 1969 seemed to presage a new realignment, a fourth major leadership change in Kilimanjaro. The new TANU activists consolidated their control over the local party by defeating their opponents within the KNCU. In other terms, the new middle class, better educated, based more on civil service and party positions than on prosperous agriculture, with a populist style, defeated the old middle class, especially the prosperous coffee farmers, and their allies, the traditional leaders. Control over the local party was incomplete without control over the KNCU, in general much more sensitive to the preferences of the local coffee farmers than to the tides of change washing through the national political system. Not until 1962 were individuals identified with TANU able to win control of the KNCU leadership.[33] And although the leaders elected then (the landed middle class) were removed from party office in the early 1960s, it was not until 1969 that the new TANU activists were successful in replacing the KNCU president. Mismanagement, which had led to the replacement of the KNCU manager by a Ministry official seconded from Dar es Salaam, had undermined the president's position. The same group that had been instrumental in his defeat as party chairman in 1965 was able to develop an alliance to oust him from the KNCU. This group secured the support of the local coffee cooperative society (the KNCU is a union of local cooperatives) leaders from Rombo, on the eastern side of the mountain—an area that had for years chafed at its relative underdevelopment, which it attributed to Lutheran and Machame/Marangu dominance in Kilimanjaro politics—by agreeing to support the MP, a Catholic, who represented that part of the mountain, for the presidency. Machame had allied with Rombo to defeat Marangu. But it seems clear that this alliance is a tenuous one, founded only for removing the former leadership.

32. For an extensive analysis of the 1965 parliamentary elections in Kilimanjaro, see Mramba, "Kilimanjaro: Localism and Nationalism." Mramba stresses the local orientation of these contexts for national office. It should be noted as well, however, that the nature of the electoral system—which admitted to candidacy only individuals who firmly supported TANU policies—required that competition between candidates be over local issues.

33. There is, unfortunately, no good study of the history of the KNCU. Important documents drawn from Tanzania's National Archives relating to the KNCU and its predecessor, the Kilimanjaro Native Planters Association, can be found in *Agriculture and Politics in Kilimanjaro,* a collection organized and mimeographed by I. N. Kimambo for teaching purposes at University College, Dar es Salaam, 1969. The KNCU minutes for the meeting at which the leadership changes took place say only that "The whole list of previous members of the managing committee was overthrown . . ." and that "Many of the Senior Staff members also resigned . . ." See Kilimanjaro Native Cooperative Union, *Thirty First Annual Report 1962-1963* (Moshi, 1966), p. 3.

Politics in Kilimanjaro

Even as the new middle class was securing power, and using that power to gain control over resources, especially land, the distinctions between it and the landed middle class began to diminish. A new grouping, still better educated, much more heavily drawn from among the civil service and party, and more in tune with the national TANU orientation, began to assert itself. In the 1969 party elections the Regional Chairman and the rural District Chairman were re-elected, but they both defeated weak opponents. The District Chairman, running against a discredited former chairman at the time involved in an ugly court case, was able to win by only a modest margin. At the 1969 TANU National Annual Conference, the Member of the National Executive Committee for Kilimanjaro Region was opposed by almost the entire Kilimanjaro delegation and was reelected only on the basis of his support outside of Kilimanjaro. His opponent, an unknown in national politics, did surprisingly well.

All of this suggests that Kilimanjaro party members, encouraged by the openness of the TANU one-party system, mounted a strong challenge against the current party leaders and began to develop a foundation for a set of alliances in support of new leaders. That, coupled with local leaders' at times less than wholehearted support of national policies and with the assessment by party officials posted from the center that Kilimanjaro party leaders are not fully committed to party policy, suggests a new turnover in the political leadership may be in the offing. The urban TANU Chairman, arguing that the pressure of his job some fifteen miles from town prevented him from being an active party leader, declined to stand for reelection.[34] He was succeeded by an individual who had a long history of party activity, but who, as a Muslim and a Pare, had not been involved in the mainstream of Chagga politics. The 1970 parliamentary elections seem to have been another step in the realignment of forces among the political leadership in Kilimanjaro. Both the District and Regional Chairmen were defeated in their bids for parliamentary seats (the former, running for the seat previously held by his brother, was outpolled eight to one by his opponent), as were the president and the vice-president of the KNCU.

Finally, it should be mentioned that during the course of 1969 the Kilimanjaro Regional Commissioner and the Area Commissioner, both former civil servants,[35] were replaced by younger men with extensive managerial experience in cooperatives and business. Although of course it is too soon to draw

34. The former Chairman was shortly thereafter convicted of accepting a bribe, in connection with his job (and not his political activity). The case was a complex one, in which personal animosity toward the former Chairman, who had replaced a European in a high position in a European-managed plantation, and whose salary was more than twice that of the Regional Chairman and Members of Parliament, played no small part. Before the arrest of the former Chairman, there were rumors, which he himself would not deny, that he intended to run for Parliament in 1970.

35. A long-time, strong-arm-style politician, transferred from another region after a conflict with the Members of Parliament there, also served briefly as Regional Commissioner in Kilimanjaro during 1969. See Chapter 3, note 7.

any generalizations from their behavior, their appointment, which came at a time when a large number of commissioners were replaced throughout the country, may indicate a need both to weed out leaders less than fully committed to party policy and to find leaders who combine the managerial and administrative skills necessary to oversee development schemes with an informed commitment to national policy.[36]

In summary, 1958 was a critical year in Tanzanian history, and it marked the success of the attempts to join local and national politics in Kilimanjaro. TANU's sweeping electoral victories demonstrated for all to see that, short of outright and large-scale suppression of opposition, and the indications were that even that would have proved fruitless, colonial rule was in its terminal phase and Tanganyika would see independence under a TANU government. In Kilimanjaro, the leaders of the antiparamountcy struggle paused long enough to ensure the victory of the TANU Legislative Council candidates. But not until the victory over the paramount chief in 1960 could national politics begin to occupy center stage in Kilimanjaro. In an atmosphere of intraparty conflict and antiparty feeling, a major turnover in the political leadership of Kilimanjaro took place in the early 1960s. Party leaders committed to little more than opposition to colonial administration were replaced by leaders who more clearly supported party policy. But by the late 1960s, as party policy became increasingly better defined in ways that seemed to threaten their (and Kilimanjaro's) privileged status, they themselves faced substantial challenges. At the same time, politics continued to have a very local focus.

Yet the disparities in development among different areas of Tanzania, at least since politics in Tanganyika began to have a national orientation, have created tension between Kilimanjaro and the rest of Tanzania. Since Independence this tension has been exacerbated by the TANU commitment to an equalization of the level of development throughout the country. While Kilimanjaro is concerned with increasing its share of national resources, especially for more schools, hospitals, and public works, national policy is oriented toward diverting some of the resources now allocated to Kilimanjaro to other, less-favored, areas of the country. In the transition to independence the Chagga, because of the earlier spread of education in Kilimanjaro, filled a disproportionately large share of the jobs left by departing British administrators, and even among the political leadership. Many Chagga are also prominent in the commercial sector in Tanzania. As a result, there has developed a resentment against a perceived substantial Chagga influence in national affairs.

36. For a perceptive analysis of the need to replace revolutionary with managerial elites after a modernizing revolution, an analysis that is premature but suggestive for the Tanzanian case, see John H. Kautsky, "Revolutionary and Managerial Elites in Modernizing Regimes," *Comparative Politics* 1, no. 4 (July 1969): 441–67.

Politics in Kilimanjaro

With this abbreviated backdrop on the development of modern politics in Kilimanjaro and overview of governmental and party structures, let us now turn to the examination of the issues, the politicians, and the party in Kilimanjaro.

PART II / *The Issues*

2

Politics of Primary Education

Introduction

The critical role of education in the complex processes of change with which African states must deal is a familiar theme to students of Africa.[1] In very broad terms education can be seen as a basic prerequisite to change: in the development of the skills necessary to produce wealth and of the desire to use it; in the development of widespread literacy, essential to national leaders in their efforts to penetrate the rural countrysides and thus to govern; and, in a society with a strong egalitarian commitment, in the development of values and norms that promote an equality of participation in the nation's production and proceeds. At the same time, education can also serve to nurture and perpetuate societal cleavages and to permit some in the society to develop and protect a favored position. In individual terms, education, and often only education, can provide access to the good life—job, wealth, security, comfort, prestige.

It is with this latter that we are concerned here, with education as the individual's key to entrance into the life he desires. In Tanzania, as in much of the world, an individual's ability to secure the job he seeks, to become wealthy, to provide for his children, and to be a person of prestige in the community, depends to a very large degree on his education. For those who were educated during the colonial period, the colonial education system "taught them that the single road of escape from forced labor, head taxes, relocation, long sessions of work with little return; and the one path to good houses, shirts and pants, bicycles, shoes, the city and money was the certificate of education. It was the sole means of breaking out of the oppressive confinement of peasant life into the glorious existence of the bourgeoisie."[2] And despite concerted attempts by Tanzania's leaders to alter this situation,

1. For useful introductions to the literature on education and development, see James S. Coleman, ed., *Education and Political Development* (Princeton, N.J.: Princeton University Press, 1965); and L. Gray Cowan, James O'Connell, and David G. Scanlon, eds., *Education and Nation-Building in Africa* (New York: Praeger, 1965).

2. Jane and Idrian Resnick, "Tanzania Educates for a New Society," *Africa Report* 16, no. 1 (January 1971): 26.

The Issues

". . . the rewards of the system still go to the educated."[3] As education expands and reaches more of the population, and as Tanzania continues to build a society in which advancement depends on individual achievement, the importance of education as a key to success will increase. Even now, for a young person to secure a job in town with a salary that permits a tolerable standard of living in the urban conditions, at least a primary education is necessary. And even now, individuals with some primary education experience difficulties in finding employment. In fact, the majority of primary school graduates—in a system in which until very recently it was assumed that all students would enter the cash economy in salaried employment—have no prospects of obtaining paid employment.[4] Thus, the determination of who gets an education, and how good an education, is an important, perhaps the most important, allocation of resources in the local political system.

This section begins the examination of local politics in Moshi by exploring several key issues. The issues selected—education, discussed here, local liquor licensing, and jobs and unemployment, discussed in the succeeding chapters—were those that were salient, that had substantial impact on the ordinary lives of the people, that were to a significant extent decided locally, and that involved challenges to the basis of authority and power. The goal, of course, is to identify such issues and then trace their resolution locally. The study of the conflict surrounding those issues can delineate much of the skeleton of local politics, and at the same time provide much of its tissue.

Key issue-area studies have their limitations, and those will be discussed in Chapter 5. The discussion here will focus on primary education, since, although secondary education is both salient and a focus for conflict, most of the decisions about secondary education are removed from the local arena. The relevant arena of conflict over educational decisions crosses urban-rural boundaries; accordingly, this analysis will draw on data from both Moshi town and Kilimanjaro rural district.

History

During the nineteenth century Christian missionaries were attracted to the snows of Kilimanjaro and, more important, to the pleasant climate of the hillsides. The Leipzig Lutheran Mission, which succeeded the British Church Missionary Society in German East Africa in 1893, opened mission stations throughout the district. At about the same time, the Holy Ghost Fathers established themselves in Kilimanjaro, at Kilema, in 1890.[5]

Both the Lutherans and the Catholics began opening schools almost as soon

3. Ibid., p. 28.

4. Idrian N. Resnick, ed., *Tanzania: Revolution by Education* (Arusha, Tanzania: Longmans, 1968), p. 8.

5. For a summary of early missionary involvement in the development of education in Kilimanjaro, see G. N. Shann, "The Early Development of Education Among the Chagga," *TNR* 45 (December 1956): 21-32.

as they arrived. Both missions clearly saw education as a fundamental tool in the propagation of the faith.[6] Since it was not until after World War II that the British colonial government in Tanganyika was willing to devote more than token resources to education, schools, and thus educational content, were largely controlled by the missions.[7]

Until the time of the British Mandate, after the war of 1914–1918, the missions were given free land in many of the Chagga chiefdoms. Chiefs saw that missionaries could be useful allies in their battles with other chiefs, and with the colonial administration, and for the most part welcomed them. But the pattern of missionary settlement was such that only one of the two major missions became established in each chiefdom. That is, because of the colonial administrations's attempts to develop missionary spheres of influence and because of the nature of the alliances between the missionaries and the Chagga chiefs, there developed a checkerboard pattern of religious influence, with each religion dominant and unchallenged in its own areas. That pattern has proved so durable that today, even though communication among the former Chagga states has been facilitated by modern roads, bridges, and, now, telephones, religious cleavages continue to coincide with geographic divisions and remain powerful influences in local politics.

The peoples of Kilimanjaro early recognized the value of the European education brought by the missionaries, and the missions, spurred by competition for allegiance, opened schools across the mountain. By 1889 the Lutherans had 170 pupils enrolled in their schools, and by 1914 Lutheran schools numbered 97 with an enrollment of over 8,000. In 1892–93 the Catholics had 87 pupils at Kilema, and by 1914 the Catholics had opened 150 schools with an enrollment of 16,000.[8] By contrast, in 1969 fewer than 10,000 pupils were enrolled in government schools in Kilimanjaro. Throughout this period Kilimanjaro residents benefited from a clear advantage over other Tanganyikans in access to schools.[9] The enrollment statistics for 1968, which show that more than

6. For an overview of ecclesiastical involvement in African education, see David G. Scanlon, ed., *Church, State, and Education in Africa* (New York: Teachers College Press, 1966).

7. Government expenditure on African education had reached only £94,500, 4 percent of total expenditures, by 1928; see Hugh W. Stephens, *The Political Transformation of Tanganyika: 1920–67* (New York: Praeger, 1968), p. 89. In 1914, for example, there were 2,500 government primary schools with an enrollment of 3,700, while some 1,800 mission schools had an enrollment of 110,000 in the same year; see J. P. Moffett, ed., *Handbook of Tanganyika*, 2d ed. (Dar es Salaam: Government Printer, 1958), p. 365.

8. For the statistics on Lutheran schools, see Shann, "The Early Development of Education Among the Chagga," p. 21, who cites mission records; and Anza Amen Lema, "The Lutheran Church's Contribution to Education in Kilimanjaro," p. 91. For statistics on Catholic schools, see Shann, "The Early Development of Education Among the Chagga," pp. 28–29; and J. Kieran, "The Origins of Commercial Arabica Coffee Production in East Africa," pp. 51–67, who cites mission records.

9. In 1947, while Kilimanjaro population was approximately 3.5 percent of the total

The Issues

Table 2.1. Kilimanjaro District Assisted Primary Schools and Enrollment, 1968, by Agency (Moshi Urban and Kilimanjaro Rural)[a]

Agency	Schools		Enrollment	
	Number	Percent	Number	Percent
Central government	5	2[b]	616	1[c]
Local councils				
Moshi Town, Kilimanjaro District	36	14	9,019	15
Lutheran (LCNT)	78	30	17,267	29
Catholic (HGF)	125	48	28,963	48
Muslim (MA)	13	5	2,758	5
Others[d]	4	2	900	2
Total	261	101	59,623	100

Source: District Education Office, Kilimanjaro District.

[a] Note that this table refers to assisted primary schools. If unassisted schools were included, the mission role would be even greater.

[b] That is, 2% of all schools in Kilimanjaro District are managed by the central government.

[c] That is, 1% of all pupils in Kilimanjaro District are enrolled in schools managed by the central government.

[d] Includes Ismaili schools. There are some discrepancies in the figures of the District Education Office; the total number of pupils may be slightly greater than that shown here.

three-quarters of the primary school pupils in Kilimanjaro attended mission-managed schools, clearly indicate the continued mission role in education (see Table 2.1). In Kilimanjaro, as in the rest of Tanzania, because the missions could build, maintain, and run schools more economically than could either the government or the local authorities, this pattern of government dependence on, and support of, mission-run schools was a fundamental characteristic of the educational system at the primary level.[10] There has developed an interdependence in the provision of primary education. Both church and state are aware of, and at times unhappy with, the need for the other's

---

Tanganyikan population, pupils in Kilimanjaro schools represented approximately 12.6 percent of the total school population. The corresponding figures for 1956 were 4.2 percent and 8.7 percent, respectively. The British government estimated that 62 percent of the children in Kilimanjaro were in school in 1951, compared to 15.5 percent of all Tanganyikan children in 1947 and 30 percent in 1953. See the reports of UN Visiting Missions to Trust Territories in East Africa, 1954 and 1957, UN Documents T/1169:4 and T/1401:64.

10. On this point, see J. Cameron and W. A. Dodd, *Society, Schools and Progress in Tanzania* (Oxford: Pergamon Press, 1970), p. 114.

assistance, but both are reluctant and perhaps unable to alter the existing relationship.[11]

As will be seen, the missions are able to maintain this dominant role in primary education in Kilimanjaro through a combination of almost exclusive access to the information necessary to run the schools, retention of much of the initiative in the development of new schools, and functional control over most of the schools now in existence. In this respect, the dependence of the Tanzania government on the missions to provide both the information and the resources necessary to run primary schools ensures the continued mission influence in educational decisions.

Over time, of course, the missions have been localized and Africanized. Although it is impossible to determine the extent of external influence in local church decisions, it is clear that by the 1960s the churches had become indigenous rather than expatriate institutions. As local rather than foreign interest groups they had become all the more closely involved in the local political process. Both the Lutheran and Catholic bishops in Kilimanjaro in 1968 had been born and raised on the mountain.

The Setting

Conflicts over who gets schools, and who gets into them, have been a feature of Kilimanjaro life since the politics of interest groups and elections replaced warfare among the chiefs. As education rapidly expanded in the 1920s it created a demand for further education, a demand at first resisted by the missions. After all, the missions were primarily interested in conversion, and, at least at that time, largely saw education as a vehicle for the propagation of the faith. They did not regard education as their basic responsibility, and although locally educated faithful were important in the conversion of other local residents, a widely extended postprimary secular education could nurture an elite that would grow distant from its tribal origins and that could become critical of its religious teaching. This conflict became especially bitter in Kilimanjaro in the 1940s when the Chiefs attempted to gain control of education from the missions and transfer it to the Native Authority (the Chiefs), even at Native Authority's expense.[12] In 1944 the Chagga Council of Chiefs assessed a two-shilling levy on each taxpayer for educational purposes. The intention of this levy was to abolish fees for primary education, and in fact the Native Authority absorbed some of the cost of primary education. Although the missions retained their dominant role in primary education, this initiative by the Chagga Chiefs was clearly an attempt to localize and integrate the schools,

11. David Abernethy makes a similar point for the church-state relationship in the provision of education in Nigeria; see "Nigeria" in Scanlon, *Church, State, and Education in Africa*, p. 240.

12. John Iliffe, "The Age of Improvement and Differentiation," p. 133, supports this interpretation.

to make them less the property of a foreign body or of a particular section of the community.[13]

This pattern—initiative in developing schools by the missions, followed by demands for, and some seizure of, control by the local government—has recurred in Kilimanjaro, with the result that initiative remains in the hands of the churches. When the burden becomes too great for them, responsibility is shifted to the local government, saddling it with such enormous operating expenses that the missions are able to retain the initiative by having a monopoly on the only resources readily available for new development.

At Independence Tanganyika found itself with an immediate need for trained manpower and a paucity of schools. Much of the modest educational expenditure made by the colonial government was directed into schools for the children of colonial civil servants and chiefs. At Independence Tanganyikans were encouraged by the government, and by TANU, to embark on self-help schemes to construct their own schools. In Kilimanjaro, this call met an enthusiastic response, and schools, constructed from local materials by the parents of the neighborhood, sprang up all over the district. In ten years, primary school enrollment in Kilimanjaro doubled, from close to 30,000 in 1956, to 35,000 in 1963, to almost 61,000 in 1966.[14] But although parents built their own schools, they could not operate them, and were dependent on the missions and on the government to provide teachers and materials, and to meet recurrent expenditures. The burden became too great for the missions, and the Kilimanjaro District Council (the successor to the Chagga Council) was pressured to assume responsibility for most of these self-help schools.

At the same time that the government was encouraging parents to build their own schools, it decided to shift basic responsibility for primary education from the central to the local (district) government. One of the major purposes of this shift of responsibility was to divert political pressure for more primary schools from the central government to lower levels of government, since the provision of universal free education was not then possible and would not be for a long time. In shifting responsibility to local government, the central government restricted its education subsidies to include only a few new schools each year and insisted that local government units open new schools and expand existing schools only when they could meet recurrent expenditures themselves. While the diversion of political pressure may have been successful in relieving the central government of some of the blame for the difficulty of access to education, the net result was to require the district councils to spend most of their funds on primary education. Since local government income is fixed

13. On this initiative see Nevil Shann, "The Educational Development of the Chagga Tribe," *Oversea Education* 26, no. 2 (July 1954): 58; and Cameron and Dodd, *Societies, Schools and Progress in Tanzania,* pp. 67–68.

14. Figures for 1963 and 1966, as well as all other educational statistics for 1961 to 1969, unless otherwise noted, are from the District Education Office, Kilimanjaro District.

by the central government,[15] heavy educational expenses leave little money in the district budget for other expenditures, and practically none for development (capital) projects.[16] Many district councils in Tanzania have experienced difficulty in meeting their financial obligations, and several were essentially bankrupt in 1969. The combination of very heavy demands for increased educational expenditures and relatively fixed incomes for local councils in Tanzania is a phenomenon not uncommon elsewhere in Africa.[17]

In Kilimanjaro, between 60 and 70 percent of the annual budget of the Kilimanjaro District Council is spent on education and culture. In Moshi town, where most schools were already government assisted at the time of the shift to local control and thus did not represent an additional financial burden on the Town Council, expenditure on education has been about 20 percent of the total budget.[18]

No sooner had the missions shifted much of the burden of primary education to the district council, than they began to respond to pressures to open new schools. But in accepting the responsibility for the unassisted schools, the council freed mission resources to open new unassisted schools. In fact, in 1969, when the central government agreed to open new primary schools in Kilimanjaro District (none had been opened in the rural areas since 1965), the conflict was over which of the unassisted schools should be converted to assisted schools.

15. The local rate assessed by the district council on taxpayers must be approved by the central government. For an extended discussion of the problem of financing local government, see Eugene Lee, *Local Taxation in Tanzania* (Dar es Salaam: Oxford University Press, 1965). In 1969 the Tanzanian government abolished the local rate and the produce cess, the major sources of income for district councils. At the same time, it assumed a greater role in the provision of health and educational services, previously left largely to the local councils. The trend seems to be toward a weakening of the district as a power center in favor of strengthening the regional apparatus. How this will work remains to be seen. Local government structure and finances will be discussed further in Chapter 5.

16. See Aart Van de Laar, "Arusha: Before and After," *EAJ* 5, no. 11 (November 1969): 16–17.

17. Writing on primary education in Kenya, L. Gray Cowan found that "The County Councils are finding that educational expenditure is not only the highest single item in their budgets, but that even to maintain present expenditure levels many are having to exhaust reserves and are operating under deficits that are so large as to threaten councils with complete financial collapse." See Cowan, *The Cost of Learning: The Politics of Primary Education in Kenya* (New York: Teachers College Press, 1970), p. 37.

18. Figures are taken from the Annual Financial Statements of the Kilimanjaro District and Moshi Town Councils. The expenditure on education includes a small amount for cultural activities. The central government, of course, provides a large portion of the funds expended on education, through payment of teachers' salaries, equipment, buildings, and administrative costs in assisted schools. In 1968, for example, the central government subsidy amounted to approximately 33 percent of the total expenditure on education by the Kilimanjaro District Council and approximately 70 percent of the Moshi Town Council expenditure on education.

The Issues

Because the District Education Office does not officially recognize the mission-sponsored bush schools, it is difficult to estimate their number. In 1969 there were officially 247[19] assisted primary schools (in theory, no unassisted primary schools were permitted to exist) in Kilimanjaro District. In the same year, there were at least 113 bush schools.[20] For every two schools at least nominally under the control of the Ministry of Education, there was another school of which the Ministry took no cognizance, and over which the Ministry had no control (see Table 2.2).

While much of the political conflict over educational decisions revolves around where schools will be located (and thus which communities will be serviced and which children will be disadvantaged by distance) and who will manage them, a related issue is the extent to which children are denied an education by the lack of available schools:

> . . . in some areas children cannot get places in schools. For four years, there have been no new Standard Is [primary schools] opened in Kilimanjaro. Even just taking care of the schools already built almost brought the council down. . . . to see the education officer is useless. . . . many children are unable to get places in schools. I have seen this myself. There are absolutely not enough schools.
>
> There are many primary-age children not in school. This is because there are not enough places. The number who are not in school is greater than the number of those who are.[21]

At the same time, others insist that primary education is Kilimanjaro is adequate, and that all children who seek places in primary schools find them. Estimates of the percentage of primary-school-aged children actually in school range from under 50 percent (quoted above) to 95 percent. The District Edu-

19. Statistics, even from official sources, are often educated estimates and approximately exact totals. In different places in the files of the District Education Office, Kilimanjaro District, for example, the number of assisted primary schools in the district in 1969 variously appeared as 245, 247, 248, 249, and 251 (exclusive of Moshi town).

20. Bush school is used as an inclusive term to denote schools not appearing in official records, staffed by unaccredited and untrained teachers, and located in substandard buildings (often simply in a house or under a tree). In Kilimanjaro, bush schools include schools registered as Primary I–II which in fact continue beyond Standard II, and unregistered Primary I–II schools. The UN Visiting Mission in 1954, with figures from the British Government, estimated there were 5,400 bush schools with an enrollment of 180,000 (half again as many as were enrolled in assisted schools) in all of Tanganyika (UN Document T/1169:5).

21. Statements from political leaders, Kilimanjaro, 1969. The study of Kilimanjaro political leadership is described in Chapter 6; Appendix 1 includes a brief discussion of the methodology of this aspect of the study, as well as the questions used. The study included extended interviews with Kilimanjaro politicians, from which these and other unattributed statements are taken.

Politics of Primary Education

Table 2.2. Assisted and Unassisted Primary Schools in Kilimanjaro District, 1968,
by Agency (not Including Moshi Town)[a]

Agency	Assisted schools				Unassisted schools[b]			Total, all schools
	I–IV	V–VII	I–VII	Total assisted	I–IV	I–II[c]	Total unassisted	
LA/KDC[d]	15	5	16	36	–	–	–	36
Lutheran	18	10	49	77	–	73	73	150
Catholic	41	13	68	122	9	27	36	158
Muslim	4	–	8	12	1	3	4	16
Total	78	28	141	247	10	103	113	360

Source: District Education Office, Kilimanjaro District, for assisted schools. Contacts with voluntary agencies for unassisted schools.

[a] As noted, statistics from official sources vary. Thus, figures shown here may not agree exactly with those shown elsewhere, but these slight differences do not affect the analysis.

[b] Since most of these schools are at least technically illegal, gathering data on them is difficult. The figures shown are approximately accurate, though other evidence suggests they may be understated for Catholic schools.

[c] Includes schools that in fact continue beyond Standard II.

[d] LA/KDC refers to Local Authority/Kilimanjaro District Council. This figure includes one school managed directly by the central government.

cation Office has calculated that there are enough places for all (100 percent) primary-school-aged children, and a similar calculation by the Ministry of Education for Standard I in Kilimanjaro District in 1969 produced a figure of 74.5 percent. That there were some places empty suggests that the percentage of those actually enrolled was somewhat smaller. An analysis of census data for 1967 shows from 60 to 70 percent were enrolled for Kilimanjaro rural and from 62 to 83 percent for Moshi town.[22] Of course, if the number of children enrolled in unassisted schools were added to the official enrollment figures, the enrollment percentage would be much higher. Perhaps the situation is most accurately summarized by suggesting that almost all parents who work hard to get their children into school find places for them in a school of one sort of another. At the same time there are a substantial number of children of primary

22. Figures on school enrollment from District Education Office, Kilimanjaro District; calculations based on the census analysis contained in Tanzania, *Provisional Estimates of Fertility, Mortality and Population Growth for Tanzania* (Dar es Salaam: Central Statistical Bureau, Ministry of Economic Affairs and Development Planning, 1968).

school age not in school, or in an inferior bush school, either because their parents have not sent them to school or because they live in an area not yet serviced by a primary school. For comparison, the government calculated that in 1968 only 47 percent of all Tanzanian children found primary school places.[23] In any case, the perception of relative deprivation by those parents who do not succeed in getting their children into school and keeping them there is heightened by their observation that almost everyone else's children are in school.

The Actors

It is a mistake to assume that politics has to do primarily with rule-making, and with the articulation and aggregation of interests related to rule-making. For rural Tanzania, formal rule-making is a distant and largely inaccessible process, and attempts to influence the authoritative allocations, attempts to determine who is serviced by the political system and who is deprived, focus on the outputs, on rule-application. In a polity in which communications between the center and up-country areas are poor, and in which the efficacy of central government control is reduced as it is transported to the peripheral areas of the country, those who apply rules tend either to become the rule-makers themselves or to surrender their power to alternative individuals and institutions. Therefore, even minor administrative decisions in the local political arena have political content. Local political conflict focuses on the governmental outputs and on the control of the administrative apparatus.

The district education officer is the Ministry of Education official charged with representing the Ministry in the District, and, in that capacity, with overseeing all schools in the district. Thus, the district education officer might be expected to play the key role in local educational decisions. It is he who has responsibility for communicating to the local area the government education plan, for ensuring that the plan is implemented, for supervising the voluntary agencies that manage schools,[24] for supervising school inspectors, and for advising the local education authority. But while it might be reasonable to expect conflict in education to center around the district education officer, in fact that was not the case at all in Kilimanjaro in 1968–69.

The district education officer does serve as the voice of the central govern-

23. Nyerere, "To Plan is To Choose," p. ix.

24. The term "voluntary agency" is used to refer to the managers of schools and includes the missions, the Muslim association (the Muslim community was in the process of reorganization in 1969, and, at least in Kilimanjaro district, the successor organization to the East African Muslim Welfare Society, BAKWATA, had not yet assumed responsibility for Muslim schools), the Asian groups which have their own schools, and any other group that manages a school. The Catholic and Lutheran missions are of course by far the largest voluntary agencies in Kilimanjaro.

ment in educational matters. He introduces governmental decisions into the local political system, and he interprets them. But even in these functions, in introducing educational policy and interpreting it, he is challenged by other individuals who have almost equivalent access to educational decision-making in Dar es Salaam: the mission education secretaries.

As a result, the major function of the district education officer is that of a go-between, a mediator, an arbiter. For example, in 1969 it was decided at the Ministry level in Dar es Salaam that Kilimanjaro District would be permitted to open several new primary schools, and, in accord with the Five Year Plan for 1969-1974, to extend some of its primary schools from Standard IV to Stand-are VII. It was left to the local education authority—the district council, through its education committee—to determine which areas should get these new and extended schools.

The decision to do this was communicated throughout Kilimanjaro more quickly by the mission education secretaries than by the education officer, so that councillors learned of it from their own contacts rather than through the governmental network.[25] The education officer then asked the education secretaries to draw up lists of priorities for new and extended schools. The education officer served to mediate between the education secretaries, to merge the separate lists into a single list. He was unable to compile the list himself because he lacked the requisite information about where people lived, where there were concentrations of children with insufficient school space, and where there were school facilities already begun (or parents willing to begin them). Because he did not have this information himself, he could only with difficulty verify the assessments of the education secretaries. The combined list created by the mission education secretaries was then presented to the education committee of the Kilimanjaro District Council for approval.

Many parents come to the education officer for assistance in getting their children into school or keeping them there, especially with requests that children be permitted to repeat Standard VII in order to have a second try at the examination for entrance into secondary school. But even in these decisions the education officer's power is circumscribed by the availability of places, and is thus ultimately contingent on the mission's and the headteacher's cooperation.

Like all government officers in Tanzania, the district education officer is a transient in Kilimanjaro, expected to spend only a few years, at most, there. While the two district education officers in Kilimanjaro in 1969 arrived in 1966 and 1968, the two mission education secretaries had spent most of their lives there.

25. Here and elsewhere in this study, unless otherwise noted, examples cited and events described are from personal observation in 1968–69.

Thus, the district education officer is a middleman, with the ability to reconcile conflicting demands for allocations of resources, with the ability occasionally to alter specific allocations, but without the ability to exercise a monopoly over educational decisions.

The people to see in Kilimanjaro for action on more schools, better schools, access to schools, are the mission education secretaries. Because of the small size and disarray of the Muslim community in 1968-69, and the small size of other groups managing primary schools, and because almost all principal political elites in Kilimanjaro rural district are identified with either the Lutheran or the Catholic Church, the two key figures are the Lutheran minister and the Catholic priest serving as education secretaries for their churches in Kilimanjaro Region. They are the local representatives of a network within each church that culminates in an education secretary-general in Dar es Salaam.[26] They are appointed by their bishops and approved by the government. And it is they, largely, who decide where new and extended schools will be located, and who will thus be served by them.

Their ability to monopolize educational decisions depends primarily on their monopoly of the basic information and resources necessary to make those decisions. Since each of the churches is exclusively dominant in its own areas of the district, it essentially runs the entire educational program in that area. The local schools, together with the local church, have primary access to the local people, access much more direct and reliable than that of the school inspectors, tax collectors, and other government officials. TANU could provide an alternate communications network, and does in some places. But in most places the overlap of local TANU and church leaders, the discontinuities in the structure linking TANU branches with the district TANU office, and the belief by TANU leaders that schools are not their responsibility, mean that reliable appraisals of popular sentiments, of demands for schools, even of population, are made only by the church, and are communicated to the education secretaries by the parish priests and ministers. Thus, since only the education secretaries can effectively collect and provide the basic information on where schools are needed, information necessary to make educational decisions, their role becomes critical. Since both churches encourage school construction and expansion contrary to government plan and engage in other irregularities in the schools, it is imperative to the churches that they retain their control of the functioning of the primary schools in their areas.

26. They represent locally the Lutheran Church of Northern Tanganyika (LCNT) and the Holy Ghost Fathers (HGF). Nationally, school managers are the Tanzania Episcopal Conference for Catholic schools and the Christian Council of Tanzania for Protestant schools. Both Kilimanjaro education secretaries regard their bishops, located in Moshi, rather than their education secretaries-general, located in Dar es Salaam, as their direct superiors.

Politics of Primary Education

As well as collecting information, the education secretaries, through their missions, have more access to resources for school construction and expansion than do local government officials. Church finances are difficult, perhaps impossible, to sort out fully, but it is clear that both major churches in Kilimanjaro can secure funds from sources outside Tanzania with little, if any, control by the government. They can expend at least some of these funds on school expansion without accounting, directly, to the government. In the mission schools an additional device is used to secure money: nuns and lay teachers employed in mission schools are often paid less than the official salary. That is, in government-assisted mission schools, where the central and local governments pay most or all of teachers' salaries, the money disbursed by the government is used to pay teachers in those schools less than the full salary, and the remainder can then be used to support unregistered and unassisted schools.[27]

Access to information and available resources, coupled with the support of the local population, enables the education secretaries to be the initiators of educational change. The churches begin bush schools, with untrained teachers in substandard facilities and inadequate materials, using their own funds and funds diverted from assisted schools. The parents support the schools, happy to have a place to send their children. As the burden on the missions becomes greater, and as parents increasingly demand schools that will enable their children to progress within the national educational system, pressure increases on the local education authority (the district council) to assume the responsibility for these schools and to regularize their status. (While it might seem that there would be pressure from government authorities to punish the missions for these schools and close them down, in fact the demand for education is so great that once a school has come into existence, it is almost impossible to eliminate it.) When the local council assumes the financial burden of these unassisted schools, it no longer has sufficient funds to open new schools, so it again falls to the missions to use their own and diverted resources to begin the cycle anew. At the time of official school expansion or construction, the local council in effect reinforces this pattern. Since the council has no money with which to construct new classrooms, when it plans for educational expansion, it looks for already well established schools, and especially those with a developed physical plant and with the better of the unqualified teachers. Thus, when the council chooses among a large number of applicants for support, it is almost invariably the mission schools that benefit the most. Although the education officers speak piously about eliminating unregistered and unassisted schools, they have been largely unsuccessful, as is clear from the number of unregistered and unassisted schools that continue to exist and that surface to apply for official status when that becomes feasible.

27. Abernethy reports the same arrangement in Nigeria; see "Nigeria," p. 226.

The Issues

Every local authority in Tanzania is a local education authority. The Kilimanjaro District Council and the Moshi Town Council are charged by law to manage the schools they control, to administer grants-in-aid, including those from the central government, and to advise the Minister of Education on educational development in Kilimanjaro District.[28] As a local education authority, the district council must establish an education committee, including district councillors, individuals named by the council, and individuals appointed by the Ministry of Education. One might expect, therefore, that basic allocations, with regard to council schools in particular, but with regard to all schools in the district in general, would emanate from the council through this committee. In fact, the basic role of the education committee of the district council is to legitimize decisions made by the education secretaries and the district education officer. In this process, councillors have an opportunity to protect the interests of their own areas. With minor alterations, the decisions of the education secretaries and the district education officer are issued as council decisions, bearing the full weight and prestige of the district council.

In the deliberations over new and extended schools in Kilimanjaro district mentioned above, the district education officer merged the two mission lists by alternating Catholic and Lutheran schools, with the few Muslim and council schools interspersed. He thus both gave official recognition to the religious balance and bound himself to the specific priorities set by the education secretaries. The merged list was then presented to the education committee for approval.

The education committee of the district council is an important arena for both religious and sectional conflict in Kilimanjaro. Since the Christian schools, because they are generally better financed, better organized, and better run, tend to be favored over Muslim schools, the education committee offers Muslims almost their only opportunity to defend and protect their access to schools. In 1969 the East African Muslim Welfare Society had been dissolved, but its successor organization had not yet begun functioning in Kilimanjaro, so that the district education officers assumed managerial responsibility for Muslim schools. Defense of Muslim interests depended on active intervention in the education committee by the Muslim councillors on the committee, one of whom held leadership positions in both the old and new Muslim organizations and was a leading political figure in Kilimanjaro.

Since religious cleavages coincide with sectional differences, and since many major political figures serve on the education committee, much of the political conflict in Kilimanjaro manifests itself in one way or another in the activities of the education committee. In the case of school expansion, because the Muslims are by and large located in the plains areas of the district, the conflict becomes one of mountain-coffee-farmers versus plains-maize-millet-and-

28. The councils, as the local education authorities, were responsible for these and other tasks as of 1969. Changes introduced in 1969 are discussed in the concluding section of this chapter.

rice-farmers. The people who live in the plains of Kilimanjaro district, both those ethnically related to the Chagga and others who have settled there, have long charged that they are inadequately represented in the Kilimanjaro District Council, and that they suffer from decisions largely concerned with the interests of Chagga coffee farmers. For example, a leading political figure, involved in both national and district politics, comments:

> The lower areas are very far behind the other areas of Kilimanjaro and even behind many other districts in Tanzania. . . . there is tribalism in the district council—the council looks upwards [up the hillsides of Kilimanjaro] and not downwards, so there is no progress in the low areas. Sometimes some project is put in the low areas to fool them—they built a dispensary, but they do not send any medicine. The remedy is for them to have their own organization—to have the Kilimanjaro District Council for the mountain and a separate council for the low areas. . . .

Similarly, the debates about school expansion reopen and reinforce other long-standing conflicts in Kilimanjaro. Machame is pitted against Marangu. The peripheral areas of the district (Rombo and West Kilimanjaro) charge that they do not receive a fair share of council services. The coincidence of these cleavages tends to exacerbate their intensity.

In this particular case of school expansion in 1969, after extended discussion in which each councillor criticized the expansion list as not giving adequate attention to his area (and thus his religion), the district executive officer, who sits in an advisory capacity to all committees, fearing that any change would destroy the compromises implicit in the list, proposed that no alterations in the list be accepted. His recommendation was approved by the committee, which meant that the allocations as originally made by the education secretaries and the district education officer were approved and legitimized. The acceptance of his recommendation also meant that the very political decisions on which areas of the district were to benefit from this extension of education were moved from the education committee, and thus the council,[29] to the ostensibly nonpolitical church education secretaries in consultation with the ministry technical officer. Thus, the basic function of the education committee is to legitimize allocations made by the education secretaries and the district education officer and to provide a forum for sectional interests.

Another function of the education committee, one in which its power is definitive,[30] is to deal with fee remissions—scholarships to children whose parents are unable to pay the fees for attendance at primary school.

29. Normal practice is for the full council to approve the recommendations of its committees with little or no discussion, though of course committee recommendations can be, and sometimes are, discussed at great length.

30. Most council decisions are subject to review by its proper officer, the Regional Commissioner, or by the Ministry charged with responsibility for local government.

The Issues

Fees in Kilimanjaro district primary schools in 1969 ranged from $2 per year for the lowest grades to $10 per year for the upper grades in day schools, and went as high as $76 per year for boarding schools. In Moshi town the fees varied from $2 to $6, plus food and uniforms for Swahili-medium schools, and from $17 to $60 per year in English-medium schools.[31] Parents unable to pay can apply to a special committee for remission of fees. Although a government policy that is moving toward universal primary education and the maintenance of primary school fees may seem contradictory, school fees remain the only effective means the local council has for collecting funds from parents. A large percentage of taxpayers all over Tanzania, and throughout Kilimanjaro, manage to avoid paying their local rates; but when a child whose parents have not paid school fees is refused entry to the school, at least in Kilimanjaro the pressure on the parents for compliance is usually sufficient to secure payment. Even nonpayment of school meal fees—in the government campaign against malnutrition and undernourishment in children, a meal eaten at school has been instituted—was formerly sufficient reason to return a child home. In 1969, however, schools were instructed to permit children whose parents had paid the school fees, but not food fees, to remain in school. Defending the fees, one of the Kilimanjaro Members of Parliament argued that payment of school fees created for the parents an involvement in the schools, and thus in the local government, that would be absent if schools were free.

In Moshi town, parents applying for school fee remissions file applications with the council education clerk, who passes them on to the town headmen[32] to verify. Parents are then given an opportunity to appear before the fee remissions committee. After parents are interviewed, the committee agrees tentatively on the amount of the remission, if any, to be granted. After all parents have been interviewed, the treasurer examines the remissions proposed to ensure that the proposed remissions comply with legal requirements. The final list of remissions is then drawn up, and approved by the Town Council education committee, with little or no discussion. This process takes place in February or March for the term beginning the preceding November.

In Moshi, in 1969, decisions on remissions were based almost entirely on the assessment by the headmen of the applicants' situations: those deemed needy by the headmen were granted remissions; those considered to have not told the truth or not needy by the headmen were denied remissions. All

---

31. Schools in which English is the medium of instruction, originally built for the children of colonial civil servants, Asians, and a few well-to-do Africans, are being phased out, and the fees are being adjusted to be identical for all schools.

32. The title "headman" is a colonial carryover from the Kiswahili word *jumbe;* "ward executive officer," corresponding to the village executive officer in rural areas, might be more appropriate. When the office of *jumbe,* established under the colonial administration, was eliminated after Independence, the Moshi Town Council decided to keep the position, and the three headmen in Moshi are paid from Town Council funds.

who met the basic criteria—living in Moshi town, having children in Standard V or higher,[33] appearing in person, if possible,[34] and considered needy by the headmen—were granted remissions. In 1969, approximately 40 percent of the remissions went to local authority schools, and 60 percent to voluntary agency schools, the reverse of the goal originally announced. Less than 1 percent of the education committee's budget for 1968 was allocated to assist just over 2 percent of the children in Moshi schools. But although approximately one-third of the funds budgeted for fee remissions were unallocated, there was no consideration of relaxing the criteria for approval of remissions or increasing some of the remissions already granted.

The school fee-remissions procedure was a cumbersome one. Deliberations did not begin until several months after the beginning of the term, parents were difficult to locate, and some parents did not appear despite several opportunities to do so. Many of those involved complained about it, but the committee and the individuals in a position to take the initiative to propose changes did not do so. This can be explained in part by the fact that those most inconvenienced by the system, the parents, have the poorest understanding of the administrative structures and are the most uncomfortable and insecure in dealing with them. Those most able to introduce change, the members of the remissions committee, are not sufficiently inconvenienced to want to take action. The treasurer was interested in streamlining the system, primarily to make his job and the accounting easier, but as an Asian in a political system dominated by Africans, and as an employee rather than member of the council, he was loath to be the initiator of change.

Thus, even in the question of the remissions of school fees, where the education committee has full decision-making powers, it functions to approve and legitimize decisions made by others.

The lowest level decision-maker in education is the headteacher in the primary school, and his power is considerable: the ability to deny access to education by refusing to admit children or by sending them home. Because parents consider primary education critical to the future success of their children, and because parents believe that headteachers can deny access to primary and future education, they are reluctant to challenge the headteacher.[35]

33. The committee limited fee remissions to children in Standard V or higher. No one on the committee could supply the source of that decision.

34. Applicants who were healthy and who did not appear in person were not considered. Where the child's father was known to be healthy and living with the family, if the father did not appear, the application was not considered.

35. Even among the local political elite, who might be expected to be more secure from retribution by headteachers than average parents, the complaints about headteachers' refusing to admit children, discriminating against them and punishing them unfairly in school, and even exchanging examination results to favor other children for admission to secondary school, were numerous.

Committees of parents have been established at each school to oversee the general running of the school—to safeguard the parents' interests in the educational system—but they either function as the tools of the headteacher or are moribund. That is, either the headteacher plays a dominant role in the school committee and uses his committee to back his demands for additional materials, new classrooms, more teachers, and other requests, or the parents are so afraid that their children will suffer if they challenge the headteacher that the committee approves whatever he recommends.[36] Thus, the decision-making chain runs from the headteacher to the education secretary, with little role for the school committees.

There are some individuals in Moshi, including the MPs and party leaders, who have regular contacts in Dar es Salaam, and who might be able to use their contacts and influence at the center to affect educational allocations in the local area. But two factors militate against this. The resources available for education in Tanzania are limited and severely strained, and the already favored position of Kilimanjaro vis-à-vis the rest of Tanzania (see Table 2.3) reduces the leverage of those who can influence decision-making at the center. To increase Kilimanjaro's share of the limited resources would defeat the government's intention to eliminate the gross inequalities between different areas of Tanzania and would be politically impossible. Kilimanjaro leaders who approach Ministry officials about increased allocations for education in Kilimanjaro are always reminded of Kilimanjaro's already favored position. As Table 2.3 makes very clear, Kilimanjaro has not suffered in allocations from the central government; and it should be noted that for much of Tanzania's first decade of independence, the Minister of Education was a Kilimanjaro Member of Parliament and the former President of the Chagga. Thus, even those with influence at the center are forced to turn to the missions for assistance when they seek to increase or improve the educational facilities in Kilimanjaro.

The local TANU organization plays no direct role in educational decisions, and even though many people seek TANU assistance in a wide range of problems, very few come to the TANU office for school problems. While the TANU regional executive secretary sits on the Moshi Town Council education committee as a nominated councillor, he and other TANU officials subscribe to the prevailing mythology that education is the concern of the technical experts, and do not become directly involved in educational matters.

In 1969 the TANU Youth League (TYL) decided, at the national level, on a fundamental reorientation, discarded all its membership rolls, and began

36. For example, at a meeting of the Kilimanjaro District Council education committee, several councillors complained about the hard work required of small children (in self-reliance projects) and about misuse of school funds by headteachers. The district education officer replied that it was the job of the school committee to correct these abuses, but there was unanimity among the councillors, including the district chairman, that headteachers would find some pretext for excluding the children of parents who protested, so that the school committee was impotent.

Table 2.3. Enrollment in Primary Schools in Tanzania by Region, 1965

Region	Assisted schools		Unassisted schools		Totals			
	Schools	Pupils	Schools	Pupils	Schools	Percent	Pupils	Percent
Arusha	164	31,040	48	3,914	212	4.9	34,954	4.6
Coast (inc DSM)	159	42,487	19	1,781	178	4.1	44,268	5.8
Dodoma	198	36,164	7	380	205	4.7	36,544	4.8
Iringa	173	31,755	12	1,934	185	4.2	33,689	4.4
Kigoma	134	22,342	1	155	135	3.1	22,497	2.9
Kilimanjaro [a]	*333*	*78,445*	*39*	*8,655*	*372*	*8.5*	*87,100*	*11.3*
Mara	171	33,748	3	484	174	4.0	36,232	4.7
Mbeya	248	48,321	98	9,534	346	8.0	57,855	7.5
Morogoro	248	43,718	6	545	254	5.8	44,263	5.8
Mtwara	378	55,263	175	10,455	553	12.6	65,718	8.7
Mwanza	290	57,529	14	2,097	304	7.0	59,626	7.8
Ruvuma	160	28,119	5	900	165	3.8	29,019	3.8
Shinyanga	170	31,497	5	1,352	175	4.0	32,849	4.3
Singida	172	30,353	–	–	172	3.9	30,353	3.9
Tabora	166	28,118	2	355	168	3.8	28,473	3.7
Tanga	274	56,360	107	6,889	381	8.7	63,249	8.2
West Lake	282	52,941	113	9,718	395	9.0	62,659	8.1
Total	3,720	710,200	654	59,148	4,374	99.1	769,348	100.3

Source: Tanzania, *Statistical Abstract 1966* (Dar es Salaam: Government Printer, 1968), p. 176.

[a] Since Kilimanjaro District has many more schools and pupils than Pare District (the other district in Kilimanjaro Region), an analysis by district would show even more clearly the favored position of Kilimanjaro vis-à-vis the rest of Tanzania.

recruiting anew through branches established only in schools. By late 1969, many schools in Kilimanjaro district had functioning TYL branches that concerned themselves with political education and the politicizing of school children, for which instructions and syllabi came from the center. They worked on developing a spirit of support for and a commitment to socialist Tanzania, largely through speeches, marches, parades, and rallies, but they had no discernible impact on educational decision-making. In the 1969 TYL Annual Conference for Moshi town a car salesman defeated the former chairman (a some-time merchant in the town market) and the principal of the cooperative college for the town chairmanship.

The Tanganyika African Parents Association (TAPA) was created to be the element of the TANU structure concerned with education, but despite repeated efforts to stimulate TAPA, it has not become a significant force in Kilimanjaro. TAPA's original purpose was to open and run schools in areas where there were no schools, not a problem in Kilimanjaro. In 1968 it was decided, at the national level, to shift the task of TAPA from that of managing schools to that of representing parents' interests on school committees. While that might have ameliorated the perceived impotence of school committees by providing them with some direct access to the political structure, and while parents called together by TAPA might have been a powerful force in influencing educational allocations, that role was neither adequately defined nor clearly understood, and the changes envisioned had not been implemented in Kilimanjaro by late 1969. TAPA in Kilimanjaro has had continuing difficulties in finding a capable leadership. Political leaders in Kilimanjaro were attempting to raise money for transport in order to hold meetings throughout the district to explain TAPA's role and increase membership, thus giving it a base from which to work. But TAPA, with no clear role and no leadership, had by late 1969 in effect ceased to function in Kilimanjaro.

Ordinary citizens, then, had little direct role in educational decision-making. Although providing an education for their children was an issue that clearly and deeply concerned most Kilimanjaro residents, neither the school committees, nor TANU, nor TAPA offered a viable channel for popular participation. It is possible that in time elections to the local councils will permit popular participation in setting some of the parameters for educational decision-making. But the continued dependence on the missions to provide and manage schools, and the popular perception, reinforced by government and TANU officials, that education is a technical matter, an element of the development plan, and thus not a proper matter for politics and elections, will continue to limit popular participation and to confine its focus to the parish clergy.

Politics of Primary Education

Summary

. A variety of factors combine to give the churches and their representatives —and not the government or TANU—the dominant role in the politics of education in Kilimanjaro.

The churches continue to rely on the provision of primary education as the major vehicle for the propagation of the faith and the primary weapon in the competition with other institutions for allegiance. The local population, assessing accurately that education is the key to the good life as it is currently defined in Kilimanjaro, resists governmental attempts to divert educational resources to other areas of the country in order to equalize development, and is thus willing to assist the missions in thwarting government education goals and priorities. The political elite themselves, though professing support for and adherence to Tanzanian socialism, and though required to swear that they will not use their leadership positions for personal or family gain, are also convinced that education is the key to the good life and are also determined to do whatever they can to ensure that their children have access to good education.[37] Thus, they too are at least tacit supporters of mission dominance in educational decision-making.

In this way, the missions, the ordinary population, and the political elite ally to control the educational administrative apparatus. At the same time, for several years this coalition of interests has effectively subverted national educational planning in Kilimanjaro. The educational goals embodied in the first Five-Year Plan (1964 to 1969), motivated by the commitment to develop self-sufficiency in high-level manpower, linked a concentration of expenditure on secondary and technical education with a restraint on the expansion of primary education.[38] Yet primary education in Kilimanjaro continued to

37. Several Kilimanjaro leaders, in explaining their compliance with Tanzania's stringent leadership code, confessed that they were able to support the leadership code in spirit now, and would support it in practice as soon as their children were educated. Others, in complaining about the difficulties their children encountered in advancing in school, spoke of sending their children out of Tanzania to continue the education denied them in Tanzania.

38. This is clear from allocations proposed in the Plan and from President Nyerere's speech introducing the plan: "If we are to do that [expand secondary and technical education] we cannot use our small resources on education for its own sake; we cannot even use them to make primary education available to all." See, United Republic of Tanganyika and Zanzibar, *Tanganyika. Five-Year Plan for Economic and Social Development. 1st July, 1964—30th June 1969* (Dar es Salaam: Government Printer, 1964), 1: xii and 65. Cameron and Dodd stress Tanzania's inability to implement the commitment to restrict the expansion of primary education; see *Societies, Schools and Progress in Tanzania*, pp. 199–208.

expand, even beyond the ability of the district council to support the new and recurrent costs.

The missions' ability to play the dominant role in educational decision-making is further enhanced by their near monopoly of the basic information necessary to run the education system. While it is true that all administrative officers are to some extent dependent on the assistance and cooperation of the interest groups within their jurisdiction, in no other issue-area in Kilimanjaro are the administrative officers more easily controlled by the very groups and individuals the officers are charged to manage. The education officers, because of the widespread demand for education, because of the interests of the major participants in maintaining the present relationships in primary education, and because of the government's difficulty in acquiring sufficient information and resources, have much less local decision-making autonomy than, for example, the health officers. The fact that the local TANU organization does not become directly involved in education and the failure of TAPA to represent the party and party policy in educational matters, or to play any substantial role at all, permit alternative organizations—the missions—to mobilize people and resources, and thus to determine and to alter educational decisions and allocations.

Although competition for allegiance is a major incentive for the missions to expand their schools, the two Christian churches manage to cooperate effectively to press their demands on the political system. While some Catholics complain that the Lutheran Church is more energetic than the Catholic Church in opening new schools, local residents are much more concerned with getting a new school than with who manages it, and neither the education officers nor any of the local political leaders have been able to utilize conflict between the churches for leverage in implementing national or local educational goals. The need to compete in a common arena and the advantages of cooperation in opposing government control have functioned to mute religious competition among the Christians.

It is not uncommon for sectional interests to support the missions' activities in opening new schools. The conflict over the opening and the location of new schools of course has a substantial impact on basic patterns of political recruitment and allocation of social roles. The eastern part of Kilimanjaro district (Rombo), for example, has long complained of inadequate representation in district decision-making and an inadequate share in district resources. This area, largely Catholic, views a restraint on expansion of primary education as a means of maintaining permanently its disfavored position, and has consistently supported the attempts of the Catholic Church to open more schools there.

Since Independence, the Tanzania government and TANU have been aware of their dependence on voluntary agencies to provide education and of the power the missions acquire as a result of that dependence. The trend, since Independence, has been to assert governmental control to replace voluntary agency control. At Independence, all schools were opened to all pupils, without regard to religion or race. Direct proselytizing has not been permitted in schools since long before control over primary education was devolved to local councils, but yet it is clear that the practice of religious rituals, in both primary and secondary schools, continues. When local councils assumed control of unassisted schools, it was thought that the mission influence would be further reduced, but in fact the change was primarily in financial responsibility, since the missions continue to manage most schools and are even able to divert public funds for their own purposes. One local government officer stressed that the missions were not unhappy with the assertion of government control, since they had essentially the same control—direct proselytizing and segregation by religion had already been forbidden—with less to pay.[39] A Unified Teaching Service was established to protect the teachers and to emphasize their role as public servants, but basic hiring, firing, and transferring of teachers in mission schools was still done in 1968–69 by the education secretaries. There has been a reorientation in the goals of primary education, with a commitment to a seven-year course equipping, and more important, psychologically preparing, children to play useful roles as farmers in rural settings, but it is too soon to see any change in the orientation toward salaried, nonagricultural urban employment. In 1969, further steps were made in this direction: a new education bill sought to reduce mission influence in education by, among other things, routing teachers' salaries through the local councils rather than through the school managers (the voluntary agencies), thus reducing the opportunity to divert funds. The central government also assumed responsibility for paying teachers previously on the payrolls of the local councils, thus freeing council funds for other purposes and shifting some power away from the local councils and into the hands of the district education officers. Both mission education secretaries in Kilimanjaro expressed concern over the restriction of their field of operations. In addition, it is likely that government education officers will be increasingly better educated and better trained, and perhaps better able to understand the formidable alliance arrayed against them and better able to deal with it. TANU continues to attempt to rejuvenate TAPA, and it is possible that TAPA will emerge as a more potent force in local educational decision-making.

But the alliance that frustrates the government's educational plans is a powerful one. And as long as the societal forces that nurture it continue—especially, dependence on missions to provide the bulk of primary education, coupled with the critical role of education as the key to the good life and a commitment by elites to the education of their children as strong as or

39. Cameron and Dodd support this assessment for Tanzania as a whole. They argue that real conflict over education between the missions and the government never developed because changes were always "carefully negotiated and reluctantly accepted . . . by the missions through their central machinery in the capital." See *Society, Schools and Progress in Tanzania*, p. 106.

stronger than their commitment to government and TANU policy—the alliance will be difficult to overcome.

Before proceeding to the analysis of the second issue-area in Moshi, it is useful to suggest briefly some of the more general implications of this study of primary education. Tanzania is legally a single-party state. But neither the party nor the government at the center exercises clear control over decisions that are central to Tanzania's development. Even the local party organization is largely ineffective in this area of local decision-making. Local government officials are similarly ineffective. And, in a continuation of the colonial pattern, major public issues are resolved by very private interests.

3

Politics of Liquor Licensing

A second key issue-area examined in the study of Kilimanjaro politics was liquor licensing. Like primary education, liquor licensing was an issue that was salient, that interested and excited the general public to a considerable extent, and that led to decisions made primarily within the local setting. The importance of the liquor trade makes this issue-area critical in studying the local economy and social stratification in Kilimanjaro. In addition, formal decision-making in liquor licensing, unlike the case of primary education, was primarily concerned with individual, rather than community-wide decisions. Liquor licensing in Kilimanjaro, then, was a specific form of governmental output that determined who was to be permitted to profit in the controlled marketplace and who was not.

In Kilimanjaro the brewing and sale of local liquor, and the sale of bottled liquor, is a widespread activity, involving most of the adult population as brewers, sellers, or consumers. In April 1969, for example, one liquor license was granted for every thousand persons in Kilimanjaro rural, while the comparable figure for Moshi town was one license granted for every 250 persons.[1] Since over 40 percent of the population was under fourteen years of age, and more than half under nineteen, the percentage of the adult population directly involved was very large. Licenses issued for the period September 1969 to March 1970 almost doubled the April to August totals, so that even though some licenses granted might never actually have been used, the number of people concerned with the brewing, sale, and consumption of liquor was enormous. The importance of the brewing and sale of local liquor in Kilimanjaro is so widely recognized in Tanzania that even casual visitors to Dar es Salaam may be told that local politics in Kilimanjaro is centered on local liquor.

Not only does the widespread involvement in the liquor trade make this a salient issue throughout Kilimanjaro, but in addition, liquor license fees

1. Calculations are made from the records of the Kilimanjaro Liquor Licensing Board, 1969. Totals include all types of licenses issued—for brewing, for sale and consumption off the premises, for restaurants, and for bars. The term "liquor" includes all alcoholic beverages.

provide an important source of income for both Kilimanjaro councils. After the changes in rural local government financing introduced in 1969, liquor license fees, together with school fees, became the major source of locally derived income for the Kilimanjaro District Council (see Table 3.1).

There are other types of licenses that are highly desired, and thus hotly contested, in Kilimanjaro—transport licenses, for example—but the formal award of those licenses is made by a national board, such as the Transport Licensing Authority, whose decisions are removed from the local arena.

Like education, liquor licensing in Kilimanjaro was an issue-area in which the formal decision-making apparatus was unable to make effective allocations and produced decisions that were often inconsistent and in conflict with its stated intentions. Also, it was an issue-area in which the regulating agency became an ally of the principal forces to be regulated.

The Setting

Liquor licenses in Tanzania are considered and awarded by boards of local individuals. The method of selection to the liquor licensing boards has varied somewhat since Independence, but the District, and then Area, Commissioner has always been the chairman, and generally, the local council has had a major role in selecting members. In 1969 new legislation combined the formerly separate licensing boards for Kilimanjaro rural and Moshi town into a single board, chaired by the Area Commissioner. The somewhat complicated formula for selecting board membership ensured that the major political forces—central government, local political leaders, and local administrative officers—were included.[2] That is, while subscribing to the norm that politics should not enter into the consideration of liquor licenses, the board was so structured that the major political leaders, including both those selected locally (the councillors) and those posted from the center (the Area Commissioner and the administrative officers), had to be included. Since this structure included both urban and rural Kilimanjaro, the analysis focuses on the district as a whole.

While the Liquor Licensing Board is responsible for both bottled (including beer and distilled spirits) and locally brewed liquor, most of the sales and consumption in Kilimanjaro are of locally brewed liquor. The local liquor in Kilimanjaro is brewed from plantains and finger millet, of which the latter provides the local name, *mbege,* differentiating it from other locally brewed beer

2. The Kilimanjaro Liquor Licensing Board in 1969 was composed of: Area Commissioner as chairman, town chairman as Board vice-chairman (the Minister responsible for local government had discretion to name the vice-chairman), two members elected by the Moshi Town Council, and four members elected by the Kilimanjaro District Council, of whom one was to be the chairman, a maximum of two chosen from the council and its employees, and one ordinary citizen. There was no specific provision in the law for a secretary to the board, but in Kilimanjaro the Moshi Town Clerk was named by the Minister to that post. Since the Executive Officer of the Kilimanjaro District Council was elected a member by the Council, the chief administrative officers, as well as the chairmen, of the two councils, were included.

Politics of Liquor Licensing

Table 3.1. Contribution of Liquor License Fees to Total Revenue of the Moshi Town
and Kilimanjaro District Councils, 1967–68

Year	Moshi Town Council		Kilimanjaro District Council	
	Liquor license fees	Percent of total revenue	Liquor license fees	Percent of total revenue
1967	240,284.20[a]	7.7[b]	748,352.00	6.0
1968	249,940.80	7.7	723,485.00	6.3

Source: Annual Financial Statements and Estimates, Moshi Town and Kilimanjaro
District Councils.

[a] Figures in Tanzania shillings. In addition, the Councils earn other income from the
liquor trade (for example, council-operated beer halls).

[b] That is, liquor license fees provided 7.7% of Moshi Town Council total revenue in
1967.

in Tanzania. Served in most Chagga homes as a regular beverage, as well as on
festive occasions, *mbege* is only mildly alcoholic when consumed shortly after
it is brewed. Because of its millet content, it is a nutritious drink[3] and is considered a normal, necessary part of the Chagga staple diet. Most of the *mbege*
sold in Kilimanjaro is brewed on a small scale by women in their homes; much
of it is purchased and transported to bars, where it is sold from large barrels
and tubs by the cup at a price substantially lower than that for bottled beer.

Since the price for coffee, the major Kilimanjaro cash crop, began to fall
in the mid-1950s, the local population has sought alternative sources of income,
of which the brewing and sale of *mbege* is an important one. In recent years
that revenue has become, for many people, an integral part of their basic income, rather than supplement to the basic income.[4] These two factors—that
the brewing and sale of *mbege* are small-scale and not the monopoly of a small
group of people, and that the trade in local liquor provides for many people

3. Local health officers in Kilimanjaro often trace the good health of Chagga
children to the consumption of *mbege*. The high caloric content and the presence
of B vitamins in millet beer clearly make it a more nourishing drink than European-
type beer or distilled spirits.

4. Most local leaders argue that *mbege* consumption has increased in recent years
and that the development of *mbege* production as an alternate source of income has
stimulated this increase. One local government officer, whose origin was outside Kilimanjaro, argued that in other coffee-growing areas, new crops, such as the cultivation
of tea in the Rungwe district, rather than local liquor, have compensated for the fall in
coffee prices. While it may be impossible, because of the nature of the commodity,
to document an actual increase in the consumption of *mbege*, the perception by the
local populace that it is an integral element of the local economy does serve to make
the competition for licenses more intense.

basic, rather than supplemental, income—help account for the intensity of the conflict over this particular governmental allocation.

At first blush, liquor licensing might seem to be a straightforward case of governmental regulation, like automobile and hawker licensing, for example, and thus of little interest in a study of community power. But in Kilimanjaro a combination of factors, including bureaucratic inefficiency and incompetence, conflict of goals, and the availability of alternative decision-making centers, renders the formal decision-making apparatus impotent to monopolize the awarding of licenses.

The Actors

The liquor licensing process seems simple enough. Prospective brewers and sellers apply to the licensing board with payment of a modest application fee, the applications are made public and objections are invited, and health officers inspect the proposed premises to ensure that they meet minimum health requirements. The licensing board, acting on its own information, on recommendations by local administrative officials, police, and health officers, and on objections filed, decides on licenses to be granted for the next six-month period. Although it receives some advice from the government and the party in Dar es Salaam, the local board is essentially free to develop its own guidelines for awarding, and denying, licenses. Formerly, applicants from rural areas were required to secure the approval of the local village development committee, but this provision was not included in the 1969 law, though apparently it continued in some areas in Kilimanjaro.

Because of the number of applications (a total of 867 in April 1969 and almost twice that number in September 1969) the deliberations of the Board are lengthy, usually involving a full day or more of meetings. The number of applications makes it impossible for each one to be discussed individually, so that most applications from previous license-holders are approved perfunctorily. Much of the decision-making, therefore, is in fact made by the local government bureaucracy, which is responsible for receiving applications, listing them accurately, receiving objections, performing health inspections, and providing supplementary information where requested. The competence of the bureaucracy is sorely tested in this process, and it is not always able to cope with the demands on it.

First, the legislation governing licensing was not fully understood by those involved. In part, this may have been due to the fact that new legislation was enacted in 1969, but an examination of the Liquor Licensing Board records indicated that even in previous years confusion over interpretation of the law led to conflicting decisions in identical cases. Because the basic law, drafted in complex English and implemented by a board most of whose members used English with some difficulty, was not adequately understood, on several occasions in 1969 the Board violated the very law it was established to implement.

Because of a confusion of categories, for example, the fee for a particular type of transfer was in some cases Shs. 5/-, while in others Shs. 500/- was assessed.

Second, records of previous decisions were usually of little use in current deliberations. Even when Board members were aware that an applicant had previously been denied a license, they could not determine the grounds for the denial. At times, it was difficult to determine even the basic guidelines previous Licensing Boards used for awarding and denying licenses. In one case dating back several years—actually a conflict between two local notables that manifested itself in opposition to a liquor license—records were so scanty and difficult to locate that a lengthy investigation by the area commissioner was duplicated. Nor were records kept by bar or location. In September 1969 three different people were awarded liquor licenses for the same building.

Third, in order to reduce public pressure on Board members and administrative officers, the public was kept relatively uninformed about the law and about the status of applications, with the result that public sentiment, rather than being channeled into Board deliberations in a coherent manner, was communicated sporadically to individual participants in the decision-making process. This meant as well that formal objections were rare. One Board member even suggested not making applications public to reduce even further public involvement and thus pressure on Board members. When objections were presented, most often they emanated from competing bar owners objecting to the loss of their monopoly. Thus, Board members, seeking to avoid pressure on them as individuals, were inclined to exclude the general public from all phases of the decision-making process; the outcome, however, was that formal objections and communications and other public pressure on the Board as a whole were reduced, while pressure on the individual Board members, often based on misinformation and misunderstanding, was increased.

Fourth, the bureaucracies involved were often in competition with each other. The urban and rural administrative officers were responsive to different constituencies and responsible to different superiors. While the bureaucratic norms did not permit open advocacy of urban or rural interests in Board deliberations, the responsiveness of the officers to their own constituencies were manifested in the treatment and presentation of applications. Urban members were in general sympathetic and rural members unsympathetic to the special conditions that applied to bars designated as night clubs, while the reverse was true for the oft-repeated proposal to be less stringent in enforcing health regulations in small rural bars. In addition, there was often conflict, rather than cooperation, within the bureaucracy itself. For several years, the administrative and health officers of one of the two Kilimanjaro councils have been in conflict, each accusing the other of chicanery in awarding liquor licenses. The administrative officers accuse the health officers of certifying, or refusing to certify, a bar without reason (corruption suggested), while the health officers accuse the administrative officers of granting licenses without their certification (corruption suggested). Precisely because several power centers were represented on the Board, aggrieved applicants could present their cases to different people, and by varying the details slightly were often successful in having the original decision reconsidered and altered. For example, an individual denied a license because the health officer refused to certify his bar as meeting health requirements could seek out his councillor and with him complain to the administrative officer that he was being harassed by the Health officer and thus get his case reheard. Finally, because no one wanted the onus of being responsible for denying a license, each sought to clear himself by blaming other Board members in his public explanations for the denial, thus reinforcing the popular belief that particularistic criteria and personalities, rather than general rules, were involved.

An additional factor that served to incapacitate the Liquor Licensing Board was a continuing conflict of goals. There was conflict between the policy goals of the Board and as a result between the principles used to guide Board deliberations.

In 1968 the Kilimanjaro TANU Regional Executive Committee called on the Liquor Licensing Board to reduce consumption of alcohol in Kilimanjaro, reaffirming a resolution of the Kilimanjaro TANU Annual Conference of 1967. There is widespread agreement in Kilimanjaro that consumption of alcoholic beverages is excessive, and many people trace all problems of social dislocation—theft, assault, rape, broken homes, corruption—to this cause. The Liquor Licensing Board regularly reiterated that its major policy goal was to reduce consumption of liquor.

At the same time, there is a strong commitment in the spirit of Tanzanian self-reliance to assert that locally brewed beer is as good as, if not better than, bottled beer (even though most of the bottled beer consumed is brewed in Tanzania, much of it under the brand name Kilimanjaro), and to promote the consumption of locally brewed beer over bottled beer. Even a Ministry circular urged local liquor licensing boards to encourage the consumption of local beer. In Kilimanjaro there is as well a general commitment to encourage the population to diversify its sources of income, especially by going into business, and to replace individual enterprise with cooperative endeavor. Both national policy and local feeling supported individuals, and especially small cooperatives, who wanted to increase their income by brewing and selling local liquor.

Thus, the policy goals of the Liquor Licensing Board included commitments both to reducing and to increasing consumption. In practical terms, this meant that the Board, which tried to reduce consumption by reducing licenses, was stymied in achieving its major policy goal. While the Board was reluctant to grant new licenses, it was also reluctant to refuse applicants who asserted they were supporting the nation's policy of socialism and self-reliance by opening bars and selling *mbege*.

Another conflict of goals involved the conflicting demands of attention to community needs (health, order) and of protection of the individual against administrative abuse and chicanery. While the adverse recommendations of health and police officials might provide a simple means of reducing the number of licenses, Board members were inclined to side with the individual applicants who felt they were being harassed by government officers using unnecessarily stringent and harsh standards. Especially in the rural area, where many bars were simply parts of private houses, with the beer served from the barrels in which it was brewed and drunk from gourds supplied by the drinkers themselves, Board members were reluctant to insist on needed improvements for a bar so marginal economically that the improvements would force the owner out of business. Likewise, police reports of law violations were often regarded as undue harassment of the ordinary peasant trying to eke out a meager living and insufficient cause for denial of license. In both cases, the lack of clear agreement on just how adverse a police or health officer's comment had to be to deny a license led to conflicting decisions in identical cases. Also, the fear of litigation by aggrieved applicants made the Board chary of denying licenses solely on recommendation of health and police officers. As a result, the most obvious and the most defensible reasons for denying licenses were rarely used, and no other causes for denial, other than rejecting new applications, were developed.

Finally, an additional conflict was that between the commitment to reduce consumption and the political repercussions of denying licenses. Individuals who feel deprived by governmental decisions are never happy, and in Kilimanjaro most people believed that license denial was a personal, not an impersonal, decision. By not differentiating decisions that were universal from those that were particular in their application, they felt singled out and sought remedy, not in the impersonal form of opposing policies and guidelines, but in the directly personal form of attempting to persuade or pressure the individual Board member believed to be responsible or to have him removed from the Board. The Board members themselves, while recognizing the standards of impartiality applicable in their decisions, were unable to escape entirely from the personal and particular obligations of family, clan, and friendship ties.[5] It was not uncommon, too, for local communities to interpret the denial of a license as the rejection of one neighborhood in favor of another. Therefore, since the personal cost of denying a license may be very high, the grounds for doing so must be very solid indeed.

Although formal decisions on the awarding of liquor licenses in Kilimanjaro are made by the Liquor Licensing Board, there are alternative ways to secure a license and to profit from the trade in liquor. The existence of these alternatives, of course, reduces the power of the Liquor Licensing Board, undermines

5. For a similar finding in Acholi, Uganda, see Colin Leys, *Politicians and Policies* (Nairobi: EAPH, 1967), pp. 46–47.

The Issues

its respect and legitimacy in the public eye, and enables individuals to defeat its intentions.

Even though the liquor licensing law clearly specifies that liquor licenses, once granted, may not be sold, in Kilimanjaro they are both sold and leased, and on occasion the original applicant's only intention is to profit from the sale or rental of his license. Since the operator of a bar can claim to be its manager, legitimately employed by the licensee, it has proved almost impossible to curtail this practice. One of the most prosperous bar owners in Moshi rents a section of his bar to a seller of "premium" *mbege* for approximately six times what his license cost for the entire six-month license period. When local rumors suggested, in August 1969, that at its September sitting the Liquor License Board would approve all applicants, several individuals applied for licenses solely for the purpose of selling them later.

Both confusion and corruption within the administrative bureaucracy permit licenses to be granted without the express authorization of the Liquor Licensing Board. In April 1969, for example, when the Board attempted to reduce the number of licenses by denying all new applications, some new applications were approved because they were listed in Board papers as renewals. While accusations of chicanery are common when such cases come to light, there is sufficient evidence of bureaucratic incompetence and error to make accidental mislisting credible. On the other hand, there is also evidence of corruption, ranging from permitting an applicant to identify herself, falsely, as a local UWT chairman and thus ensuring preferential treatment, to issuing a health certificate without ever visiting the prospective bar, to forging a superior's signature in the issuance of a license. Proof of corruption is difficult to obtain in such cases, especially since TANU policy considers the offerer of a bribe as guilty as the recipient, and it is rare that a license is denied or revoked because it was obtained illegally. In addition, the difficulty of enforcing licensing regulations in rural areas provides another path for operating a bar without Liquor Licensing Board approval.

Still another channel for circumventing the Liquor Licensing Board is to apply pressure on the Area Commissioner, its chairman, and even on the Regional Commissioner. As the representatives of the central government in the district and region respectively, and as direct appointees of the President, these two officials wield extensive powers. Although government circulars define the limits of their operations, it is widely believed that they are able to delay or alter directives emanating from the center and that they can exercise at will the ultimate coercive power—to jail an individual without reason indefinitely.[6]

6. The abuse of their power by some commissioners supports these perceptions, though TANU and the government are increasingly successful in educating people about the limits of commissioners' power and methods of appeal against abuse. See the United Republic of Tanzania, *Annual Reports of the Permanent Commission of Enquiry, June 1966–June 1967* and *July 1967–June 1968* (Dar es Salaam: Government Printer, 1968 and 1969).

Politics of Liquor Licensing

The new liquor licensing law of 1969 specified hours for the sale of liquor, introducing changes widely opposed in Kilimanjaro. Opposition focused on closing bars between 2 and 5 PM—the time a farmer returns from his field and is accustomed to drinking *mbege* with his meal—and on keeping bars open until 11 PM or midnight—believed to be the cause for an increase in antisocial behavior. This opposition developed just after the arrival in Kilimanjaro of a new Regional Commissioner, an individual transferred from another region where he had been supported by the party in a dispute with the local Members of Parliament.[7] As is the custom in Tanzania, the new Commissioner toured the mountain and held public meetings both to introduce himself and to give people an opportunity to present complaints. After several weeks of meetings that focused largely on opposition to the new beer law, the Regional Commissioner suspended implementation of the new law and announced that in regard to bar hours the old law would remain in effect, thus bringing to a halt both the demonstrations against the new law and its enforcement by the police. At first stymied by the Town Clerk, the Regional Commissioner won support for this action from the new Liquor Licensing Board. But after several more weeks, during which the Town Clerk and perhaps others pointed out the illegality of the suspension of the new law to the Ministry,[8] a high-ranking Ministry official was dispatched to Kilimanjaro to ensure that the hours in force were those specified in the new law.

Another example of the power of the commissioners to intervene in the functioning of the Liquor Licensing Board involved a leading European bar owner in Moshi who was denied a license because the Board, instructed by a Ministry circular, restricted licenses to Tanzanian citizens. The bar owner appealed to the Regional Commissioner, who telephoned the Area Commissioner and instructed him to issue the license under a clause in the law exempting bars serving the tourist trade from the citizenship requirement. In this case, the Area Commissioner brought the matter to the Board (the applicant had by then appealed directly to the Minister), which, assessing the situation accurately,

7. For details of this dispute, see H. U. E. Thoden van Velzen and J. J. Sterkenburg, "The Party Supreme," *Kroniek van Afrika* 1 (1969): 65–88. The dispute was perhaps more complex than this article suggests, and involved a basic clash over the necessarily conflicting roles of Member of Parliament and Regional Commissioner. After acrimonious exchanges in the Parliament, a TANU committee was sent to the region to investigate, and it supported the Regional Commissioner. The MP's were subsequently dismissed from the party, and thus lost their seats in Parliament. The Regional Commissioner was shortly thereafter transferred to Kilimanjaro, and after a few months in his new post, was retired. Subsequently, one of the dismissed MPs became an officer of the Moshi Town Council, and the former Regional Commissioner was appointed chairman of a national licensing authority. For the full report of the TANU committee, see Tanganyika African National Union, *Taarifa ya Tume maalum iliyokwenda Mkoa wa Ziwa Magharibi kusikiliza Matatizo juu ya Wabunge wa Mkoa huo na Mkuu was Mkoa huo* (Dar es Salaam: Government Printer, 1968).

8. Although of course cause and effect cannot be established, this was widely believed to be a major factor in the sudden demotion and transfer of the Town Clerk to a less prestigious rural post shortly thereafter.

after some acrid comments approved a six-month terminal license, to permit the bar owner to close out his business or find a citizen to purchase it. When the time for the next application came, the bar owner indicated he had applied for citizenship, Board files contained no record that he had ever been notified that his license was a terminal one, and the license was granted without comment. Because of this power to intervene in the functioning of the Board, aggrieved applicants often approached the commissioners directly to influence or alter Board decisions.

Finally, applicants dissatisfied with Board decisions are permitted by law to appeal directly to the Minister, who, apparently, upheld all appeals to him from Kilimanjaro in 1969. There were widespread allegations of corruption involved in these reversals of Board decisions, and charges that the Minister, from a neighboring, rival ethnic group, acted out of dislike for the Chagga. Privately, the Liquor Licensing Board was unanimous in its condemnation of the Minister's actions, and all agreed it made the Board purposeless. If all who were denied licenses by the Board could secure them from the Minister, the Board felt that it might as well approve all applications in the first place and thus avoid antagonizing people. It was in large part this feeling that led to the approval of nearly twice the number of licenses awarded in September 1969.

Thus, although the Liquor Licensing Board was formally the locus for authoritative decisions on who would be permitted to engage in the liquor trade and who would not, in fact several viable alternative means existed for profiting from the brewing and sale of liquor, and they were often used.

Public opinion plays little direct part in the politics of liquor licensing in Kilimanjaro. The popular reaction to the bar hours of the new liquor licensing law—which resulted in several demonstrations and refusals to leave bars for the midday closing—has already been mentioned. Through the Regional Commissioner public pressure was temporarily successful in altering the impact of the law in Kilimanjaro, but the suspension of the new rules was ultimately thwarted in Dar es Salaam. Public attitudes on the subject were contradictory. A strong religious ethic, supported almost fervently by both Christian and Muslim leaders, that alcohol is evil and individuals must be kept from its evil influences by societal restraints, was opposed by the importance of *mbege* in the local diet, and, perhaps more importantly, by the extent to which the local populace profits from the liquor trade.

For liquor licensing, then, mass public opinion is recognized only when it is manifested in large public outbursts. In addition, for most aspects of liquor licensing public opinion is rarely united or cohesive, since no organized group is successful in mobilizing public opinion on this issue. There are also few direct channels for incorporating public opinion in the decision-making process.

Before the new liquor licensing legislation of 1969, the Moshi Town Council had set limits on the number of bars to be approved within the different

sections of town. But the Council, unsure of its authority under the new legislation, declined, at the election of its representatives to the new Liquor Licensing Board, to instruct them to implement these limits. Thus, the only specific
policy of the Town Council in regard to liquor licensing fell casualty to the
new legislation. Other than this election of its representatives to the Board,
the Town Council took no official cognizance of liquor licensing, though individual councillors did confer with each other and with the Town Clerk as Liquor Licensing Board secretary on licensing problems.

In Tanzania, party policy frowns on the formation of interest groups in
general, and economic interest groups in particular. Except for trade unions,
cooperatives, and social and charitable organizations, it is assumed that the
interests of any particular section of the population can be adequately represented by TANU and its auxiliaries, and that adherence to bureaucratic norms
assures individuals fair and just treatment without the need for recourse to interest group protection. In other words, it is assumed that the political functions performed by interest groups in other polities—especially interest aggregation, articulation, and communication—are performed by TANU and its
auxiliaries, and that interest groups, which could be used to form competing
centers of power, are both unnecessary and dangerous. In addition, it is assumed that interest groups with a primarily economic orientation represent
antisocialist elements in the society and therefore should not be tolerated. This
party policy, coupled with the other factors discussed here, have largely prevented the emergence of a strong interest group of beer brewers and bar owners in Kilimanjaro.

Attempts have been made to organize individuals involved in the liquor
trade, but dissensions and splits among those concerned have further eroded
their already limited ability to influence authoritative allocations. A national
association of local beer brewers was formed in Tanzania in the early 1960s,
but by 1969 it had become an association of brewers and bar owners with its
headquarters, and apparently its only activity, in Kilimanjaro. And even there,
it has been unsuccessful in recruiting the majority of bar owners and in obtaining official recognition as the representative of brewers and bar owners. In
fact, it was widely believed that the president and major officers operated the
association as a profitable, and perhaps only quasi-legal, business. Apparently
the president was able to collect fees from uninformed bar owners to intercede in their favor with the Liquor Licensing Board. Once decisions have been
made by the Board, but before they are made public, he manages to secure advance information on the outcome of Board deliberations. He then visits the
applicants, claiming an additional fee for his intervention from those who were
successful and collecting money from those who were unsuccessful to finance
appeals in Dar es Salaam. Local police have conducted a lengthy investigation
of the association, and the Board itself is sufficiently convinced of his dishonesty
to refuse to consider objections filed by the president. On the other hand,

many people in Kilimanjaro, including several leading political figures, are convinced of the power and influence of this individual, who also maintains an office as a Public Writer (he writes letters for illiterates, completes applications and forms, offers general advice on business ventures, personal problems, and everything else, and functions as a lawyer in quasi-legal and legal disputes, all for a fee). He himself claims that he has been instrumental in several instances in influencing government liquor licensing policy.

Although local politicians refer to the power of bar owners and their association, their power stems not from a formal organization and organizational activities, but from concerted action to pressure decision-makers individually and to discourage and weaken competition, and from the availability of sufficient resources to fight court cases, to fly to Dar es Salaam to press appeals, and to direct some of their funds into the hands of cooperative public servants. Thus, the formal economic interest group has been diverted to serve the interests of its officers and is not recognized as a legitimate participant in the local political system, and the bar owners influence allocations by marshalling their considerable economic resources and acting in concert.

A major focus for UWT activities in Kilimanjaro has been to encourage women to go into business, both as a supplement to farm income, and, because of the land shortage and low coffee prices, as an alternative source of income. Among the most attractive business opportunities are bars, where the capital investment required is minimal and profits are high. By 1969 there were several women's groups running bars, some as UWT branches and some independently, as well as individual women running bars and maintaining stalls in the town beer market. The Liquor Licensing Board, anxious to support UWT activities and in accord with a Ministry circular directing it to favor cooperatives over individual applicants, acted favorably on almost all applications from women's groups. And even in cases of competitive bidding to manage local-government-owned bars, the Town Council has accepted low bids, and thus reduced its own revenue, to assist the women's groups. But it should be noted that women's groups active in the liquor trade in 1969 functioned as shareholding companies and not as cooperatives. That is, women bought shares in the joint venture and expected a return on their investment, but the consumers were not shareholders and did not benefit (either by reduced prices or by distributions of dividends) from the operation. Despite the assistance of the government commercial officer and other officials, there were many complaints by members that the bars were unable to show a profit and that individuals had not received their shares of profits made. Several groups obtained permission, as well, on the grounds of the economic marginality of their bars, to pay their employees less than the minimum wage. In most cases, then, the women's groups were neither replacing private ownership with cooperatives, nor eliminating the long hours and low wages of employees for which private ownership is regularly criticized. Thus, the UWT was in the position of publicly condemning the consumption of alcohol and at the same time devoting extensive energy within the political system to ensuring that women's groups were assisted in entering the liquor trade.

The local TANU organization was not directly involved in liquor licensing. Both the TANU Annual Conference and the TANU Regional Executive Committee had called for a reduction in the consumption of alcohol, and in so doing may have represented the views of the general citizenry. But TANU itself took no specific, direct action to ensure implementation of that call. While all of the members of the Liquor Licensing Board, save the citizen elected at large, can be considered TANU leaders, TANU, as TANU, was not specifically involved in their deliberations. In fact, on several occasions, party influence was specifically cited in decrying the Minister's reversals of Board decisions. When it was suggested that this problem be raised at the TANU National Annual Conference, one Board member, who held both a TANU and government post, argued that taking the issue to TANU was absolutely useless.

Conclusions

Formal awards of liquor licenses are made by the Liquor Licensing Board in Kilimanjaro. But it is clear that the Board has little real control over the liquor trade.

The major method of control chosen by the Board, reduction in the number of licenses granted, cannot seriously be expected to achieve its major goal, a decrease in drinking. On the contrary, it is more likely to strengthen the position of the major entrepreneurs.

In fact, because of the various pressures on the Board discussed here, very few licenses are actually denied. Likewise, raising the cost of the licenses (also proposed to reduce their number), while it may produce additional revenue for the local councils, is unlikely to reduce drinking. It is possible that at some threshold point reducing the number of bars will make it so difficult to obtain liquor that some people will be discouraged from drinking. But Kilimanjaro District now is so saturated with bars that a reduction in the number of licensees, or a freeze, simply favors those who retain their licenses, making their bars larger and more profitable, and gives forces opposed to a reduction in consumption a monopoly position in the liquor trade. Indeed, one might argue that a more rational strategy for socialist Tanzania would be to attempt to attack the economic base of the large entrepreneurs by granting licenses to anyone who applies.

Moreover, the channels available to reverse Liquor Licensing Board decisions—appeal to the Minister, pressure on political figures and Board members, corruption—are all more easily utilized by the larger, richer bar owners than by their less affluent, small-scale competitors. Thus, by favoring the larger, richer entrepreneurs at all stages of the liquor licensing process, in the legislation, in Board decisions, and in enforcement, the Board

The Issues

becomes the ally of those elements that dominate the trade it seeks to regulate.

An additional factor that enables the larger liquor entrepreneurs to use their regulating agency in this way is the extent to which the center involves itself in this primarily local issue, limits the local Board's freedom of action and ability to deal with the problems it perceives, and overrides and reverses local decisions. While greater local autonomy in liquor licensing might seem an obvious remedy, most, though not all, participants in the liquor licensing process oppose greater local autonomy. They do so both because they find it difficult to conceive of basic policy and control not emanating from the center and because they feel that maintenance of Dar es Salaam as the ultimate source of power protects them from what they fear would be intolerable local political pressure. At the center, greater local autonomy is opposed because it would defeat one aim of the new law—to curb arbitrary action by local commissioners—because it is felt that coordinated development can only be achieved by direction from the center, and because it would make one more circumstance in which Kilimanjaro was accorded special treatment in Tanzania.

For all of these reasons, then, the Liquor Licensing Board does not control the trade in liquor. Bureaucratic incompetence and corruption distort the decision-making process. Conflicts among the goals and guidelines used by the Board for granting licenses produce decisions that are at times inconsistent and contradictory. The existence of alternative means to obtain licenses and the ability of external forces to influence Board decisions permit individuals unsuccessful in the formal, official decision-making process to obtain liquor licenses nonetheless. Public opinion—a combination of vocal condemnation of alcohol and pressure on Board members to grant licenses—has not been effectively mobilized and plays no significant direct role in Board decisions. And the contradiction between condemnation of the evil influence of alcohol and support for individuals and groups involved in the liquor trade is manifest even within TANU and its auxiliaries.

Local liquor is a major element of the Kilimanjaro economy. In addition, it has become a major vehicle for the development of local capitalist entrepreneurs. Until it is recognized and addressed in those terms, it is difficult to see how this situation, in which the formal decision-making apparatus makes few significant decisions, can be fundamentally altered.

This study of liquor licensing in Kilimanjaro complements and supports the findings of the study of primary education. In both cases the official, formal decision-making structure was thwarted in its efforts to promote orderly local development in accord with national plans. In both cases the regulating body was largely manipulated by the very groups and individuals it was charged to regulate. These findings have two more general implications.

Politics of Liquor Licensing

One concerns the party. In both primary education and liquor licensing the local party organization has at best a modest role in formal decision-making. Church groups and major brewers and bar owners are largely able to disregard it. Thus the party, expected to manage change in Tanzania, has been able to exercise little influence in two of the most important allocations made within the local political system. And ordinary citizens, when they participate in these arenas at all, do not do so through the party.

The second implication concerns the nature of political change in up-country Tanzania. Decisions made in both primary education and liquor licensing have served to reinforce economic and political structures that are inconsistent with the socialist development described in party policy. Not only have they not promoted a more equitable distribution of societal resources and benefits, but they have nurtured a pattern of economic differentiation inimical to a more egalitarian distribution. And they have strengthened both the norms implicit in capitalist development and the very set of local entrepreneurs who are in direct conflict with national policy.

4

Politics of Jobs

Introduction

The study of local politics in Kilimanjaro has thus far focused on participants and outcomes in conflicts over primary education and liquor licensing. A third issue-area considered important by Kilimanjaro residents is jobs and unemployment. Conflict over jobs and unemployment meets the criteria of salience and concern and, in addition, involves decision-making that differs from the patterns already described in that there are no specific, clearly defined decision-points. It is important to examine this issue-area, at least briefly, because it is suggestive of the types of conflict in Kilimanjaro that do not revolve around or culminate in clearly defined decisions and because it is a corrective to the institutional bias implicit in studies that focus primarily on clearly defined decision-making and decision-makers. This overview of the conflict over jobs and unemployment in Kilimanjaro will also provide some insight into other elements of Kilimanjaro politics to be discussed in more detail later, especially development planning and coordination and the role of the local TANU organization as an expediter in local politics.

Background

The shortage of land in Kilimanjaro and the fall in coffee prices in recent years have reinforced the strong drive among Tanzania's youth for salaried employment. Furthermore, a large number of students, unable to proceed beyond Standard IV or Standard VII, leave the school system each year oriented toward the wage economy. In 1968, for example, because of limited places at the higher levels, almost 3,000 children in Kilimanjaro District were unable to advance from Standard IV to Standard V, and another 7,900 ended school at Standard VII (see Table 4.1). Thus, almost 11,000 students finished their schooling in Kilimanjaro in 1968, most of them expecting to find salaried employment.[1]

1. President Nyerere has argued that this orientation toward salaried employment is one of the major shortcomings of the Tanzanian system of education. In his paper "Education for Self-Reliance," he notes that "Individually and collectively we have in practice thought of education as a training for the skills required to earn high salaries in the modern sector of our economy," reprinted in Resnick, *Tanzania: Revolution by Education*, p. 49.

Politics of Jobs

Table 4.1.   School-leavers in Kilimanjaro District, 1968

	Number who sat			Number selected			
	Boys	Girls	Total	Boys	Girls	Total	Percent
	Standard IV Examination						
Kilimanjaro rural[a]	4905	3998	8903	3502	2523	6025	63[b]
	Standard VII Examination						
Kilimanjaro rural	4994	3140	8134	368	133	501	6.2[c]
Moshi town	192	156	348	42	38	80	23.0

Source: District Education Office, Kilimanjaro District.

[a] Does not include Moshi town, where in 1968 almost all children enrolled were admitted to Standard V.

[b] That is, 63% of the pupils who sat for the Standard IV Examination in Kilimanjaro District in 1968 were selected to enter Standard V.

[c] That is, 6.2% of the pupils who sat for the Standard VII Examination in Kilimanjaro District in 1968 were selected to enter secondary school.

Since the total number of employees in all of Kilimanjaro Region (including Pare as well as Kilimanjaro District) in 1968 was some 26,000,[2] it is clear that only a small percentage of the more than 10,000 school-leavers in 1968 were able to find salaried employment. Even though some Kilimanjaro school-leavers were still too young to be looking for jobs immediately, and even though some could find jobs elsewhere in Tanzania, with more than 10,000 school-leavers yearly for the past several years, clearly there is a large number of young people in Kilimanjaro who expect to obtain jobs and who are unable to do so.

The actual number of unemployed in Kilimanjaro is difficult, if not impossible, to ascertain. Local estimates in 1969 ranged from 1,000 (Labour Office), to 5,000 (NUTA District Office), to 20,000 (Town Clerk's Office), to 30,000, plus 90,000 more who would take jobs if they were available (NUTA Regional Office). NUTA figures actually showed a total employment for Kilimanjaro Region of twice the Central Statistical Bureau figures. While it may be that the error in the NUTA figures simply resulted from the inclusion of Arusha Region figures in the total (the NUTA office in Kilimanjaro served both regions), the point here is that local officials were often unaware of statistics compiled by the central government and in dealing with their day-to-day responsibilities were only rarely motivated to search for a more detailed picture of the overall situation.

A survey of the Tanzanian labor force in 1965 found unemployment rates

2. See Tanzania, Ministry of Economic Affairs and Development Planning, Central Statistical Bureau. *Survey of Employment and Earnings 1968* (Dar es Salaam: Government Printer, 1969), Appendix X. This figure includes almost 7,000 casual workers.

The Issues

of 3.9 percent in rural and 7.0 percent in urban areas, and underemployment (the full-time equivalents of individuals working less than full time) rates of 14.8 percent for rural and 4.2 percent for urban areas.[3] Applying these percentages to Kilimanjaro District and Moshi town suggests as crude figures some 7,400 unemployed and 26,750 underemployed for the district as a whole. Because in the design of this survey people actually unemployed but who had not previously had work, or who were not actively seeking work, were more likely to be left uncounted, these figures probably seriously underestimate the actual number of people who considered themselves unemployed and looking for work, especially in the town. In summary, then, there are certainly a large number of people actively looking for jobs in Kilimanjaro, and an even larger number who would seek jobs if they thought salaried employment were more readily available.

Thus, a severe shortage of land, successive years of poor return on the major cash crop, and an annual output of more than 10,000 young people from an education system oriented toward salaried employment create a high rate of unemployment and underemployment in Kilimanjaro. The inability to create jobs quickly enough to meet the demand for them is recognized by local political leaders, who cite unemployment as one of the most important local problems and who recognize that other problems they mention, theft and prostitution, for example, are related to unemployment. But the difficulties in obtaining accurate statistics and a narrow view of possible solutions combine with the unwillingness of any individual or institution to assume major responsibility for dealing with this problem to produce a disjointed and largely ineffectual reaction to the widespread demand for jobs.

The Actors

Although Kilimanjaro political leaders are almost unanimous in their agreement that the shortage of jobs is a critical problem, there is little coordinated or direct action to deal with it. Most local leaders regard construction of additional factories by the central government as the only viable solution to unemployment. Even those who recognize the cycle—that low coffee prices make enterprises dependent on the local market unable to expand and thus unable to create new jobs—confess they do not see anything they can do about it.

The Regional Labour Office registered about six hundred people each month looking for employment during 1968–69, and labor officers indicated there were many more looking for employment on their own. Labor officers did not consider it their responsibility to be concerned with the general employment situation in Kilimanjaro, and were both unable to provide statistics on employment and unfamiliar with major reports and studies, such as the

3. Robert S. Ray, *Labour Force Survey of Tanzania*, mimeographed (Dar es Salaam, January 1966). See pp. 60ff for Ray's discussion of unemployment and underemployment, and p. 83, Table 5.8: Unemployment Rates and Underemployment.

Politics of Jobs

Labour Force Survey of Tanzania and the annual *Survey of Employment and Earnings*. Nor did they consider themselves responsible for dealing with unemployment: their only efforts to assist job-seekers were to request, occasionally, work from local employers, and they stressed that the pressure on jobs makes that an unrewarding approach. And when new factories are opened in Kilimanjaro, job-seekers come from as far as Uganda and southern Tanzania. Some local employers did use the Labour Office when hiring: an employer who needed temporary labor might hire by sending a lorry to collect men sitting around the Labour Office, and the Moshi Town Council sometimes requested names of individuals with specific skills needed. But in general, labor officers did not consider unemployment in Kilimanjaro as serious as in other areas of Tanzania where land is less fertile and agriculture able to support fewer people. They did not regard unemployment as a problem about which they could do very much, nor did they consider the large number of individuals who unsuccessfully sought work a social, as opposed to simply a labor, problem. To explain and justify their inability to do anything to remedy the unemployment situation, labor officers emphasized that other institutions, including the local councils, NUTA, TANU, TYL, and UWT, were also unable to do anything about unemployment.

The second major institution concerned with the problems of work and workers, NUTA, also offered little assistance to people seeking jobs. Official NUTA policy, at least as interpreted and implemented in Kilimanjaro, was that in general the unemployed were a problem for the Labour Office, or someone else, but not NUTA. NUTA assumed responsibility only for NUTA members, which meant individuals who had had jobs, and even for them, NUTA offered assistance in finding jobs only in unusual cases. For example, some effort was made to find jobs for agricultural employees laid off because of the contraction of the sisal industry, but that effort was largely unsuccessful because sisal workers, interested in half-day jobs to leave time for work in their own fields, were largely reluctant to move into industrial employment. Since NUTA had no institutionalized means of assisting individuals looking for work, when NUTA officials were willing to help, they relied on informal contacts with employers. While they could not adequately service the twenty-five to thirty people who came to NUTA each day looking for work, for a few members, or relatives or friends of members, NUTA officials were successful in finding employment. Like the Labour Office, NUTA did not regard unemployment as its problem, except for occasional cases of NUTA members laid off previous jobs and occasional assistance to friends and relatives of NUTA members. Nor did NUTA consider the existence of massive unemployment, which it recognized, a social problem. While it may be common for trade unions to limit their concerns to the immediate and work-place interests of their members, it is clear that in Tanzania NUTA, perceived by TANU leaders as one of the main pillars on which the party stands, is expected to have a broader view of the needs of workers and the society in general. According to NUTA rules, for example, no more than 50 percent of income is to be spent on administration, leaving half the organization's income to be spent for social services or invested; a NUTA-operated Workers Development Corporation has been established to invest union funds in development projects.[4] Yet NUTA officials in Kilimanjaro insisted that unemployment was not their concern.

Nor did the Moshi Town Council assume any responsibility in dealing with the shortage of jobs. Although both councillors and Council officers were aware of the problem (an advertisement announcing six posts in the town fire brigade, for example, brought six hundred responses, and the Regional Land Officer, a nominated councillor, reported that construction in town, and thus related employment, had dropped by 50 percent), the Council did not formally consider the creation of jobs in the formulation, definition, and implementation of its plans and programs. The Kilimanjaro District Council began an ambitious and at least initially successful program to provide training in the use of hand tools. But while both councils recognized the pressure of unemployment created by land shortage, low coffee prices, and the massive annual primary school output, both Councils, forced to expend most of their income on education, social services, and salaries, had little money to commit to dealing with this problem. In fact they concentrated their efforts on assisting individuals to settle in other parts of Tanzania and on training programs reaching a few people at best. Neither council considered the creation of jobs—as opposed to the provision of training—a top priority or incorporated the creation of jobs in an overall strategy to deal with these problems.

Thus, none of the formal institutions that might be expected to assume responsibility and exercise local initiative in dealing in a comprehensive way with the shortage of jobs in fact assumed that responsibility or exercised that initiative. There were some efforts by private institutions to deal with this problem, but none has thus far had noticeable success. The YMCA operates a farm training school, designed to take Standard VII school-leavers and equip them to be modern farmers, able to set an example and lead other farmers in their communities. But difficulties in administration, inability to secure places for farm school graduates in government settlement schemes, and confusion over the extent of government participation in the management of the school have meant that the first graduates have returned home to the very plots they knew were too small to support them and their families before they went off to school, with an unfulfilled expectation of prosperity and prestige as a result of their training. The Catholic mission operates a typing and secretarial course, but the graduates of the six-month course are not sufficiently skilled to emerge successful in the tight competition for office positions. They too must return home, their expectations unfulfilled. A crafts training program is planned, to be managed by the Catholic mission and supported by the Town Council, but it is not at all clear that the young men who will complete this six-month car-

4. Tordoff, *Government and Politics in Tanzania,* Chapter 5.

pentry course will be able to find jobs. A more sophisticated plan, organized by two Kilimanjaro Members of Parliament, to train girls to manufacture children's clothing using remnants from Tanzania's textile factories would train fewer than twenty girls annually. Although more than a year had elapsed since the plan was announced, nothing concrete had been established by the end of 1969. A committee on unemployment, organized among local notables by these same two MPs, in effect ceased to function almost as soon as it was constituted. As in the public sector, private institutions considered unemployment someone else's problem, and individual attempts to deal with it were not incorporated into a coordinated plan.

Thus, a picture emerges of wide agreement that shortage of jobs is a serious problem, institutions unwilling to assume prime responsibility for dealing with it, and individual efforts that are spasmodic, uncoordinated, and often unproductive. What responses there are focus on training, rather than creating jobs, and rely on informal networks rather than institutionalized relationships.

Other than NUTA, none of the TANU auxiliaries played a substantial role in dealing with the shortage of jobs. By encouraging women to go into business, and by providing sewing instruction for a small group of girls in Moshi, the UWT did assist some women to find productive employment. But in general these efforts were not directed toward alleviating the problems of those seeking jobs, but functioned rather to encourage some women who would not normally be seeking jobs, and who thus would not normally be considered unemployed, to seek remunerative work. As has already been mentioned, TYL in 1969 turned its attention toward schools and away from school-leavers.

The local TANU organization itself provided a form of job referral service, and in doing so may have assisted more people in getting jobs than all of the other institutions combined. Individuals seeking work could come to the local TANU office and obtain a letter from the TANU secretary asking the NUTA or Labour officers, or an employer, to assist the individual. Although NUTA and Labour officers and employers insisted they treated all applicants equally, it is clear that an individual who could produce a letter from the TANU office did have a slight advantage over other applicants.

Finally, one might look to the Regional and District Development Committees to initiate a coordinated attack on this problem. The Development Committees provide a framework within which officials from the government technical departments meet with local party and council leaders to propose, consider, and implement development plans. The combination of problems—land shortage, exacerbated by low prices for the major cash crop and coupled with an output of over 10,000 school pupils a year—clearly demands a coordinated approach. The reaction of local political leaders, and of the Development Committees, to this combination of problems, however, has been to focus on relocating Kilimanjaro residents in other areas of Tanzania. After extensive surveys of available areas, a comprehensive plan was begun in 1969 to move two thousand people from Kilimanjaro to Mwese, near Mpanda in western

Tanzania. Over eight hundred people had been moved by the end of 1969; they were to be supported by the government until the first harvest, at which time it was expected that their success would enable them to bring their families to join them and would encourage others to migrate, thus relieving the pressure in Kilimanjaro. The functioning of the Development Committees will be discussed in more detail in the next chapter, but for our purposes here it suffices to note that the concentration of efforts on this response to the combination of overpopulation, low prices, and unemployment has the effect of diverting attention from other, and perhaps more immediately productive efforts. In fact, a comprehensive and detailed report on development prospects for the region went virtually unnoticed.[5] This report stressed more efficient use of manpower in agriculture, expansion of industries servicing agriculture and facilitating food consumption, and industrialization based on the expansion of existing technology and capabilities. It also criticized the Regional Development Committee view that pressure on the agricultural resources of Kilimanjaro should be remedied by settling some of the population on new agricultural lands:

> This view ignores the structural changes which agricultural development promotes. A more technical analysis of the situation is that there is insufficient division of labour in the area, and that human resources now in agriculture should be moved into non-agricultural pursuits. This programme of specialization of labour needs to be accompanied by a programme of diversification in the use of land now under coffee cultivation. The returns from capital expenditure on improving the quality of the human resource and making more economic use of existing agricultural land are likely to outweigh the returns from bringing new land under cultivation.[6]

Although this report emphasized that the economy of northern Tanzania had reached a take-off point that would enable it to alleviate the pressures of overpopulation and unemployment, and included detailed recommendations for achieving these objectives, only a few local officials, most of whom said they were unable to do anything about unemployment, were aware of the report. Only one had actually read it. The Development Committees primarily concerned themselves with relocating people elsewhere and did not attempt to deal with these problems by developing the local economy.

Nepotism and corruption compounded the problems of the shortage of jobs in Kilimanjaro. It was widely understood that a job applicant must have a "cousin" in the plant or be friendly with the personnel manager in order to

5. See Max B. Ifill, "Perspectives for Regional Economic Planning in Kilimanjaro Region," mimeographed (Dar es Salaam, 1969). This comprehensive report on development in Kilimanjaro Region was prepared for the Ministry of Economic Affairs and Development Planning during the formulation of the Tanzania Second Five-Year Plan.

6. Ibid., p. 6.

obtain employment. Preference for relatives, friends, and people from the same local area was common in hiring. Common as well was low-level corruption: a "gift," usually money but occasionally beer, a goat, or other consideration, to the manager as a prerequisite to employment. In one local factory the payoff was so well organized that job applicants, informed by clerks that they should not come empty-handed, presented their "gifts" to a taxi driver intermediary before appearing in person. In another plant which employed women, only young, pretty, and willing girls were employed. In addition to this petty corruption in the employment process, employers took advantage of the demand for jobs by retaining new employees on temporary terms for extended periods, which meant that they received neither the full salary nor the welfare benefits of regular employment and that they could be easily dismissed if they complained. Not only private owners, but also the managers of publicly owned plants, perhaps interested in showing increased profits by holding down the total wage bill, behaved similarly. And these practices, which are common in many countries and which have certainly been noted elsewhere in Africa, flourish in Tanzania, despite a monolithic trade union structure presumably able to apply the power and sanctions of both the government and the single party.[7] Most local political figures in Kilimanjaro charged that NUTA and Labour Office officials participated in the payoff. But even were that wholly untrue, the importance of his job to an individual makes him unwilling to jeopardize it: he is ready to go into debt and prepared to participate in the corruption in order to obtain a job, and willing to work under illegal conditions in order to keep it. Jobs are so scarce, and the formal institutions so unresponsive to complaints of exploitation, that individuals are not willing to risk their jobs to complain. In Kilimanjaro at least, where the government owns an important or controlling interest in many of the large factories, this was no less true in publicly owned than in privately owned plants.

In Kilimanjaro, NUTA has proved so unresponsive to workers' complaints about these and other practices that the local TANU organization itself has absorbed some of NUTA's trade union functions. Especially in cases of alleged corruption and complaints against small urban employers, many workers with grievances sought assistance at the TANU, rather than NUTA, office, and TANU officials usually dealt with the complaints directly:

> . . . NUTA cannot do anything and just sends [the complainant] to TANU anyhow. There is no point in sending him to NUTA—that just makes him angry by sending him on pointless trips all over town.

---

7. In fact, the incorporation of NUTA within the TANU structure and the reduction of its operating autonomy in order to prevent the emergence of a competing power base have clearly hampered its ability to defend workers' interests. See Tordoff, *Government and Politics in Tanzania,* especially pp. 152–53. The NUTA-TANU relationship is discussed in more detail in Chapter 10.

In this regard, it is important to note once again the manner in which the local TANU organization functions to expedite action within local institutions without seeking or bringing about major change. Individuals could utilize TANU to improve their chances of getting and retaining jobs, but TANU did not provide the major initiative in dealing with the problems—either the large problem of unemployment or the small one of bribes to get jobs—of which its official indicated they were aware. In this way, TANU served individuals who did not have "cousins," and absorbed the responsibilities of other institutions people found unresponsive.

Conclusions

We have briefly surveyed the shortage of jobs in Kilimanjaro and the local responses to that shortage. Local managers continue to be able to take advantage of their economic power and the scarcity of jobs to exploit employees and, perhaps, public institutions as well. Attempts to deal with unemployment have made little use of public power and formal institutions, but have relied instead on informal networks so that traditional relationships continued to play a critical role in what is usually considered an index of modernity—salaried employment. The recommendations of the central government's planning adviser, suggesting a locally based strategy to deal with overpopulation and unemployment, have neither been adopted nor even carefully examined locally and little has been done about them. Although it was recognized by most local leaders as a serious problem, unemployment and its ramifications for planned development in an agricultural society have at best been only poorly understood. Local responses to this problem, both public and private, except for modest programs to train and a substantial effort to relocate people, have not thus far been characterized by concerted, direct action.

Two observations are important here. First, although local resources and expertise for dealing with unemployment are sorely limited, and although any general strategy to deal with unemployment must be nationwide in its focus, Tanzania's planners did conclude that local action could have major payoffs in dealing with this problem. A major role for the local-level development committees could be the coordination of efforts and resources to deal with unemployment. The increasing unemployment is rendered even more serious by the rapid expansion of the public sector, which has thus far proved no more successful in dealing with this problem than has the private sector. Indeed, recent evidence suggests that the nationalization of expensive housing has been accompanied by a contraction in the construction industry, a significant source of employment in this prosperous local area.

Second, the rapidly expanding numbers of young people seeking salaried employment and not finding it are not effectively represented by either governmental or party institutions. For some job-seekers and workers TANU does provide assistance, expedite requests and applications, and attempt to deal with grievances. It is recognized as legitimate, and it is trusted. But in general, the response of the local TANU organization has proved reactive, not innovative. A large pool of unemployed, relatively well educated in Tanzanian terms, who see few local solutions, who see restraints on action by local entrepreneurs, and who see little substantial action by public institutions is a potential source for serious political unrest.

5

Issues in Moshi

Introduction

The studies of the conflict over key issues have served to introduce local politics in Kilimanjaro. To complement the insights of these issue-area studies, this chapter will take a more detailed look at the formal institutions of local government in Moshi. First, however, a word about the selection of issue-areas is in order. Before moving on to the study of the major actors in the local political system, it is appropriate as well to comment on some of the limitations of the issue-area perspective.

The criteria for the issue-areas selected were: (1) they had to involve key, rather than routine, decisions—challenges to the fundamental bases and structures of authority; (2) they had to be issues that clearly concerned and excited both local leaders and, at least in part, substantial segments of the local population; and (3), since the study is concerned with the politics of Moshi, issues had to be town-centered and to culminate in decisions essentially within reach of the local political system.

Especially because of the demand that the decisions be local in nature, few issue-areas in Kilimanjaro met all these criteria, and in fact those studied were almost the only ones available. Unlike education, health (hospitals, rural medical stations, medicine) has been defined locally as a primarily technical issue, with major decisions reserved for technical experts. That is, although of course there was local conflict over the location of new medical installations and over the allocations of resources, in general the health officers had a much more determinative say in ultimate decisions than did the education officers. In addition, despite the large sums spent by the local councils for health services, the councils were much less free to make their own decisions about those allocations than they were in regard to educational expenditures. Likewise, decisions about communications, including the roads so vital to farmers with cash crops to transport to town, and the provision of water supplies were largely monopolized by technical officials and were largely made, following the advice of ministry experts, in Dar es Salaam. In fact, the local Members of Parliament and other leaders with contacts in the capital devoted extensive efforts to influencing allocations of this sort—the location of rural dispensaries, the construction of roads, and the provision of water. But they were not issues largely debated and decided locally. Partly, this different treatment of ostensibly similar issues stems from central government initiatives. Both the colonial administration and the independent Tanzanian government have made primary education and liquor licensing local responsibilities. Partly, it is the case that local resources can be used to build schools, and even to staff them, while that is not true for hospitals. Partly, this different treatment stems from the fact that local interest groups, with available resources and a local power base, have mobilized around these issues. Local interests have simply not organized around the provision of roads. Partly it reflects the widespread acceptance that health and communications are technical matters. Long after key administrative positions in education, for example, were localized, Tanzania continues to rely on foreign expertise for water supply (the substantial feats of hydraulic engineering in Kilimanjaro notwithstanding). Partly, as well, it is the critical role of education in individual achievement and of liquor licensing in the local economy that makes them so hotly contested locally.

The study of community power through the prism of the participants and outcomes in selected local conflicts, which owes much to the work of Robert Dahl,[1] provides a tool with which to attempt to sort out the intricacies of power and influence in a local setting. It has outlined some of the major peaks of the Kilimanjaro political landscape.

The major criticisms of this approach—that it fails to distinguish routine from key decisions, that it takes little account of nongovernmental decision-making, and that it is unable to assess the power exercised in narrowing the range of issues that are considered by formal decision-makers—have been persuasively presented elsewhere.[2] The issue-areas selected for this study, and the analyses of those issue-areas, have been informed by these criticisms of that approach. Decisions in the issue-areas selected are key, not routine, in that each involves a fundamental challenge to the basis and organization of authority. In all three, substantial attention was devoted to nongovernmental decision-making, precisely because nongovernmental decision-making was clearly a significant element in the allocation of resources at the local level in these issue-areas. And in all three the analysis has dealt with the ability of some groups in Moshi to pursue their own goals by preventing some issues from ever coming to a formal decision and with the ways in which the mobilization of bias operates

1. The basic work, Robert Dahl's study of New Haven, Connecticut, is *Who Governs?* (New Haven, Conn.: Yale University Press, 1961).

2. For a forceful critique of this approach, see Peter Bachrach and Morton S. Baratz, *Power and Poverty,* Part One; and Todd Gitlin, "Local Pluralism as Theory and Ideology," *Studies on the Left* 5, no. 3 (1965): 21–45. Both studies contain useful bibliographies on the pluralist approach to the study of community power. See also Nelson W. Polsby, "How to Study Community Power: the Pluralist Alternative," *Journal of Politics* 22, no. 3 (August 1960): 474–84; and Polsby, *Community Power and Political Theory* (New Haven, Conn.: Yale University Press, 1963).

locally: "the dominant values and the political myths, rituals, and institutions which tend to favor the vested interests of one or more groups, relative to others."[3] The missions, for example, were successful in maintaining their dominant role in primary education by using the prevailing demand for education to prevent their initiatives from coming to formal decisions where they might be defeated. Likewise, in liquor licensing, the extent of the involvement in the liquor trade worked to benefit those who were involved by opposing clear decisions to reduce it. And even in regard to jobs, the workers and the unemployed remained relatively powerless to the degree they were unable to bring pressure to bear on formal institutions to accept basic responsibility for dealing with their problems.

Although it is not the purpose here to provide an extensive critique of this approach, several other problems with it need to be mentioned to indicate its limited usefulness for the study of local politics in Moshi. The study of decision-making focuses attention on the process by which legislation and rules are created, both for the operational ease of execution of the study and because of the commonly held notion that popular demands are funneled into rule-making institutions and that bureaucracies enforce impartially the rules made. But in so doing, it diverts attention from the application of the legislation and the enforcement of the rules. Not only is most formal rule-making distant from the mass of the rural population in Tanzania, but also the links that do connect the up-country populace with the rule-making process are few and fragile and, as a result, function only intermittently. To concentrate on legislation and rule-making is to assume that the important political processes are those that characterize the functioning of formal rule-making institutions and those that in some way associate nonelites with specific legislation and rules. To concentrate on legislation and rules is surely to overlook much of what politics is all about in up-country Tanzania. Much of what people are interested in has to do with enforcement and not legislation. Demands for a place in secondary school, or a waiver in licensing requirements, or a delay in the implementation of an eviction, are pressed on the political system when distant rule-making is about to be translated into immediate action by local officials. Clearly, ". . . the nature of most political demands in transitional nations is such that they are simply not amenable to the legislative process."[4]

3. The term "mobilization of bias" is taken from E. E. Schattschneider, *The Semisovereign People* (New York: Holt, Rinehart and Winston, 1960), p. 71: "All forms of political organization have a bias in favor of the exploitation of some kinds of conflict and the suppression of others because *organization is the mobilization of bias* [original emphasis]. Some issues are organized into politics while others are organized out." This term is used here following Bachrach and Baratz, *Power and Poverty,* p. 43.

4. James C. Scott, "Corruption, Machine Politics, and Political Change," *APSR* 63, no. 4 (December 1969): 1142–43. Scott's perceptive analysis supports the argument made here that to concentrate on legislation is to exclude from consideration much of the essence of politics in Tanzania.

Another problem with this approach is its incorporation of the Weberian notion of bureaucracies and bureaucrats that stresses the impersonality of their operations. Although the norms of impersonality and objective, rational decision-making have been accepted by most Tanzanian officials, their behavior, because of the imperatives of their responsibilities, rarely conforms to those norms. As has already been mentioned, most bureaucrats, and politicians as well, are still heavily influenced by the social obligations of their local society.[5] But beyond that, these norms are to a large extent inappropriate where officials are charged with managing the extent and direction of economic and political change. Tanzanian civil servants who are responsible for using their discretionary power to achieve a set of both general and specific goals tangential to usual bureaucratic concerns must reject the insulation demanded of bureaucracies by these norms. Instead, they must move out into the community as leaders to develop the formal and informal contacts necessary to coordinate the flow of resources to achieve these goals.[6]

Still another problem is the equilibrium point implicitly assumed in most decision-making studies, the set of structures and relationships defined as normal, through which specific patterns are examined. In Tanzania, formal governmental institutions have yet to become stable because they are still being built. The modification of institutions is both frequent and often self-conscious. The rapidity of change precludes the distribution of power around a stable point of equilibrium.[7] And certainly it is a conflict theory, and not the equilibrium orientation that is central to the functionalist approach, that underlies the analysis offered here.[8]

Decision-making studies also may unnecessarily narrow the boundaries of the relevant political arena. Surely several of the outcomes in local conflicts noted in the preceding chapters would make little sense without attention to the intrusion of national politics and national influence into the local political system and the lack of clarity in the delineation of national versus local government powers and responsibilities.

Finally, many decision-making studies embody a notion of government inappropriate to the Tanzanian context. The depiction of government as a neutral arbiter, as the manager of conflicts, as the registrar of political outcomes, distorts the theoretical framework where the government has self-consciously

5. The impact of these obligations on decision-makers in the liquor-licensing process has been noted. For a humorous and moving treatment of this pattern, see Chinua Achebe, *A Man of the People* (London: Heinemann, 1966).

6. The conception of bureaucracy as an institution for the impartial implementation of policy, and the reliance on bureaucracy to manage change, will be considered more fully in Chapter 11.

7. Seymour J. Mandelbaum makes this point for New York in the nineteenth century in *Boss Tweed's New York* (New York: Wiley, 1965), p. 4.

8. On functionalism as a conscious alternative to conflict theory, see W. G. Runciman, *Social Science and Political Theory* (Cambridge: Cambridge University Press, 1965), especially Chapter 6.

adopted a set of goals toward which it is working to move the society. This notion of government neutrality, presented both analytically and normatively in decision-making studies, makes it difficult to deal with the ways in which government always serves some interests more than others, and is inapplicable and misleading in Tanzania, where goals, albeit at times vague and contradictory, are expressed explicitly.

One important supplement to the issue-area studies, then, is to examine in more detail the formal institutions of local government in Moshi. It is necessary to proceed beyond the perspectives that were drawn from the issue-area studies. At the same time, lest the examination of those structures be focused on formal prescriptions to the exclusion of political behavior, it is essential that this analysis of these institutions, the Moshi Town Council and the development committees, be informed by the insights of those issue-area studies.

Issues in Moshi: Local Government

The Moshi Town Council is a largely representative body, modeled after British local government, charged with governing the town of Moshi.[9] In 1968–69 it was composed of nineteen councillors elected to represent the six town wards and nine councillors nominated (appointed) by the President, and was chaired by the chairman of the TANU urban district. Subventions from the central government accounted for approximately 35 percent of Council revenue (see Table 5.1), and expenditures on public health and education comprised more than half of all funds spent (see Table 5.2). Urban councils in Tanzania follow a chain of authority different from that of the more numerous district councils, and supervisory power over their activities, especially control over their finances, is vested not in the office of the local Regional Commissioner, but in the Ministry responsible for local government in Dar es Salaam.

The Moshi Town Council is organized into six committees, in which most of the substantive work of the Council is done. Committee decisions are usually approved with little or no discussion by the full Council, although of course on occasion matters decided in committee are debated in full again at a meeting of the entire Council. The Finance Committee, which is chaired by the town chairman, and which includes the chairmen of all of the other committees, functions as the Council Executive Committee. The fact that it normally meets monthly, while other committees and the full Council usually meet four times a year, together with its control over funds, gives this committee a key role in Council decision-making.

The chief administrative officer of the Town Council is the Town Clerk. The term *Clerk* is rather a misnomer, since the Town Clerk, with his cabinet of department heads, has the responsibility, power, and authority of a town manager, and is considered by most local political figures to be more powerful

9. For an overview of local government in Tanzania, see William Tordoff, *Government and Politics in Tanzania,* Chapter 4; and Stanley Dryden, *Local Administration in Tanzania* (Nairobi: EAPH, 1968), especially Chapter 7.

Table 5.1. Moshi Town Council Principal Sources of Revenue,
as Percentage of Total Revenue, 1968

Licenses and permits	
Liquor	7.7[a]
Other	5.8
Market dues and rent	7.1
Central government subventions	
Vehicle licenses, health, salaries	20.0
Schools	15.9
Site rates and urban house tax	26.2
Other	17.3
	100.0

Source: Moshi Town Council Financial Statement, 1968.

[a] That is, Liquor License fees provided 7.7% of the Shs. 3,227,338.54 total revenue
in 1968.

Table 5.2. Moshi Town Council Expenditures, by Committee, 1963–69 (in percentages)

Committee	1963	1964	1965	1966	1967	1968	1969[a]
Public Health[b]	39.1	31.7	33.3	33.3	37.6	37.5	34.1
Communications and Buildings[c]	33.0	25.9	25.8	24.6	23.8	18.4	18.7
Urban Planning	–	–	–	–	–	3.6	3.3
Finance[d]	22.3	20.7	17.3	16.8	14.1	16.5	12.3
Education	–	20.7	22.3	20.5	20.1	20.4	17.5
Industrial Development	–	–	–	–	–	0.0	0.1
Total recurrent expenditures	94.4	99.1	98.7	95.2	95.6	96.4	86.0
Capital expenditures	5.7	0.7	1.3	5.5	4.3	3.6	14.4
Total expenditures	100.1	99.8	100.0	100.7	99.9	100.0	100.4

Source: Annual Financial Statements, Moshi Town Council.

[a] Figures for 1969 are estimates. The Minister responsible for local government refused
a request to increase the site rate and ordered the budget reduced; most capital expenditures were subsequently eliminated in order to secure approval of the 1969 budget.

[b] In 1968 this became the Public Health and Markets Committee.

[c] This committee, established in 1968, combined the former Buildings and Works and
Highways Committees; the figures for 1963 to 1967 are the combined totals for these
two committees.

[d] The expenditures for the Finance Committee include the salaries for the principal
Council employees.

and influential than the elected town chairman. For the individual citizen, it is the Town Clerk who has access to state power and public funds, and it is he who will determine the impact of governmental decisions. The Town Clerk and all senior town officials are appointed by the Tanzania Local Government Service Commission, and may be posted and transferred throughout the country without reference to the Moshi Town Council. The unification of local government service in Tanzania provides the central government a means for making a rational distribution of scarce skilled manpower and offers local government civil servants possibilities of advancement they would not have if they were limited to service with a single council. But it also means that local councils must be dependent on officers who are not chosen locally, and who, as a result, are often not very responsive to the demands of the local situation in which they are serving. That town officials are often more responsive to Ministry than to Council reactions is a source of considerable discontent among Moshi councillors.

To what extent, then, is the Moshi Town Council a locus for authoritative allocations and to what extent does it have a monopoly on decision-making in the local arena?

That Council decisions are constrained by Ministry action has already been noted. For example, although the Moshi Town Council is constituted by statute as a Local Education Authority, most of the major allocations for education are limited by the education plan prepared by the Ministry of Education, by policies and rules set at the center, and by the control on expenditures exercised by the local education officers. The requirement that the Town Council budget be approved by the Ministry responsible for local government makes the Council subject to both policy and executive decisions that are largely beyond its reach. A national policy decision to restructure the financing of local councils in 1969, for example, led to a rejection of the request of the Moshi Town Council to increase the site rate (a tax on the unimproved value of land in town that is the major single source of Council income) in order to embark on an ambitious program of capital development. The complexity of the approval process itself is a further obstacle to local initiative. The annual Council estimates are prepared in October and submitted to the Ministry in November. Ministry comments on the proposed estimates, usually including instructions to reduce expenditures, are often not received by the Council until April. Final approval, after the cuts have been made, was not received in 1969 until October. Most of the year had passed before the Council received final approval for its expenditures. Since the Council is required not to exceed the spending level of the previous year and not to begin capital projects until its estimates have been approved, most of the year is over before expansion can take place and projects can begin. As a result, major projects may take several years from conception to completion, even when they involve tasks as routine as road resurfacing. Ministry control of Council finances has an especially limiting effect on capital (development) expenditures, because they are the most easily cut once the fiscal year has begun.

Thus, the limitations imposed on Council authority by the need to refer major decisions to Dar es Salaam make the Council a legislative and executive agency for only very low-level local issues, such as public sanitation, maintenance of roads and cemeteries, and management of town markets. And in fact the delays in the budgeting process, together with the heavy demands of recurrent expenditures, are major impediments to any development spending at all.

These limitations, coupled with the lack of technical skills among town councillors, ensure that the Town Council itself is not a major source of initiative for change in the local area. With few exceptions, major proposals are made by Council officers, and not councillors, and the form taken by resulting projects is also largely determined by Council officers. For example, in 1968–69 the Town Clerk proposed that the Town Council become involved in the construction of a factory to brew and bottle the local Kilimanjaro beer, *mbege*. After the Council Industrial Development and Finance Committees approved the idea, which had been discussed for many year in Kilimanjaro, the Town Clerk pursued contacts with a major brewing concern in Dar es Salaam and with the Ministry. The Council accepted, largely without comment, the major elements and subsequent changes in the plans, from method of financing to location. Although the project had foundered by the end of 1969, it is clear that the Council was limited to legitimizing proposals by its officers and perhaps exercising a vague and rarely used veto.

The budgeting process—the annual statement of priorities and allocation of resources to specific individuals and groups—is also dominated by Council officers. To obtain specific allocations from the Town Council Moshi residents most often seek out the Town Clerk and other Town officials, rather than their ward councillors. To stress that initiative in most matters lies outside the Council is not to overlook the substantial efforts of those few active councillors who do propose new programs to the Council, nor is it to suggest that this pattern of initiative outside the Council is either dysfunctional or uncommon for elected local government bodies. But it does suggest that the Moshi Town Council is not the major source of authoritative allocations in Moshi and that its power is severely limited by internal and external constraints.

Just as urban councils in Tanzania do not fit into the hierarchy of regional administration and rural local government, so too are urban areas excluded from the chain of development committees that link the rural areas with the politicians and development planners in Dar es Salaam. Urban ward development committees are occasionally mentioned in party statements and Town Council records, but none were functioning in Moshi in 1968–69, and apparently none had ever played a substantial role in Moshi town. Moshi town is not represented in the Kilimanjaro District Development and Planning Committee (DDPC), and does not formally come under the purview of the

Kilimanjaro Regional Development Committee (RDC), though the Moshi chairman and Town Clerk do attend Regional Development Committee meetings. For example, during the preparations for Tanzania's Second Five-Year Plan, a five-year plan for Moshi, drawn up largely by the Town Clerk, was neither submitted to nor debated by the District Development Committee; it was distributed to members of the RDC for their information, but was not discussed by them. Nor are Moshi town projects eligible for support from the Regional Development Fund, and town representatives are not involved in decisions on the aloocation of the Regional Development Fund. Thus, both in the structure of local government in Tanzania and especially in the structure of development planning, Moshi town functions as an island, whose lines of communication to the center are often more direct than those to its rural neighbors. As a result Moshi town, and the Moshi Town Council, are only indirectly involved, at best, in development planning.

Though the Moshi Town Council primarily serves to provide official approval and legitimacy for decisions actually taken by its officers, it does have a limited ability to veto proposals placed before it. It also serves at times as a buffer between the urban population and its officers, absorbing criticism of their actions, albeit rarely able to alter them substantially. Since the Council is both responsible for administering some central government programs and limited by the central government in its own action, it occasionally serves as a lightning rod for the central government, absorbing criticism directed toward it. For example, many individuals unhappy with educational decisions direct their criticisms to the Town Council even though the Council's range of alternatives is severely limited by government action. We have also found that the Moshi Town Council does not normally function as a local legislature with the power to make significant rules for the town, and that the Council, although it is largely elected, is at times unresponsive to its electorate and only occasionally the prime arena for political conflict, because it is constrained by the central government and dependent on its officers.

Perhaps an example will help sharpen this picture of the behavior of the Moshi Town Council. In 1969 the Council decided that sidewalks in the commercial areas of town had become dirty and unsightly, and decided to eliminate commercial use of the sidewalks. The sidewalks in Moshi had long been used by merchants to display their wares, ranging from cloth to pots and pans to beds and mattresses, and by artisans—tailors, shoemakers, watch repairers—unable to afford to rent places of their own. The decision to clear the sidewalks originated in a proposal by the assistant to the Regional Commissioner who represented him (as a nominated councillor) in the Council. It was approved by the Urban Planning Committee, and was implemented by Council officers even before it was presented to the full Council. When the committee resolution became known around town, but before it had been implemented, many of the tailors went, as a group, to the Town Clerk, several town councillors, the Area Commissioner, the Regional Commissioner, and to the TANU office to complain that they would be forced out of business. On the one hand, the tailors were paying exorbitant fees to local merchants for storing their sewing machines overnight and thus could ultimately benefit from pressure to make other arrangements. But on the other hand, much of their trade depended on contact with customers as they left the shops where they purchased cloth. As these grievances were being presented the decision was announced publicly, and town officers, accompanied by police, made a sweep of the sidewalks, confiscating goods found displayed and chasing off artisans.[10] Several lengthy, and often heated, meetings ensued. The Town Clerk agreed to suspend enforcement of the committee resolution for the tailors—but not for other artisans—to permit the TANU office to work with them to make other arrangements. Six months later a projected cooperative of tailors had not yet been formed (an earlier tailors cooperative had continuing trouble surviving economically, despite preferential treatment in contract bidding from government units), and the tailors were still on the sidewalks.

The point of this lengthy excursion is that it is a typical, and clear, example of the Moshi Town Council role in those low-level local decisions it is charged to make. The original initiative was by a government officer serving as a nominated councillor. The decision was made in a Council committee and subject to Council review only after it had been implemented. The Town Clerk, who could have enforced a long-standing law without having a Council committee baptize it, was able to enforce the decision selectively, without formal Council authorization to do so. And at least for a period following the decision, it was not enforced on one of the groups against whom it was directed.

In summary, there is in Moshi a council which is roughly two-thirds elected and one-third appointed, with an organizational pattern that ensures that most Council decisions are made in committee rather than in the full Council, a set of centrally appointed officers responsive to Dar es Salaam, as well as to the Moshi Town Council, and a limited range of Council authority that is subject to extensive review and control by the center. The Council does not normally function as a local legislature with the power to make significant rules for the town. And although it is largely elected, because it is constrained by the central government and dependent on its officers, it is at times unresponsive to its electorate and only occasionally the prime arena for political conflict.

---

10. It should be noted that this decision represented an indirect form of rule-making by the Urban Planning Committee. Although the Committee resolved to clear the sidewalks, in legal terms a long-standing law that required Council permission to use the public sidewalks was to be enforced. This suggests, of course, that the Town Clerk could have acted on his own, but instead sought Council legitimacy for what was to be an unpopular act.

Development Committees

Another major governmental institution in Kilimanjaro is the chain of development committees, which function at the village, district, and regional levels. Since there were no functioning development committees in Moshi town in 1968–69, and since for development purposes Moshi town was treated as an island, not directly related to its rural hinterland, this analysis will concentrate on the Kilimanjaro District Development and Planning Committee (DDPC) and the Kilimanjaro Regional Development Committee.

Tanzania is firmly committed to planned development, and in 1969 began its second Five-Year Development Plan. Development targets are projected as far as the 1980s. Tanzania has attempted to deal with the problem of reconciling local participation in decision-making with the need for efficient and rational management of national resources by creating a chain of development committees designed to link the rural population with Dar es Salaam decision-makers in planning for development.[11] The district and regional development committees unite in a single institution popularly elected representatives, TANU leaders, representatives from major institutions (cooperatives, trade union), and government administrators and technical experts. In theory, development proposals are to originate at the village level and to be considered first at the district and then at the regional level to assess their importance and feasibility and the availability of resources to support them. Only after careful consideration at each of these levels are they to be submitted to development planners in Dar es Salaam for inclusion in the national development plan. This procedure is designed to maximize popular participation in the planning process and to ensure that the proposals submitted to Dar es Salaam fit into a coordinated local development scheme.[12] In practice, however, the development committees have been serving somewhat different purposes.

The development committees have been hampered by the lack of a clear association between structure and purpose. The Village Development Committees (VDC), for example, designed to facilitate a two-way flow of communication between the government and the mass of the population, have in fact

11. Useful analyses of the philosophy and organization of development planning in Tanzania can be found in the following: Bienen, *Tanzania: Party Transformation,* Part III; Dryden, Chapter 3; Reginald H. Green, "Four African Development Plans: Ghana, Kenya, Nigeria, and Tanzania," *JMAS* 3, no. 2 (August 1965): 249–79; G. K. Helleiner, "Tanzania's Second Plan: Socialism and Self-Reliance," *EAJ* 5, no. 12 (December 1968): 41–50; Goran Hyden, "Planning in Tanzania: Lessons of Experience," *EAJ* 6, no. 10 (October 1969): 13–17; R. Cranford Pratt, "The Administration of Economic Planning in a Newly Independent State: the Tanzania Experience 1963–1966," *Journal of Commonwealth Political Studies* 5, no. 1 (1967): 38–59; and Knud Erik Svendson, "The present stage of economic planning in Tanzania," in *Nation-Building in Tanzania,* ed. A. Rweyemamu (Nairobi:EAPH, 1970), pp. 79–80.

12. See Bienen, *Tanzania: Party Transformation,* p. 323.

Table 5.3. Membership of the Kilimanjaro District Development and Planning
Committee, 1969

Area Commissioner, Chairman	District cooperative officer
District Chairman	District commercial officer
Kilimanjaro District Council Finance Committee (9 members, including Council vice-chairman)	District labour officer
	District health officer
	Water engineer
District rural development officer	District executive officer
District veterinary officer	Area secretary
District probation officer	Representative, Tambarare Cooperative
District building and works officer	Representative, Kilimanjaro Native Cooperative Union
District forestry officer	
District agriculture officer	Representative, NUTA
District policy commander	Representative, UWT
Prisons officer	TANU district executive secretary
District education officer	

Source: Kilimanjaro District Development and Planning Committee. (Note that where
the district representative of a Ministry is specified, that Ministry may not have a district
office in Kilimanjaro, in which case a regional officer attends.)

Note: This list differs slightly from that in Paul D. Collins, "A Preliminary Evaluation
of the Working of the Regional Development Fund," p. 9. Collins notes that the DDPC is
authorized to coopt members.

largely been limited to applying for approval and assistance for self-help
projects, with little two-way flow at all.[13] The link between village and district level development committees is a weak one, and research in 1968 indicated that there was little awareness at the lowest level of the development
committee chain of the Regional Development Fund, a mechanism specifically designed to encourage local initiative and participation.[14]

The structure of the DDPC is an anomalous one, since it is formally a committee of the District Council and yet its chairman and most of its members
are not councillors. (See Table 5.3 for membership of the Kilimanjaro District
Development and Planning Committee.) Since many District Council programs
are officially considered development programs as well, the jurisdiction of the
DDPC is often broader than that of the Council itself. And since the Area
Commissioner and Ministry representatives are included in the DDPC and not
in the Council, many local leaders in Kilimanjaro consider it a more powerful
body. Because of this inclusive membership on both the district and regional

13. For an incisive analysis of the functioning of Tanzania's development committees, see Paul D. Collins, "A Preliminary Evaluation of the Working of the Regional Development Fund," mimeographed (Dar es Salaam, 1969). See p. 11 for comments on Village
Development Committees.

14. Ibid., p. 12.

Table 5.4.   Membership of the Kilimanjaro Regional Development Committee, 1969

Regional Commissioner, chairman	Town Clerk, Moshi
Administrative Secretary	District executive officer, Kilimanjaro
Regional agriculture officer	District Council
Regional commercial officer	District executive officer, Same District
Regional community development officer	Council
Regional cooperative officer	Regional chairman, TANU
Regional education officer	Regional secretary, NUTA
Regional forest officer	Representative, UWT
Regional information officer	Representative, Chamber of Commerce
Regional land officer	Representative, farmers' association
Regional medical officer	Representative, Kilimanjaro Native Co-
Regional engineer	operative Union
Regional mines inspector	Representative, Tambarare Cooperative
Regional police commander	Union
Regional superintendent of prisons	Representative, Vuasu Cooperative
Regional veterinary officer	Union
Regional water engineer	Representative, factories
Regional labour officer	Regional secretary, TAPA
Senior welfare officer	Representative, National Agricultural
Head postmaster	Products Board
Regional accountant	Member, National Executive Committee
Area Commissioner, Moshi	of TANU
Area Commissioner, Same	Members of Parliament

Source: Regional Office, Kilimanjaro Region.

Note: In addition to those listed here, the Chairmen of Kilimanjaro and Same Districts participated as members.

planning committees (see Table 5.4 for the membership of the Regional Development Committee), and because they are more responsive to central direction and control, they often deal with local problems and programs that have little direct relationship to development plans. That is, because they include both popular representative and technical advisers and both government and TANU officials, problems that require coordinated action and problems in which the center is especially interested are brought to the development committees, even though formally those problems may be the direct responsibility of the district council and only indirectly, if at all, related to development. The research in 1968 found that one-fourth of the items discussed by DDPCs in Tanzania dealt with development, while most DDPC time was spent on public festivities, social services, education, school-leavers, famine, and land problems.[15] This was certainly the case in Kilimanjaro, where much of the deliberation of development committees was devoted to relocating Kilimanjaro residents in Mwese and to discussing famine and malnutrition resulting from a poor growing season.

15. Ibid., p. 10.

Issues in Moshi

Although development committee efforts and resources are to be directed only toward development projects—those that will directly increase production, such as seed nurseries or cattle dips—most of the members of the development committees were more concerned with social services, such as schools and clinics. And in fact, if the development committees are to have real power in the allocation of resources locally, they are the logical focus for popular pressure for social services. But the result of the concern with social services is that of the few projects that originate at the bottom of the chain, many are rejected because they are not concerned with development. At the same time there is a continuing effort to divert development resources into social service projects which the District Council is unable to support by itself. The situation was further complicated in Kilimanjaro by the differing views on the nature of development planning held by the key figures on the development committees. The overriding tendency was to consider the development plan a statement of goals, a listing of good ideas that could not be implemented immediately. The effect of this prevalent viewpoint was that the difficult choices involved in establishing priorities and rejecting some projects in favor of others were rarely made by the development committees. The lack of funds available locally for development projects nurtured this attitude that the development plan was a statement of goals and not a working document to be implemented.

The poor articulation of the links between the levels in development planning, and the bureaucratic imperative to avoid responsibility where rules and precedents were not clear, function to nurture a tendency to shift decisions to higher levels and thus to limit local participation in development planning. Each level comes to believe that its proposals are not evaluated fairly at the next level, with the effect that much of its attention is diverted from assessing specific proposals to determining how to protect whatever proposals are passed on. Members of the Kilimanjaro DDPC, for example, felt that they had not received a fair share of regional resources in 1968, and they attributed the large allocation to Pare District to influence by the minister responsible for rural development, whose origin was in Pare District.[16] As a result, when projects for 1969–70 were considered, the major focus of deliberations was the attempt to ensure that Kilimanjaro should receive its share of regional funds. Consequently, although Shs. 1,000,000 were again expected for the Regional Development Fund, Kilimanjaro projects proposed for support by the Fund totaled Shs. 1,300,000. Later, when the Kilimanjaro DDPC was asked to establish priorities for its projects, it agreed to aim for a total of Shs. 800,000 to 900,000. When the District Executive Officer attempted to establish a priority order for these projects, DDPC members insisted on submitting them as a block, fearing that to order them would enable the RDC to reduce them. The refusal to set

16. Of the Shs. 1,000,000 Kilimanjaro Regional Development Fund for 1968–69, Shs. 652,872.65 were allocated to Pare District, and Shs. 302,650.00 to Kilimanjaro District.

priorities at the district level resulted in shifting decision-making to the regional level, thus reducing local participation in the determination of which projects were to be supported and which were not.

This leads to what is, perhaps, the most critical problem in the functioning of the development committees: their dependence on, and as a result their domination by, government officials and technical experts. Although the chain of committees is designed so that projects will originate at the bottom, most projects approved originated in the various ministry offices.[17] In theory, projects should stem from popular initiative at the lowest level, they should be evaluated by the technical advisers, and then they should be assigned priorities by political leaders in coordination with technical advisers. In practice, however, projects originate in Ministry offices, and popular representatives at the local level have little to say about them. It is true that the popular representatives on the development committees (the elected chairman and councillors) do not have the training and skills necessary to evaluate projects on a technical basis, but it is also the case that Ministry officials neither define their role as technical advisers to political leaders nor present their projects in a form suitable for evaluation by the less educated committee members. It was common for Kilimanjaro DDPC meetings to begin by considering several VDC proposals and rejecting them as not related to development (for example a new school). The water engineer then presented his proposals for irrigation projects. Although councillors might object that supplying water to place Y was more urgent than supplying it to place X, they were usually reluctant to challenge Ministry officers, and the Ministry proposal was approved with little or no modification. In another case, a Ministry representative proposed that cattle dips be located in certain areas, elected members of the DDPC argued that they were more needed elsewhere, and the Ministry proposal was approved. The process is identical at the regional level, where popular representatives are even more outnumbered by Ministry officials, and where the RDC has only advisory authority. In 1969, for example, after the Kilimanjaro DDPC approved its five-year plan for 1969 to 1974, the plan was submitted to Ministry officials for their comments (they had of course already been involved in the initial deliberations on plan proposals). At the subsequent meeting of the Regional Development Committee, the Kilimanjaro plan existed in two documents, one as approved by the DDPC and the second as revised and amended by Ministry officials. It was the latter that was formally considered by the RDC. That several of the Ministry officials were expatriates with little knowledge of Swahili, and that communication between the DDPC and Ministry offices was so poor that Ministry comments often were not received in sufficient time to incorporate them into DDPC documents, both served to further the exclusion of popular representatives at the regional level. Allocations of the Regional Development Fund,

17. Collins, "Preliminary Evaluation of the Regional Development Fund," p. 19, found this to be generally true in Tanzania in 1968.

intended specifically as seed money for local projects not included in Ministry plans, are even more dominated by Ministry officials, and are ultimately made by very few officers (see Table 5.5).

Table 5.5.   Membership of the Kilimanjaro Regional Development Subcommittee on the Regional Development Fund, 1969

Regional Commissioner, chairman	Administrative Secretary
Regional agriculture officer	Regional chairman, TANU
Regional building and works officer	Area Commissioner, Moshi
Regional rural development officer	Area Commissioner, Same
Regional cooperative officer	District Executive Officer, Moshi
Regional veterinary officer	District Executive Officer, Same
Regional water engineer	Members of Parliament
Regional commercial officer	District chairman, Moshi [rural]
Regional information officer	District chairman, Same
Regional economic secretary	

Source: Kilimanjaro Regional Office.

Note: This list differs from that of Collins, "A Preliminary Evaluation of the Working of the Regional Development Fund," p. 7, who characterizes this committee as primarily a technical body, and does not include the key political and administrative leaders. In Kilimanjaro at least, although the Regional Development Fund Subcommittee remains dominated by government officers and advisory, several popular representatives have been co-opted.

The development committees, then, are significant governmental institutions in the local area, and their structure and functioning might well be expected to surmount some of the problems that make the local councils relatively impotent. Their membership, including technical advisers, overcomes the lack of skills that hampers the local councils. By including the commissioners and Ministry representatives they have more direct access to the center than do the local councils. And they link the rural population with the central government in a way that local councils cannot. In fact, however, they are dominated and controlled by government officials, and they function largely to legitimize government proposals placed before them. Thus, the decentralization of decision-making power and control over finances by locating them in the development committees does not lead to increased local participation and involvement, but rather to strengthening the hands of government officials at regional and district levels.[18] It is certainly true that a broad range of decisions in development planning must ultimately depend more on technical expertise than on popular sentiment. But it is also the case that Tanzania's party and its leaders have committed themselves to widespread public participation in the planning process. Equally important, because the government's implementation capabilities in up-country Tanzania are limited, popular cooperation and support are necessary to successful plan implementation. Nonetheless, the point here is that

18. Collins, ibid., concludes that this was generally true for Tanzania in 1968.

there was in fact in Kilimanjaro, as in much of Tanzania, little popular participation in the creation and initiation of local projects and little direct popular input into the discussions about resource allocation within the planning framework. It should be noted as well that TANU, as TANU, was little involved in this aspect of development planning. Although of course many of the members of the district and regional development committees were TANU leaders, the local TANU organization played little significant direct role in development planning at those levels.

Conclusions

The chapters of this section have provided an introduction to politics and community power in Moshi by focusing on several key local issues. They have delineated the ability of the missions, the bar owners, and other forces in the community not formally represented in decision-making institutions to marshal economic resources, popular support, key alliances with local officials, and local mores and values to exert strong influence on the local decisions that concern them. And they have stressed the power of government officials not subject to popular elections and the relative impotence of several governmental institutions in the local arena.

This preliminary view suggests a plural power structure, not dominated by a cohesive elite. Only a few individuals are able to influence decisions and determine outcomes in more than one issue-area. In fact, there are several loosely structured groupings, each seeking to mobilize support to deal with the issues with which it is most concerned. This suggests that those few individuals who are most able to influence outcomes—especially the commissioners and the chairmen—depend on informal networks of these factional groupings for their power. This also suggests that what might be a relatively stable pattern of factional alignments organized into networks to support the key leaders must be frequently unbalanced by the transfers of officials into and out of the area. What cannot yet be discerned, however, is the extent to which those who exercise local power are drawn from a narrow and perhaps self-perpetuating stratum of the local populace. This plural system may in fact involve the circulation of a very limited set of elites.

Let us now turn our attention to a second approach to an understanding of local politics in Moshi, a study of its politicians.

PART III / *The Politicians*

6

Political Leadership

The focus on key issues outlined some of the major peaks of the Kilimanjaro political landscape; the brief analysis of local government rendered more distinct the ridges linking those peaks. To explore the flatlands and tortured valleys we turn here to the study of the major participants in the political life of Moshi. Who are they? What are their backgrounds? How do they interact? What is their picture of local politics? To answer these questions, to explore local politics from the perspectives of its major participants, the political leadership of Moshi was interviewed in depth. Political leadership in this context refers simply to those individuals who, either by virtue of some official or unofficial leadership position in the community (to be specified shortly), or by nomination by other leaders as a "powerful" or "influential" person in the community, or by observation a major figure in key local issues, could be expected to play a significant role in determining how resources are allocated and which individuals and groups benefit, and which do not, from the outputs of the local political process.

It is of course a common technique in studies of community power to attempt to locate the local influentials and describe the political process in terms of the characteristics, attitudes, and actions of those individuals. The shortcomings of that method of analysis have been discussed at length elsewhere and need not concern us here.[1] But it should be stressed that in interviewing the political leadership of Moshi, it was not assumed that the individuals interviewed constituted an exclusive elite, that they were cohesive or organized, that they shared goals or even a common value structure, or that they were somehow more powerful, or influential, than other members of the community.[2] Rather, it was expected that the perceptions and observations of the

1. For a critical review of the literature on community power that focuses on local elites, see Polsby, *Community Power and Political Theory;* Bachrach and Baratz, *Power and Poverty,* Chapter 1; and Geraint Parry, *Political Elites* (London: Allen and Unwin, 1969), who stresses the advantages of combining decision-making and elite studies in understanding local politics. For the use of elite studies in African urban settings, see William John Hanna, "Influence and Influentials in Two Urban-Centered African Communities," *Comparative Politics* 2, no. 1 (October 1969): 17–40; and Dick Simpson, "The Political Evolution of Two African Towns" (Ph.D. diss., Indiana University, 1968).

2. For useful distinctions between influence and authority, see Bachrach and

major participants in the local process would be a valuable adjunct to other information available, and that an analysis of the backgrounds and attributes of the political leaders would enhance our ability to make some general comments about the local political process. In addition, these interviews are important tools in understanding local political institutions, such as the Moshi Town Council, and in determining the importance, if any, of association with the party, the government, or other institutions.

Therefore, the bulk of Part II is devoted to more detailed examinations of the Moshi Town Councillors, the Moshi town TANU cell leaders, and the networks of support that form the foundation of the local political process. To explore the dynamics of that process, special attention will be paid to the origins and patterns of recruitment of local leaders, their perceptions of their own power and influence, the linkages among them, and their ability to perpetuate elite status by ensuring that their children have continued access to power and influence. But first, a brief explanation of the methodology used.

Methodology

During the field research in Kilimanjaro in 1968–69, interviews were conducted with 107 political leaders.[3] Because of the small size of the community, and to avoid distortions caused by sampling from such a small number, an attempt was made to interview all individuals who could be considered political leaders. The approach was inclusive: anyone whose role seemed important, even though remotely so, was interviewed. As was noted earlier, the relevant political arena has, throughout this work, been defined by the nature of the issues and the behavior of the participants, rather than by any geographic, administrative, or temporal space. Therefore, although this study is concerned with politics in Moshi, those individuals who seemed to be key in town politics, even though officially they were more concerned with the rural district, or with the regional or national levels, were also interviewed. In this way, 78 individuals were interviewed in depth. The interviews ranged from forty-five minutes to almost six hours, using a format in which questions were open-ended, but always phrased identically to ensure comparability. That is, individuals interviewed were encouraged to discourse at length on their views about local politics—major issues, their own roles, the roles of key individuals and institutions, their understanding of integration and nation-building, and their assessments of party and government activity. In order to cross-check information, they were also asked to comment on the assessments of other leaders. The standardized questions were intended to guide, but not constrain, the conversation. In addition, a random sample of cell leaders, the lowest level of the TANU structure,

Baratz, *Power and Poverty,* Chapter 2, and the comments by William J. Hanna in *Conference on The Government of African Cities, 1968* (Chester, Pa.: Lincoln University, 1968), pp. 89–95.

3. For a more detailed discussion of the methodology, and the complete interview schedules, see the Appendices. The discussion here will be limited to a brief summary.

Political Leadership

covering 20 percent of all cell leaders in town, was interviewed, using an adapted version of the same question schedule. For all of the individuals interviewed, biographical data, ranging from parents' education and occupation through the respondent's own life to the education and occupation of his children (somewhat abbreviated for cell leaders), were also collected.

To compile the list of individuals to be interviewed, leaders were first selected on the basis of positions held. Then, individuals determined by observation to be important participants in the decision-making in the three issue-areas studied were included. Seven other individuals, principally the leaders of the major religious and ethnic communities, whose community role made them important figures in the local political process, were also included. All individuals interviewed (except cell leaders) were asked to name persons they considered powerful or influential. But all of those individuals nominated by 10 percent or more of those asked—indeed a minimum standard for assessing influential-by-reputation—turned out to be included already under one of the other categories. (See Table 6.1 for a breakdown of the 107 individuals interviewed.)

Local tax records were consulted in an attempt to determine the economic leadership of the community, but that proved impossible with the resources available. Records were incomplete, names were confused, many properties were listed to companies and joint holdings, and, more important, taxes were computed on unimproved land values, so that individuals who had small but highly profitable plots (bars, for example) could not be identified from those records. Also, individuals whose income was derived from several sources, or whose income was not reflected in landholdings, or whose income was not fully reported, could not be identified from local tax records. Finally, most of those individuals listed as major property holders, at least by inspection of their names, were either Asian or European and were clearly not directly involved in the local political process. They did not hold major political or other significant community leadership positions, they were not major participants

Table 6.1.   Political Leadership Interviews: Summary by Category

Selection criteria	Number	Percent of total (107)
Position held	69	64[a]
Major participants in one or more issue-areas	36	34
Significant community role	7	7
Reputation (nomination by 10% of leaders)	10	9
Economic leaders	2	2
Cell leaders	29	27

[a] That is, of the 107 individuals interviewed, 64% were holders of key political positions in 1968–69. Since these categories are not mutually exclusive (a holder of a key position might also be named by 10% of the other leaders as an influential person), the sum of these percentages exceeds 100.

in the contested local issues, and for the most part they were not described by leaders as "powerful" or "influential." That is not to say that they were unable to protect, and further, their interests in Moshi, though it is the case that the political power of Europeans and Asians in Tanzania is increasingly limited. It is rather to suggest that their point of intervention in the Tanzanian political system was in general outside Moshi and that only rarely were they directly involved in local political conflicts. Two individuals named by others as major economic leaders were interviewed.

Local TANU and council party invitation lists were consulted to determine the social leadership of the community, but an analysis of those lists revealed that social status in Moshi, by that measure, was a derived category. Only individuals thought by local council and party officers to be politically powerful were accorded the social status of invitation to major parties and celebrations; accordingly, social status was not used as a criterion to supplement the list of interviewees.

Thus, using a very broad and inclusive definition of political leadership, almost all individuals who could be considered political leaders in Moshi town were interviewed.

Overview

In the study of the political leadership of Moshi, it is clear that there is no single, cohesive elite group that rules. Despite the overlaps of institutions and despite the fact that many individuals hold several leadership positions, various factions among the political leaders are continually in conflict. Yet that observation should not be overdrawn. While it is true that what might be termed the aristocratic elite of the colonial period has been displaced by a set of generally younger and more educated individuals, an entrepreneurial and administrative elite, it seems also the case that the new leadership has proved increasingly able to entrench itself. The flow of events in 1968–69, the Arusha Declaration notwithstanding, seemed to render that leadership even more secure in its position of advantage. That is, while the evidence suggests substantial competition for leadership positions, this circulation of elites may well be restricted to a narrow stratum of the Kilimanjaro populace. That stratum, though still defensive in a fluid situation, and though ostensibly circumscribed by the norms of Tanzanian socialism embodied in the Arusha Declaration, nonetheless may be able to control political recruitment sufficiently to exclude the mass of the local populace from effective access to leadership positions.

Thus far the political leadership has been treated largely as an undifferentiated whole. The concern of the succeeding chapters of Part III, therefore, will be to examine separately several of the subsets of the political leadership to explore who they are, where they come from, and how they conceive of the local political process. First, however, it may be useful to make some general comments about the political leadership as a whole.

Perhaps the most striking observation about the local political leadership in Moshi is the extent to which institutions overlap and individuals occupy more than one position. Branch chairmen are also local councillors. TANU leaders hold government positions. And individuals at all levels serve as cell leaders. The distinction between government and party is blurred by the fact that many principal government officials hold positions in TANU. Distinctions of level are also blurred, as branch leaders hold district and regional positions and regional officials serve on the local councils. Even elected versus appointed leadership is not an easy distinction to make, since several individuals hold multiple positions, of which some are elective, some appointive.

This supports and helps explain the finding in the studies of decision-making in key issues that local institutions are multifaceted,[4] and that the local political process is multichanneled: individuals frustrated in their approaches to one institution can pursue their goals through another. Tailors unhappy with a Moshi Town Council decision, for example, could take their grievances to several different individuals, representing ostensibly different political structures, and have them heard. To the extent that positional overlaps maintain TANU influence throughout the spectrum of political activity, this finding also provides some empirical support for the conclusion that the party is unwilling to permit the emergence of politically strong and independent institutions that might provide a foundation for competition with the party. This finding highlights also the difficulty in attempting to separate policy formulation and implementation. Administrators not only have the power, influence, and authority that always accompany responsibility for implementing policies, but many administrators in Moshi have direct access to the policy-making process as well.

Who, then, are the political leaders in Moshi, and what are they like?[5] The political leadership is largely (79 percent) from thirty to fifty-four years old, and almost all leaders are male (90 percent). Most leaders (62 percent) were born locally. Yet although many leaders (40 percent) are long-time local residents (twenty years), because both government and party officials are highly transient, more than one-fifth of the local leaders are newcomers. This transience is reflected in the fact that one-fifth of the political leaders have held their current positions for less than one year, and more than one-quarter have been in their current jobs for less than two years.

The political leadership reflects the general population of Moshi town in its ethnic and religious composition (see Table 6.2). The political leadership is better educated than is the general population (61 percent have had more than a primary education), largely in Christian schools; in addition, almost all

4. Norman N. Miller explores the multifaceted nature of the local party in one area of rural Tanzania in "The Rural African Party: Political Participation in Tanzania," *APSR* 64, no. 2 (June 1970): 548–71.

5. Statistical analysis of interview data was completed at the University of Wisconsin Computing Center, with support from the University of Wisconsin Graduate School Research Committee and the University of Wisconsin Computing Center.

The Politicians

Table 6.2.   Moshi Political Leadership and General Town Population: Ethnicity and
Religion (in Percentages)

	Political leadership	Moshi town
Ethnicity		
Chagga	44[a]	37[b]
Neighboring tribe[c]	12	13
Other African	34	38
Religion		
Christian	60	54
Muslim	35	38
Other world religion	4	4

Source: Moshi Political Leadership Survey (1969) and Tanzania 1967 Population Census. (There is no reason to believe there were significant nonrandom changes in the town population from 1967 to 1969.)

[a] That is, 44% of the political leaders reported their tribe as Chagga.

[b] That is, 37% of all heads of households in Moshi reported their tribe as Chagga.

[c] Neighboring tribes for Moshi town are: Arusha, Masai, Meru, Pare, and Taveta-Teita.

of the political leadership seem able to ensure a much higher level of schooling for their children than is currently the general average for all of Tanzania.

The Moshi political leadership is not dominated by long-time political activists. About half of the Moshi political leadership in 1968–69 reported they had not been active in early nationalist politics (though some 22 percent did indicate they had held leadership positions in the early phases of nationalist agitation), and almost three-fourths came from families that were not politically active. While nearly one-third had joined TANU by 1956 and three-fifths had become TANU members before independence, about one-tenth (13 percent) indicated they had joined TANU since 1965 or were not TANU members in 1968–69.

About one-quarter of the Moshi political leadership was employed by the government in 1968–69, while a tenth had no formal employment. In general the political leadership was widely traveled—fully 70 percent indicated they had spent extended periods in areas of Tanzania other than their places of birth, and half reported they had spent some time outside Tanzania.

The political leadership of Moshi, then, is a fairly heterogeneous lot, largely local in origin and similar to the local populace in ethnic and religious make-up, but clearly differentiated from the local citizenry in what might be called access to modernity, for example, education and travel.

7

Moshi Town Council

Introduction

. . . there must also be an efficient and democratic system of local government, so that our people make their own decisions on the things which affect them directly, and so that they are able to recognize their own control over community decisions and their own responsibilities for carrying them out. Yet this local control has to be organized in such a manner that the nation is united and working together for common needs and for the maximum development of our whole society.[1]

The development of Tanzania cannot be effected from Dar es Salaam; local initiative, local co-ordination of plans, and local democratic control over decisions are also necessary.[2]

The studies of decision-making in three key issue-areas in Moshi, and the brief analysis of structures of local government, have developed a composite picture of the Moshi Town Council: rarely the locus for authoritative decisions on significant issues and most often an institution that functions to legitimize decisions made elsewhere. Much of the detail of that composite view can be delineated by exploring the perspectives and backgrounds of its members and officers. And the image can be further refined by examining the Council in the context of urban local government in Tanzania.

Most of the study of local government in Tanzania has paid careful attention to the British colonial heritage and to constitutional, legislative, and administrative structures and institutions.[3] It is only recently that attention has

1. Julius K. Nyerere, *Socialism and Rural Development* (Dar es Salaam: Government Printer, 1967), p. 11. This pamphlet and other major papers by President Nyerere defining Tanzanian socialism are reprinted in Julius K. Nyerere, *Ujamaa—Essays on Socialism* (Dar es Salaam: Oxford University Press, 1968); henceforth citations from these papers will be to this volume. This quotation is from p. 119 of the book.
2. Nyerere, "To Plan is To Choose," p. 34.
3. For a selection of such studies see the Bibliography, below in this book, and Taylor, *The Political Development of Tanganyika*, Bibliography. For a study of the origins of Chagga local government, see Johnston, "Chagga Constitutional Development." For an early attempt to go beyond the narrow confines of studies of transplanted British local government, see J. Gus Liebenow, "Tribalism, Traditionalism and Modernism in

begun to be focused on the changing tasks of local government and the inter-relationships of government and party at the local level in Tanzania.[4] The aim here, then, is to supplement the findings of the Moshi decision-making studies and of studies of local government in Tanzania by concentrating on the participants themselves, the Moshi Town Councillors, both those elected by the residents of the town and those nominated (appointed) by the President (see Table 7.1), and the officers of the Moshi Town Council.

Table 7.1. Membership of the Moshi Town Council

1	Chairman[a]
19	Councillors elected to represent 6 town wards[b]
9	Councillors nominated by the President[c]
	Representative of the Regional Commissioner
	Head Postmaster
	Regional Secretary, NUTA
	Regional Land Officer
	Regional Medical Officer
	Regional Engineer
	Regional Secretary, TANU
	2 individuals by name

[a] The individual elected to be Chairman of the TANU urban district is automatically the Chairman of the Moshi Town Council. For the purposes of this analysis, he has been included among the elected councillors.

[b] There were two vacancies in 1968–69; one of the former councillors was interviewed.

[c] These councillors were nominated by both name and office by the President, in General Notice No. 669 of 31 March 1967. It was presumed in Moshi in 1968–69 that the office was determining, so that when a named officer was transferred, his replacement was welcomed as a nominated councillor, without further action by the President. One of the councillors nominated by name had resigned, and was unavailable for interview. Two different holders of the post of Regional Executive Secretary, TANU, were interviewed in 1968–69, and both are included in this analysis as nominated councillors. The representative of the Regional Engineer who actually served on the Council was interviewed.

In general, the elected town councillors are similar in basic demographic characteristics to their constituents, the residents of Moshi town. They are mostly individuals who became active in nationalist politics very early and who today serve largely as representatives to, rather than from, the government. Not only do they have little actual power to deal with the problems of the town and to make authoritative allocations, but by and large they see themselves as powerless to deal with both the problems they see as important and

Chagga Local Government," *Journal of African Administration* 10, no. 2 (April 1958): 71–82.

4. For example, Bienen, *Tanzania: Party Transformation,* especially Chapter 9; Dryden, *Local Administration in Tanzania,* especially Chapters 7 and 8; and Tordoff, *Government and Politics in Tanzania,* Chapter 4.

Moshi Town Council

the problems brought to them by their constituents. The nominated (appointed) councillors, however, who are mostly government officials selected apparently for their technical and managerial expertise, are able to assume a more active role in determining Council policies and decisions, at least in their own
special areas of competence. Council officers, whose responsibilities are divided between the Council they serve and the Local Government Service Commission that appoints them and that largely determines their future careers, are
most often the key decision-makers in town affairs. The role of the local
TANU organization is a complex one, and ranges from control to impotence,
depending on the nature of the conflict, the specific form it takes, and the desire and ability of party officers to insert themselves into the decision-making
process.

Councillors and Town Population

The political leadership of Moshi is similar to the population of the town
in regard to national origin, religion, and ethnicity. With few exceptions, that
is also true for a major subset of that political leadership, the Moshi Town
Council and its officers. The Council and its officers in 1969 generally reflected the town population in national origin: primarily African (see Table 7.2).[5]
Although there were a few Europeans serving in technical and administrative
posts in Moshi, and although Asians were involved in local commercial enterprises, Tanzanian Africans held almost all key posts in local government.

As has been noted, Christian missionaries were attracted to Kilimanjaro
and have been established throughout the district for more than fifty years.
In Moshi town, however, as in most towns in Tanzania, travelers and traders,
as well as indigenous administrators brought by the colonial powers from
coastal regions, carried Islam with them.[6] More recently, TANU, at least in its
early phases, was identified with the swahili culture, including Islam.[7] It is not
surprising, therefore, to find that while more than half of the town population
is Christian, more than half of the elected Moshi town councillors were Muslim
(see Table 7.3). This suggests that the Muslim-Christian division is one of the
major cleavages dividing Moshi town from its rural hinterland, or rather, dividing the elevated areas of the Kilimanjaro foothills from the lower plains areas.
More than half of the nominated councillors and Council officers were Christian, indicating simply that Tanzanians in areas of missionary penetration had
earlier and better access to education, and thus were more likely to be selected
for civil service posts.

5. In evaluating the percentages in this and other tables in this chapter, careful attention must be paid to the small number of cases: for Nominated Councillors, for example, where N=9, one councillor is represented as 11 percent of the total. The absence of
Europeans in Table 7.2 is explained in notes b and d.

6. See J. Spencer Trimingham, *Islam in East Africa* (Oxford: Oxford University
Press, 1964), especially pp. 22–30.

7. On this point, see Bienen, *Tanzania: Party Transformation,* pp. 43–46.

The Politicians

Table 7.2. Moshi Town and Its Council: National Origin

	Moshi town	Elected councillors (N=19)	Nominated councillors (N=9)	Council officers (N=9)
African	89%[a]	95%	100%[b]	89%
Asian	8	5	0	11
Arab	0[c]	0	0	0
European	1	0	0	0[d]
Not ascertained	3	0	0	0
	101%	100%	100%	100%

Source: Moshi Political Leadership Survey and Tanzania 1967 Census (Moshi town percentages refer to heads of households).

[a] That is, 89% of all heads of household in Moshi in 1967 were African.

[b] An African assistant to the Regional Engineer (a European, later replaced by an Asian) represented him on the Council.

[c] Less than 0.5%.

[d] A European volunteer serving temporarily as Town Engineer was not interviewed. He spoke little English and no Swahili and consequently was unable to participate in most Council deliberations. His views had little discernible impact in local decisions.

Table 7.3. Moshi Town and Its Council: Religion

	Moshi town	Elected councillors (N=19)	Nominated councillors (N=9)	Council officers (N=9)
Christian	54%[a]	38%	66%	55%
Lutheran	–	16	22	22
Roman Catholic	–	11	33	0
Anglican	–	11	11	33
Muslim	38	58	22	22
Other world religion[b]	4	5	0	11
Local belief	1	0	0	0
Not ascertained	4	0	11	11
	101%	101%	99%	99%

Source: Moshi Political Leadership Survey and Tanzania 1967 Census (Moshi town percentages refer to heads of households).

[a] That is, 54% of all heads of households in Moshi in 1967 were Christian.

[b] For example, Hindu.

Moshi Town Council

Table 7.4.   Moshi Town and Its Council: Ethnicity

	Moshi town	Elected councillors (N=19)	Nominated councillors (N=9)	Council officers (N=9)
Chagga	37%[a]	58%	0%	33%
Neighboring tribe[b]	13	11	22	11
Other African	38	26	78	44
Other[c]	10	5	0	11
Not ascertained	2	0	0	0
	100%	100%	100%	99%

Source: Moshi Political Leadership Survey and Tanzania 1967 census.

[a] That is, 37% of all heads of household in Moshi in 1967 reported their tribe as Chagga.

[b] Arusha, Meru, Masai, Pare, Taveta-Teita.

[c] Coded "Not Applicable" in Tanzania 1967 Census; includes Asians, Europeans.

The Chagga are the major ethnic group in Moshi town,[8] and the proportion of Chagga among the elected town councillors is even greater than the proportion of Chagga among the total town population (see Table 7.4).[9] This suggests that while the Swahili culture may continue to be an important element of local politics in Moshi, many individuals identified as Swahilis were local in origin and not immigrants from coastal areas. Since the nominated councillors and Council officers were appointed from Dar es Salaam and subject to frequent transfer,[10] most serving in Moshi were not local people. In other words, although the elected councillors had strong local roots and did not include as many foreigners as the high percentage of Muslims might suggest, nonetheless, many individuals with key roles in Council activities not only were not subject to a local electorate, but also were not local in origin and were often unknown to local people before their arrival in Moshi. In addition, nominated councillors

8. While it may be anthropologically inaccurate to treat Chagga-speaking peoples as a single ethnic group, under certain circumstances these people of Kilimanjaro recognize a common ethnic identity—call themselves Chagga—and so are grouped in that way here.

9. Note that in the collection of census data in Tanzania in 1967 information on ethnic groups was gathered from heads of households, which could introduce distortions in the data if there were many multiethnic households, or if there were many errors by census takers in the numerous multihousehold houses in Moshi town. The general direction of the results, which is what we are concerned with here, is sufficiently accurate for the purposes of this discussion.

10. That is, individuals serving as nominated councillors were appointed to their posts by government or party offices in Dar es Salaam, and while serving in those posts were nominated to the Moshi Town Council.

The Politicians

and Council officers were younger and better educated than the elected councillors (see Table 7.5).

Elected Leadership

That the Moshi Town Council does not have a determining role in the allocation of resources locally, and the frequency with which the Council is included in the decision-making process, principally to legitimize decisions made outside the Council itself, have already been noted. Assessed from that perspective, the Council as a whole, and especially the elected councillors, cannot have a major impact on many of the decisions that are ostensibly within Council competence. The elected councillors are aware of this, and comment on it frequently. Further, when asked specifically about the problems they see as important in Moshi and about the problems brought to them by their constituents, many describe themselves as unable to do anything at all about these problems. There is, among the elected Moshi town councillors, a pervasive feeling of subjective incompetence.[11]

Political leaders were asked to indicate what they thought was the most important problem in Moshi. The question was open-ended, and responses covered a wide range of problems.[12] There was no substantial agreement among

Table 7.5. Moshi Town and Its Council: Education

	Moshi town	Elected councillors (N=19)	Nominated councillors (N=9)	Council officers (N=9)
No formal schooling	40%[a]	5%	0%	0%
1–3 years of school	12	5	0	0
4–7 years of school	31	47	11	33
8–11 years of school	13	21	33	0
12–13 years of school	3	16	33	22
14 or more years of school	1	5	22	33
Not ascertained	0	0	0	11
	100%	99%	99%	99%

Source: Moshi Political Leadership Survey and Tanzania 1967 Census.

[a] That is, 40% of the Moshi population in 1967 had no formal schooling. Note that this refers to the entire population; 46.9% of those over five years of age had no formal schooling.

11. For the pioneer discussion of the sense of civic competence, see Gabriel A. Almond and Sidney Verba, *The Civic Culture*, abridged ed. (Boston: Little, Brown, 1965), Chapter 6. Almond and Verba dealt with the sense of competence of ordinary citizens, while the discussion here concerns the sense of competence of the political leadership. Note also that Almond and Verba dealt with subject and object competence, referring to an individual's assessment of his roles as subject and object of the political system, while subjective competence here refers to a leader's own assessment of his power.

12. For the complete question schedule used, see Appendix 1.

Table 7.6.   Moshi Town Council: The Most Important Problem in Moshi

	Elected councillors (N=19)	Nominated councillors (N=9)	Council officers (N=9)
Education	0%[a]	0%	11%
Unemployment	21	11	22
Land shortage; overpopulation	21	22	11
Quality of leadership; corruption	16	11	11
Social dislocation (crime, etc.)	0	0	11
Development (business, housing problems)	21	33	11
Other	21	11	22
Not ascertained	0	11	0
	100%	99%	99%

Source: Moshi Political Leadership Survey (Question 1).

[a] That is, none of the elected councillors regarded education as the most important problem.

Moshi town councillors and Council officers that any single problem was indeed the most important (see Table 7.6). Leaders were then asked what they were doing, or could do, about the problem they had mentioned. More than half of the elected town councillors said they could do nothing at all about what they considered to be the most important problem in Moshi, and another quarter said they could do nothing more than explain to their constituents government action that dealt with the problem (see Table 7.7). Fewer than one-fifth of the elected councillors, compared to about one-half of the nominated councillors and Council officers, felt they could play a part in resolving what they saw as the most important problem facing their town.

Leaders were asked to list several other problems they considered important in Moshi, and were asked specifically if they thought unemployment, primary education, and corruption in local licensing were serious problems in Moshi. Again, almost half of the elected councillors reported that they could do nothing at all about the other important problems in Moshi, and another third said they could do little more than explain to citizens government programs and plans. In other words, more than three-quarters of the elected councillors said they were unable to have a substantial impact on the whole range of problems they regarded as important in Moshi. (See Table 7.8.) It should be noted that even a majority of Council officers felt themselves incompetent to deal with what they regarded as serious problems.

To get another perspective on this self-perceived incompetence of local councillors, leaders were asked to describe the problems brought to them, problems in which local people sought the assistance of their councillors and Council officers, and their responses to those problems. None of the elected councillors, compared to almost one-half of the nominated councillors and

The Politicians

Table 7.7.   Moshi Town Council: Action on the Most Important Problem in Moshi

	Elected councillors (N=19)	Nominated councillors (N=9)	Council officers (N=9)
Able to do nothing at all	58%[a]	22%	44%
Can do nothing to solve the problem, but represents government to citizens, explains	26	11	11
Takes general remedial action (action actually taken−not simply proposed or possible; respondent's own explanation of how this action was remedial was accepted)	16	44	0
Takes specific remedial action	0	11	44
Cites no problems	0	11	0
	100%	99%	99%

Source: Moshi Political Leadership Survey (Question 2).

[a] That is, 58% of the elected councillors reported they could do nothing at all about what they considered to be the most important problem.

three-quarters of the Council officers, reported that he was able to solve the problems brought to him by himself. Indeed, only one-half of the elected councillors thought that the problems brought to them by their constituents could be dealt with adequately within town governmental and party structures (see Table 7.9).

Thus, even for the kinds of problems for which local citizens seek out their councillors, a majority of the elected councillors themselves felt they were

Table 7.8.   Moshi Town Council: Action on Other Important Problems in Moshi[a]

	Elected councillors (N=19)	Nominated councillors (N=9)	Council officers (N=9)
Nothing at all	42%[b]	22%	67%
Nothing to solve the problems mentioned, but represents government to citizens, explains	37	22	11
Takes remedial action	21	44	22
Cites no problems	0	11	0
	100%	99%	100%

Source: Moshi Political Leadership Survey (Questions 3–6).

[a] The major thrust of respondent's response to all other problems mentioned was coded.

[b] That is, 42% of the elected councillors reported they could do nothing at all about the other major problems they mentioned.

Moshi Town Council

Table 7.9.   Moshi Town Council: Action on Problems Brought by Local Individuals and Groups

	Elected councillors (N=19)	Nominated councillors (N=9)	Council officers (N=9)
Respondent can solve problems by himself	0%[a]	44%	78%
Respondent cannot solve problems alone, but they can be solved at his level (e.g., cell, branch, district)	53	44	22
Problems cannot be solved by respondent alone or at his level, but can be solved at next higher level, to which respondent has some access (e.g., for cell leader, at branch level)	37	11	0
Problems cannot be solved at a level where respondent has an official role (e.g., at regional level for town councillor)	11	0	0
	101%	99%	100%

Source: Moshi Political Leadership Survey (Questions 14–16).

[a] That is, none of the elected councillors reported that he was capable of solving by himself the problems brought to him by his local constituents.

unable to be of much assistance. Of course, this process is a reciprocal one, in that local citizens are likely to attempt to seek assistance from people who they feel can help them. As they find that their elected councillors are unable to help them, or that they are more successful if they take their problems elsewhere, they are less likely to bring their problems to their elected councillors in the first place. But the general finding is very clear: for the whole range of problems with which the elected councillors must deal, both the problems they regard as important and the problems their constituents bring to them, the elected councillors feel they are unable to have a significant impact:

I cannot do anything. Assessors [lay assistants in the primary courts] are powerless to do anything.

This problem can be solved only by money; the Council cannot do that. I cannot do anything.

I cannot do anything because it is in the hands of the Public Works Department.

There is nothing to do—it is all up to the government. There is nothing we can do.

Me myself, I cannot do anything.

I cannot do anything. I have no land myself.

What can I do?

The Politicians

It might be argued that this finding reveals nothing more than that councillors listed major problems of such scope and importance that very few individuals in any society could feel able to do much to resolve them. But councillors were asked to describe problems affecting the town in which they constitute the leadership, and clearly far fewer other political leaders (both the nominated councillors and Council officers shown in these tables and other political leaders surveyed) projected this subjective incompetence. This finding does indicate, however, that both the prevailing sentiment and the objective realities in Tanzania serve to convince local leaders that only action initiated at and supported from the national level can possibly cope with the range of problems perceived in up-country Tanzania.

To examine the possibility that respondents simply believed that all significant problems could be resolved only at the national level, responses were examined to ascertain whether or not the problems leaders saw as significant could be resolved locally.[13] For the problems described as most important, the other significant problems mentioned, and the problems brought by local citizens to the councillors and Council officers, most councillors and officers thought that local solutions were possible. For this entire range of problems, then, most Council leaders thought that local action could be efficacious. Most elected councillors, when describing how they might influence decisions affecting Moshi, reported also that they would see local level leaders (see Table 7.15, below). The general finding is supported: when discussing important local problems, most of which they believe can be resolved locally, elected councillors think that they themselves can do little.

A further verification of this finding of subjective incompetence is found in the responses of local leaders concerning the Arusha Declaration. TANU leaders, meeting in Arusha in 1967, approved a statement of party (and thus national) policy that subsequently became a rallying cry, an explanation of policy in terms comprehensible to ordinary peasants, and a standard against which progress toward Tanzanian socialism could be measured.[14] Political leaders in Moshi were asked to describe what they themselves were doing to implement the Arusha Declaration. A summary of their responses indicates that more than half of the elected councillors were either doing nothing specific to implement the Arusha Declaration or were concerned primarily with

13. Questions were open-ended, and respondents were encouraged to expand on their responses. When a respondent mentioned a problem, he was asked what he could do about it. If his response to that second question did not indicate how he thought the problem he was discussing could be resolved, he was asked to discuss it further until the full nature of the problem and its solutions, as the respondent saw them, were clear. It was then usually not difficult to determine whether or not the respondent thought the problem(s) he was discussing could be resolved locally.

14. See Nyerere, *Ujamaa-Essays on Socialism.* For an overview of the Arusha Declaration and related policy statements, see Henry Bienen, "An Ideology for Africa," *Foreign Affairs* 47, no. 3 (April 1969): 545–59; and Bienen, *Tanzania: Party Transformation,* Chapter 13.

the restrictions imposed on leaders. (Leaders were required to limit themselves to a single source of income derived from their own efforts. Earning several salaries, absentee landlordship, and shareholding were thus forbidden to leaders.) Several leaders, while describing their sacrifices in complying with these leadership requirements, complained that they were left with an inadequate source of income (see Table 7.10).

Thus, both the studies of issues and the interviews of the participants make it clear that not only are locally elected councillors largely excluded from the critical stages of local decision-making, but also that most of the councillors considered themselves (rather accurately) unable to deal effectively with the problems they regarded as important and with the problems brought to them by their constituents.[15] Their subjective incompetence complemented their objective incompetence. They reported that what action they did take was largely confined to explaining policy and action to their constituents and representing their constituents to government and party.

Table 7.10. Moshi Town Council: Implementation of the Arusha Declaration

Respondent's role in implementing the Arusha Declaration[a]	Elected councillors (N=19)	Nominated councillors (N=9)	Council officers (N=9)
Does nothing, since Arusha Declaration had no impact on him	26%[b]	11%	44%
Does nothing, since was implementing the principles of the Arusha Declaration even before it was announced	5	0	0
Became more self-reliant	5	0	11
Took up, or substantially increased, farming	11	0	11
Made changes required by leadership code	26	44	11
Became involved in some group activity (including cooperatives)	11	0	0
Other (including encouraged, led others) and combination of several of the above (equal emphasis)	16	33	22
Not asked	0	11	0
	100%	99%	99%

Source: Moshi Political Leadership Survey (Question 9).

[a] Assessment by the respondent of his own role; where several were mentioned, the role described as most important was coded.

[b] That is, 26% of the elected councillors reported they were doing nothing to implement the Arusha Declaration because it had no specific impact on them.

15. For a discussion of political elites who consider themselves unable to influence government policy, see Victor T. LeVine, *Political Leadership in Africa* (Stanford, Cal.: Hoover Institution, 1967), Chapter 4.

The Politicians

Table 7.11.   Moshi Town Council: Place of Birth and Length of Local Residence

	Elected councillors (N=19)	Nominated councillors (N=9)	Council officers (N=9)
Born in:			
Kilimanjaro Region	79%[a]	11%	56%
Elsewhere in Tanzania	16	89	44
Outside Tanzania	5	0	0
	100%	100%	100%
Has lived in current residence for:			
Less than 1 year	0%[b]	33%	22%
1–2 years	0	22	11
2–10 years	11	44	22
10–20 years	32	0	11
More than 20 years	58	0	22
Not ascertained	0	0	11
	101%	99%	99%

Source: Moshi Political Leadership Survey.

[a] That is, 79% of the elected councillors were born in Kilimanjaro Region.

[b] That is, none of the elected councillors had lived at his current residence for less than one year in 1969.

What, then, is the nature of the elected leadership (in the Town Council) in Moshi? What sorts of people become elected councillors? If they do not have a monopoly on local decision-making, and if they consider themselves unable to deal effectively with major local problems, where do they concentrate their efforts? These questions themselves suggest the paradox involved in the call for dynamic local leadership that is implicit and explicit in national policy and the inability of the local council to attract capable and energetic local leaders who are willing and able to do something more than forward complaints to the government and party hierarchies.

The elected town councillors in Moshi in 1969 were mostly local people, individuals who had lived in Moshi for some time. Four-fifths were born in Kilimanjaro Region, and more than half had lived at their current residences for more than twenty years in 1969. Nominated councillors and Council officers were more often born outside Kilimanjaro Region and lived in Moshi for much shorter periods of time (see Table 7.11). Elected councillors had a longer record of political activity than did nominated councillors and Council officers: they joined TANU earlier and they had served in political positions longer. More than half of the elected councillors joined TANU before 1956 and had served in political positions for more than ten years (see Table 7.12). Elected councillors in 1968–69, then, were largely local people who had very early become involved in TANU activity, and who had continued their political activity through membership in the Moshi Town Council.

Nearly half of the elected councillors in Moshi in 1968–69 had no formal employment,[16] and another third were either farmers or operated small shops

16. Income was derived from a variety of sources: the modest allowance to town councillors, farms maintained by wives and relatives, support from grown children,

Moshi Town Council

Table 7.12.   Moshi Town Council: History of Political Activity

	Elected councillors (N=19)	Nominated councillors (N=9)	Council officers (N=9)
Joined TANU:			
Not a TANU member	0%[a]	11%	0%
Joined TANU since 1963	0	22	33
Joined TANU 1957–62	47	33	33
Joined TANU 1954–56	42	33	11
Was active in a pre-TANU nationalist organization[b] and subsequently joined TANU	11	0	11
Not ascertained	0	0	11
	100%	99%	99%
Political service:[c]			
No political service	0%[d]	0%	44%
Less than 2 years of political service	0	44	11
2–5 years of political service	21	22	11
5–10 years of political service	26	11	22
More than 10 years of political service	53	22	0
Not ascertained	0	0	11
	100%	99%	99%

Source: Moshi Political Leadership Survey.

[a] That is, all of the elected councillors were TANU members in 1969.

[b] For example, Tanganyika African Association.

[c] Political service means holding a position in which a substantial portion of the individual's time and energy were devoted to political activity. Thus, depending on an individual's description of his own background, service in a government or trade union post might or might not be coded as political service.

[d] That is, all of the elected councillors (by definition) had had some political service.

(see Table 7.13).   Thus, three-quarters of the elected town councillors were individuals with a great deal of time available for political activity. Service on the Council can be very time consuming, especially for those councillors who devote most of their energies to being available to their constituents. Communication in Moshi is largely by word of mouth, and they are in the neighborhood, ready to listen to complaints, accompany people to the TANU office or the Town Hall, and intercede in disputes. These councillors often reported that their constituents expected them to be available and to be able to drop what they were doing to deal with a constituent's problem.

---

the small allowance for service as primary court assessors. Many townspeople and some leaders believed that several councillors also had quasi-legal or illegal sources of income: fees charged for intervention with the bureaucracy or legal or business advice, unlicensed taxi services, and rental income from property officially listed to relatives.

The Politicians

Table 7.13. Moshi Town Council: Employment

	Elected councillors (N=19)	Nominated councillors (N=9)	Council officers (N=9)
Farmer	16%[a]	0%	0%
Salaried:			
government	0	44	100
TANU	5	22	0
trade union	0	11	0
parastatal	5	0	0
cooperative	5	0	0
commercial	5	0	0
other	0	22	0
Self-employed:			
professional	5	0	0
commercial	16	0	0
Unemployed[b]	42	0	0
	99%	99%	100%

Source: Moshi Political Leadership Survey.

[a] That is, 16% of the elected councillors reported their occupation as farming.

[b] No major income-producing activity. Income derived from farms maintained by wives and relatives, support from grown children, councillors allowance, and, in some cases, quasi-legal or illegal activities (see note 16).

In 1969, however, there were indications that this councillor role—to be available locally to hear complaints and represent constituents—was becoming less viable. First, the leadership provisions of the Arusha Declaration make it difficult for such individuals to find adequate means of support. Formerly, many councillors were able to acquire homes, in which they then rented one or more rooms, and land, which they either rented out or employed others to farm, but both of these sources of income, income not derived by the efforts of the individual himself, are specifically forbidden to leaders in Tanzania. Although it was difficult to secure reliable information, it is clear that some councillors in Moshi continued to receive income from these sources in 1969. At the same time, there was continuing pressure by the councillors to increase their Council allowances. A second obstacle to this councillor role is the attempt to find better educated and more highly skilled councillors. Individuals with skills and education are likely to be found in government service, or working for cooperatives, trade unions, parastatal organizations, or large businesses, and in general they do not have the free time or accessibility that unemployed or self-employed councillors have.

In 1968–69 two seats on the Moshi Town Council became vacant when councillors resigned for reasons of health and unwillingness to comply with the leadership provisions of the Arusha Declaration. Three separate attempts to fill the vacancies by election in 1969 were unsuccessful, as each time only a

Moshi Town Council

Table 7.14.   Moshi Town Council: Local Contacts

	Elected councillors (N=19)	Nominated councillors (N=9)	Council officers (N=9)
Very many (11 or more a day)	21%[a]	33%	67%
Many (6–10 a day)	16	22	0
Average (1–5 a day or at least 25 a month)	32	11	22
Few (2–7 a week or at least 8 a month)	11	0	11
Very few (2–7 a month)	11	11	0
Only occasionally (1 a month or fewer)	11	22	0
	102%	99%	100%

Source: Moshi Political Leadership Survey (Question 13).

[a] That is, 21% of the elected councillors reported that "very many" (11 or more) people brought their problems to them every day.

single candidate successfully filed nomination papers.[17] Although both Council and party officers expressed dismay about the continuing vacancies, neither group took any action to promote candidacies. The inability to fill these two vacancies, despite three attempts, highlights the contradiction between the perceived powerlessness of the Council, the restrictive leadership requirements of the Arusha Declaration, and the meager rewards (both symbolic and other) for Council service on the one hand, and the need for dynamic locally elected leadership on the other.

Another dimension of this paradox of local leadership is that, although the elected councillors did receive complaints and did represent their constituents, they did not provide effective two-way links between the urban populace and the larger polity. By representing their constituents they provided ties to the local government structures. But elected councillors in general received fewer complaints from urban residents than did other political leaders. By the leaders' own analysis, local citizens were more likely to bring their problems to Council officers than to elected councillors (see Table 7.14). Moreover, most elected councillors, because they traveled so rarely outside of Moshi, had little opportunity to establish links between Moshi residents and other areas of Tanzania. More importantly, when asked who they would see if they wanted to influence decisions affecting Moshi (both those made locally and those made in Dar es Salaam), most local councillors reported they would seek out local level people, regardless of where the decision in question was made (see Table 7.15).

17. Prospective candidates were unable to secure the signatures of twenty-five voters registered in the ward to be represented. One candidate who secured signatures sufficiently far in advance of the filing date to verify them in the registration rolls could not be seated because election rules require that the number of candidates be at least equal to the number of vacancies before the election can be held.

The Politicians

Table 7.15.   Moshi Town Council: Contacts to Influence Decisions

	Elected councillors (N=19)	Nominated councillors (N=9)	Council officers (N=9)
To influence the outcome on a local matter, respondent would see:[a]			
No influence; can do nothing	5%[b]	0%	11%
Local government official	16	0	33
Councillor or take to Council	32	0	11
Local TANU officer	21	22	33
Area Commissioner	0	0	11
Regional Commissioner	5	22	0
Member of Parliament, or Member of TANU National Executive Committee	5	0	0
Other person or combination of above	16	33	0
Not asked or not ascertained	0	22	0
	100%	99%	99%
To influence the outcome on a matter in which the decision has been made or will be made in Dar es Salaam, respondent would see:[c]			
No influence; can do nothing	5%[d]	11%	22%
Regional ministry or department official, or person at district level or lower	63	11	67
Regional commissioner	0	11	11
Regional Chairman or TANU at Regional level	0	22	0
Member of Parliament	10	0	0
Person in or from Dar es Salaam	21	11	0
Other person or combination of above	0	22	0
Not asked	0	11	0
	99%	99%	100%

Source: Moshi Political Leadership Survey (Questions 7 and 8).

[a] Leaders were asked whom they would see if they wanted to influence the decision on a local matter.

[b] That is, 5% of the elected councillors reported they could do nothing to influence a local decision.

[c] Leaders were asked whom they would see if they wanted to influence a decision made or to be made in Dar es Salaam on a matter that affected Moshi.

[d] That is, 5% of the elected councillors reported they could do nothing to influence a national decision that affected a Moshi problem.

Moshi Town Council

Table 7.16. Moshi Town Council: Responses to Problems Brought by Constituents

	Elected councillors (N=19)	Nominated councillors (N=9)	Council officers (N=9)
Respondent is:[a]			
General source of assistance	21%[b]	0%	11%
Pacifier, reconciler, arbitrator	5	0	33
Able to assist only because of the nature of respondent's job (e.g., education officer who gets only school problems)	0	56	44
Representative to government[c]	42	22	0
Representative to TANU (including to TANU and government)	16	0	0
Representative from government	5	0	11
Representative from TANU (including from TANU and government)	5	11	0
Representative both to and from government and/or TANU	5	11	0
	99%	100%	99%

Source: Moshi Political Leadership Survey (Questions 14–16)

[a] Coded from all problems brought to respondent, according to respondent's own description of his behavior, into mutually exclusive categories, beginning from the bottom.

[b] That is, 21% of the elected councillors reported that they were able to be of general assistance to people who came to them with problems.

[c] Means to carry messages toward; an individual whose response to problems brought by constituents was to bring the problems up in a Council meeting was coded as a representative to government, while an individual whose response was to explain Council action was coded as a representative from government.

As they described themselves, then, councillors offered at best a one-way link to local institutions. When asked what they did about the problems their constituents brought them, two-thirds of the elected councillors described themselves either as general sources of assistance (helping individuals to find jobs, for example) or as representatives to the government or TANU or both (carrying complaints to the Council, for example; see Table 7.16). Thus, three-quarters of the elected councillors concentrated their efforts on carrying messages to, rather than from, party and government.

In summary, then, elected councillors in Moshi in 1968–69 were local people who had long been involved in politics, who served primarily as representatives to the government, transmitting problems and complaints to Council and other officials. At the same time, the Town Council had little substantial direct impact on local policies and allocations, and many councillors considered themselves to be unable to deal effectively with what they regarded as important local problems. Elected councillors were confined largely to the local arena in representing their constituents, in that they rarely sought out officials outside Moshi, even on issues in which they believed that the critical decisions were made in Dar es Salaam, and in that they rarely had occasion to travel outside Kilimanjaro. Many elected councillors, because they were unemployed or self-employed, could be readily available to their constituents. But the increasing need for better-educated local councillors in Tanzania, coupled with the requirement that leaders' income be derived from their own efforts, nurtured a contradiction between the two different types of councillorship, a contradiction that contributed to the inability to fill two Council vacancies.

Appointed Leadership

The nominated Moshi town councillors in 1968–69 were not local people. Primarily administrators, they were apparently appointed to the Council because of their managerial skills and technical expertise. In their own special areas of competence their voices carried great weight in Council deliberations— the opinion of the Regional Health Officer on health matters, for example. In Moshi town, at least, the position of nominated councillor has clearly not been used as a device of patronage, a means of rewarding political activists and faithfuls, nor has it been used to ensure TANU dominance in Council affairs by appointing only TANU stalwarts. Although, of course, there is no clear boundary between what is political and what is not in Tanzania, the nominated councillors in Moshi (except the NUTA and TANU secretaries) consciously attempted to avoid becoming involved in what they saw as political matters, and in 1968– 69 at least one was not even a TANU member.

The Council officers have already been discussed. It is clear that in most issues in which a decision is actually made locally, the Council officers, and especially the Town Clerk, are the key people. It is they who make most decisions. It is they who make recommendations to the Council and its committees, recommendations usually adopted with little modification. And it is they, with control of the communications link between the Council and the Ministry responsible for local government and with primary responsibility for implementing Council decisions, who can alter decisions in the communication and implementation processes. Moreover, local people are more likely to seek assistance from Council officers than from their councillors, both because the officers in the Town Hall are the primary symbols of local government and authority and because town residents are aware that it is the officers, and not the councillors, who can make the decisions in which they are interested. Even when people seek assistance from their councillors, the common course of action for the councillors to follow is to represent or intercede on behalf of their constituents with Council officers. The officers themselves, at least in Moshi in 1968–69, were quick to deprecate the skills and abilities of the councillors and the political process in general. Perhaps, like administrators almost everywhere, they were sure they could run the town more smoothly if there were no politics and politicians at all.

As has been noted, Council officers have divided responsibilities (and allegiances). They are directly responsible to the Town Council, and are generally accountable to it for their actions, but they are appointed, promoted, and transferred by the Local Government Service Commission. In addition, the Town Clerk, as the executive officer of the Town Council, is responsible to the Ministry of Local Government for the actions of the Council. Thus, it is not uncommon for an officer to evaluate a proposed course of action in terms of the anticipated response, not of the Council, but of his superiors in Dar es Salaam. It is also not uncommon for the local councillors to feel frustrated by their inability to control the actions of their officers. For example, in 1969 a former Member of Parliament who had been expelled from both TANU and Parliament after a conflict with the Regional Commissioner in his home area was appointed an officer of the Moshi Town Council. Anxious to demonstrate both his skills and his commitment to party policy, he announced, publicly, several new Council initiatives, including takeovers of some aspects of local commerce. His announcements preceded Council debate. Before he had been in his post for a month, councillors expressed concern with his independent decisions and statements to the press, and about his unresponsiveness to the Council.

TANU

In waging the independence struggle, TANU was a national movement that drew its strength from locally based groups organized around local problems and grievances. When the TANU government replaced the colonial government after Independence, it became the focus for some of those local grievances, and TANU was confronted with opposition in several local councils.[18] To offer the local electorate a democratic alternative TANU rebels and independents were permitted to oppose party candidates and were occasionally successful in defeating them. The dilemma for TANU was to encourage responsibility to the local electorate by providing for competitive open elections, while at the same time ensuring that national policy would guide local action. To deal with this problem the Presidential Commission on the Establishment of a Democratic One Party State recommended that the TANU District Executive Committees be included in District Councils (and likewise in urban areas). Among the changes that developed from those recommendations was the decision that the elected TANU District Chairman automatically become the Chairman of the

18. The Kilimanjaro (rural) case—so many independents were elected in 1963 that TANU, even with its clear majority, formed an elected members organization to caucus before council meetings—has already been mentioned; another was in Buhaya. See Bienen, *Tanzania: Party Transformation,* pp. 103–6; Tordoff, *Government and Politics in Tanzania,* pp. 114–16; and Hyden, *Political Development in Rural Tanzania,* pp. 131–39.

relevant district, town, or municipality.[19] Moreover, all candidates must be TANU candidates, approved by both the local party and the Central Committee.[20] Thus, both the elected councillors and the Chairman must be approved and supported by the local TANU organization; the early affiliation with the party and long party service of many elected councillors have already been noted.

And yet, the studies of decision-making in several key issue-areas and the examination of councillors' understanding of the local political process suggest that the local TANU organization does not dominate Council activities. The missions, the bar-owners, and some employers are able to subvert, or at least avoid implementing, TANU policy. The administrative officers in fact make many Council decisions. The local TANU organization is successful in altering some Council decisions, but unsuccessful in altering others.

The councillors themselves, in dealing with what they consider to be important problems in the local area, do not often turn first to TANU. The comments of councillors and Council officers on how they deal with what they consider to be important problems in the local area show clearly that only a few councillors respond in ways that directly involve TANU (see Table 7.17). And yet, an objective assessment of those problems as they are defined by the councillors and Council officers suggests that local political action—deputations, petitions, group pressure—could well be effective. The point here is simply that TANU dominance in Tanzania does not mean that the local TANU organization directly controls the deliberations and actions of the Town Council. Nor does it mean that when councillors and Council officers confront problems they automatically turn first to the local TANU organization. In fact, in 1969 one councillor complained loudly at a committee meeting that town residents were taking local government problems to the TANU office instead of to their councillors and Council officers, and he suggested that the TANU office should refuse to hear such problems. He was warmly supported by other councillors.

As has been stressed several times, the overlaps between the structures of local government and party in Moshi are extensive. The TANU urban Chairman is automatically the Council Chairman. Elected councillors are all TANU candidates. Four of six TANU urban branch chairmen were elected councillors, and one Town Clerk served as a branch chairman. The TANU Regional Executive Secretary was a nominated councillor. One elected councillor

---

19. See Tanzania, *Report of the Presidential Commission on the Establishment of a Democratic One Party State* (Dar es Salaam: Government Printer, 1968), pp. 24–25. The provision that the TANU Chairman be the local government Chairman is included in the TANU Constitution (which is itself the First Schedule of the Interim Constitution of Tanzania, 1965), Article IV, Section C.

20. The procedure for election to local government councils mirrors the Parliamentary election procedure, for which see Belle Harris, "The Electoral System," Chapter 2 in Cliffe, ed., *One Party Democracy*.

Table 7.17. Moshi Town Council: Important Problems—Action Involving TANU

	Elected councillors (N=19)	Nominated councillors (N=9)	Council officers (N=9)
Action on most important problem:			
Respondent takes action directly involving TANU[a]	0%[b]	11%	11%
Respondent takes action not directly involving TANU	16	44	33
Respondent cites no problems or takes no action	84	44	56
	100%	99%	100%
Action on other problems:			
Respondent takes action directly involving TANU[a]	5%[c]	22%	0%
Respondent takes action not directly involving TANU	16	22	22
Respondent cites no problems or takes no action	79	55	78
	100%	99%	100%

Source: Moshi Political Leadership Survey (Questions 1–6).

[a] Action involving a TANU officer or the TANU organization at any level. Does not include action involving government officer who happens to be a TANU member or official.

[b] That is, none of the elected councillors takes action that directly involves TANU on what are considered to be the most important problems.

[c] That is, 5% of the elected councillors take action that directly involves TANU on the other problems they consider important.

served on the TANU Regional Working Committee, and he and another elected councillor served on the TANU Regional Executive Committee (where both the TANU and NUTA Secretaries, who were nominated councillors, also served). Two elected councillors and the Town Clerk served on the TANU Urban District Executive Committee. One of the two urban branch secretaries served as an elected councillor—in fact, he lived in one ward, represented a second in the Council, and was the TANU branch secretary in a third.

Confusion among councillors as to what the local TANU role should be both contributes to and helps explain the overlapping roles. When councillors were asked what they thought the role of TANU should be in the local area, there was a wide spread of opinions and no substantial agreement among elected councillors on what the local TANU organization should be doing. (See Table 7.18.) Among the nominated councillors and Council officers there was more agreement, but their consensus, that the primary TANU role was to express national policy in the local area, defined a role that largely excludes TANU

Table 7.18.   Moshi Town Council: TANU Role in the Local Area

	Elected councillors (N=19)	Nominated councillors (N=9)	Council officers (N=9)
TANU is the defender of the people; TANU helps little people; TANU oversees the leaders	11%[a]	0%	0%
TANU's role is general assistance; receives local problems; expedites action	21	0	0
TANU's role is decision-making; TANU decides on local matters	5	0	11
TANU legitimizes; TANU enables the government to do its job; TANU is "mother" of government	5	0	0
TANU reconciles, brings conflicting groups together, builds unity	11	0	0
TANU is the local expression (mouth) of national policy (incl TANU's job is propaganda, political education, exhortation, party maintenance)	37	67	67
TANU mobilizes; TANU gets the masses to implement policies, promotes development	5	33	0
TANU is/does combination of the above[b]	0	0	11
Not ascertained (includes opposition to TANU)	5	0	11
	100%	100%	100%

Source: Moshi Political Leadership Survey (Question 20).

[a] That is, 11% of the elected councillors said that TANU's role in local matters is to defend the people, ...

[b] Although many individuals mentioned several roles for TANU in local matters, almost all stressed one; that role was coded.

from direct involvement in local decision-making and government. When local leaders were asked to differentiate the party and the government, fully one-third could find no clear differences. (See Table 7.19.)

An example may help give substance to the complex nature of the inter-twined relationship between the Council and the local TANU organization. A councillor (who was also a Council committee chairman and a TANU branch chairman), responding to complaints about high rents in his ward (branch), wrote to the Town Clerk to seek redress. The Town Clerk forwarded the letter to the Senior Resident Magistrate, who was the vice-chairman of the local Rent Tribunal, which has the power to approve, or disapprove, rental charges. The Senior Resident Magistrate forwarded both letters to the TANU District Executive Secretary. In doing so he enclosed a letter from the Dar es Salaam-based chairman of the Rent Tribunal encouraging local Rent Tribunals to make

Table 7.19.   Moshi Town Council: Differentiation of TANU, Government

	Elected councillors (N = 19)	Nominated councillors (N = 9)	Council officers (N = 9)
No difference	37%[a]	33%	44%
TANU decides, government implements	16	11	22
TANU persuades, government uses force	11	11	0
TANU creates and legitimizes government	16	11	0
TANU corrects government, is people's watchdog; TANU is the people's organ (government is not)	16	11	22
Other; combination of the above	5	22	11
	101%	99%	99%

Source: Moshi Political Leadership Survey (Question 21).

[a] That is, 37% of the elected councillors said they saw no difference between TANU and the government, or were unable to explain any difference between TANU and the government.

house-to-house visits to ensure that rents charged were fair. The TANU Regional Executive Secretary (who was both a nominated councillor and a member of the local Rent Tribunal) then wrote to the Town Clerk, supporting action by the Town Council. Ultimately, a subcommittee of the Council Urban Planning Committee was selected to look into the matter. Thus, in this case the initiative by a party branch chairman (and councillor) was to the Council, and a Council subcommittee assumed by default the role of the local Rent Tribunal, with the encouragement of the local TANU organization.

The extent of TANU control over local government actions and of TANU participation in local government decisions varies widely, depending on the specific issues involved, the nature and the locus of the conflict generated, and the initiative of local TANU officials. In fact, while most of the elected councillors regarded the party as supreme over the Council, administrators tended to regard the Council as supreme:

> [TANU's] role should be, if they want to be more effective, purely advice. If TANU tries to pop their noses into administration problems, then things will be in a muddle.

> The government people are stronger than party officers. . . . the government is supreme: the party can propose and the government can refuse, but not the reverse—the government cannot propose to TANU and be refused.

What is clear, then, is that the overlaps between the local council and the local TANU organization, both institutional and through service in multiple leadership positions, are extensive. Within the limitations of national policy, and it should be stressed that major policy emanates from the center, the local council and the local TANU organization both complement each other and serve as alternatives to each other. Both the Council and the party organization are involved in local allocations, and each is used to appeal the decisions of the other. In the ultimate confrontation, the party is, of course, supreme, but in the day-to-day affairs, that challenge does not frequently develop, and the two function interdependently.

Conclusions

The evidence here supports the finding that the principal role of the Moshi Town Council is to provide legitimacy for decisions either taken by Council officers or made at other levels above the Council in the hierarchical chain that links it to the Ministry in Dar es Salaam. A second role is to provide, in a limited way, a forum to which the complaints and demands of urban residents can be brought. This forum, though severely constrained in its ability to influence local decisions, is nonetheless heavily used.

This leads us to look again at local government in Tanzania. The case for strong local government has been made on three separate, but related, grounds. It is argued that only strong local institutions can mobilize the up-country population to the extent necessary for development to take place. It is also argued that development efforts cannot be directed from Dar es Salaam and that effective local government structures are necessary to implement national policies and programs successfully. And, finally, it is widely believed that for an up-country Tanzanian, participatory democracy within the framework of the one-party state has meaning primarily through participation in and control over local decisions. At the same time, there is a growing trend in Tanzania to regard local government as inimical to coordinated development and national integration: by aggregating and articulating local parochial interests, local government reinforces and entrenches opposition to national policies and programs. This trend is manifested in the strengthening of functionally specific institutions (ministry offices, cooperatives) at the local level.[21]

In 1969, spurred by the continuing failure of local government to shoulder a substantial share of the development effort and by the financial insolvency of many local councils, Tanzania began a fundamental reevaluation of local government. The local rate and the produce cess were eliminated. The central government assumed greater responsibility for education and health. The commissioner system (individuals serving simultaneously as government and party officers, already functioning at regional and district levels) was extended down to the ward level. Regional ministerial offices were strengthened. Development funds were made available for allocation at the regional level. And a broad study of local government, conducted by foreign experts, apparently recom-

21. For an analysis of this trend, see Fred G. Burke, "Research in African Local Government: Past Trends and an Emerging Approach," *Canadian Journal of African Studies* 3, no. 1 (Winter 1969): 73–80.

mended reducing the role of the unsuccessful district-level institutions and strengthening the regional level apparatus.

Views on the future role of local government among the political leadership in Moshi varied widely. Some major leaders thought that district councils should be eliminated completely, in favor of strengthening the office of the Area (District) Commissioner and the regional level apparatus. Others, arguing that the mass of the population is effectively represented only at the district level, recommended strengthening the district and urban councils. Still others thought that merging party and government at all levels would solve the problem.

How has the Moshi Town Council performed these tasks assigned to local government? Our overview of the Council, its members, and its officers suggests not well at all. The Town Council has rarely directly attempted to mobilize the urban populace, other than for parades and celebrations, and has certainly not been successful in mobilizing people for development projects. The Council has also not taken an active role in the implementation of national policy and programs. Councillors have been largely unable to translate national policy into urban terms. Local officials cannot agree on what the Arusha Declaration means in the urban setting, and their general assessment is that it has had little impact in Moshi. Excluded from the local development committees, the Council has no real development program, other than to attract new industry to the town. The functioning of the Moshi Town Council provides local residents with few clear, direct, accessible avenues for participating in, and controlling, local decisions. It even proved impossible to generate enough enthusiasm about service on the Council to fill two vacant Council seats. And yet, if the Council has not been active in promoting development goals and programs and national integration, it is clearly not because the Council has become the vehicle of local discontent and concerted opposition to national strategies.

But local government in Moshi should not be equated with the Moshi Town Council. The relationships that link the Town Council and the local TANU organization are extensive, and much of the local leadership holds positions in both. Although the local party organization has not been much more active than the Council in mobilizing the urban populace or in implementing national policy, the party does provide additional avenues of participation in local decision-making. By appealing to the party, and by pressuring the party to intercede with the Council, local groups have been successful in getting some decisions, albeit very low level ones, altered and reversed.

What all of this seems to suggest is that local government, including the party, is at something of a crossroads in Tanzania. Thus far it has had little success in meeting the broad developmental charges placed on it by the national leadership, though perhaps it has served to extend participation in the political process far beyond the boundaries of the colonial period. Yet it is not at all clear that to move in the direction of relying more heavily on technical experts and administrators, even when they are nominally party members, will promote *ujamaa* in Tanzania.[22]

Two more general comments are in order here. The evidence in Tanzania since Independence suggests that for local government to be viable and to play a substantial role, national leaders may have to be willing to tolerate some tension between national and local interests.[23] Strong local governing institutions, in which the local populace can participate and over which they can exercise substantial control, can provide the sense of identification, and ultimately allegiance, necessary to incorporate disaffected parochial interests and can induce compliance with and support of national goals and programs.

Second, the extensive interdependence and overlaps of the Town Council and the local TANU organization suggest that it may be misleading to treat the local party organization as a single unit. The local party is an alliance of several different sets of interests and people—a coalition of factions. There is tension between those who associate themselves with Christianity and with Chagganess and those who feel they represent the non-Christian, the non-Chagga, and the more transient segments of the urban population. There is tension between those who have a long history of party activity but who do not fully support the policies of Tanzanian socialism and the largely younger, better-educated individuals more firmly committed to the goals of *ujamaa*. This is not to suggest that these tensions and the factions within the local political leadership, which will be examined more fully in Chapter 9, inhibit development and integration in Tanzania. Rather, it is to suggest that they may provide a rational, though perhaps at times unconscious and reluctant, strategy for incorporating conflicting pressures and molding them into viable developmental institutions.

22. See Chapter 10, note 17.

23. Goran Hyden argues that more local autonomy and control over plan formulation and implementation are necessary in "Planning in Tanzania: Lessons of Experience," pp. 13–17.

8

Moshi Cell Leaders

Introduction

A major concern of this study has been the nature of the contact between the government and the party on the one hand and the ordinary population in an up-country urban setting in Tanzania on the other. One group of locally responsible leaders who link government, party, and people are the elected Moshi town Councillors, examined in Chapter 7. A second group of local leaders, elected by their immediate neighbors and forming the lowest level of the party structure, consists of the cell leaders. Who are those cell leaders in Moshi, and what do they do?

First contemplated officially in 1963, cells were established in Dar es Salaam at the end of 1964, and have subsequently been instituted throughout the country.[1] As of 1965 cells were formed in about half of all TANU branches.[2] The spread of cells in Tanzania is still uneven. Although the dense population of the urban area makes it especially amenable to the organization of cells, in Moshi in 1969 there were many homes, and people, not incorporated into a functioning cell.

The 1965 TANU Constitution defines the cell, to consist of ten houses grouped together, as "the basic organ of T.A.N.U."[3] In practice, however, cells vary greatly in size. In rural areas where houses are widely scattered, the cell may include fewer than ten houses, while in densely populated urban areas either fewer or more than ten houses may constitute a cell. There was no uniform pattern of cell size in Moshi in 1968–69, and in several cases both the branch chairman and the cell leader were unsure about the extent of the cells under their jurisdiction.

Cells were established to facilitate communication between the mass of the population and the local and national leadership, to manage tasks of party

1. For the origins of the cells, see William Tordoff, *Government and Politics in Tanzania*, pp. 166–69.
2. Estimate attributed to Second Vice-President Rashidi Kawawa in Bienen, *Tanzania: Party Transformation*, p. 359.
3. Interim Constitution of Tanzania, Act No. 43 of 1965, First Schedule (Constitution of the Tanganyika African National Union), Article IV, Section A.

maintenance, to assist in maintaining security (identification and control of both foreign elements and local troublemakers), and, more recently, to mobilize people for development purposes.[4] (In rural areas, the Village Development Committee, constituted largely of the local cell leaders, has marked a formal merging of party and government.) In practice, the local cell leader, who flies the party flag at his house, can function as a repository for local problems and grievances, and at the same time can keep local party leadership and government officials informed on activity and attitudes among the residents of his cell. Although the TANU Constitution stipulates that the cell be composed of TANU members, in practice all adults living in the houses grouped into a cell are expected to participate in cell activities, including election of the cell leader. On occasion, even the cell leader himself is not a TANU member.

The cell, then, is designed to be the lowest level of the political structure,[5] and it is expected to provide the key point of contact between the population and political leadership of Tanzania. Therefore, to supplement the study of the district level leadership in Moshi, a sample survey of the cell leaders in Moshi town was conducted.[6] The survey had three basic purposes: to develop a better understanding of linkages and allocations—a better feel for what politics was all about—at the local level; to explore further the overlap of party and government and the grafting of new party structures onto existing institutions; and to study the basic party cadres themselves.

Moshi Town

In the discussion thus far, Moshi town has been treated largely as a single unit of analysis, but, as in most towns, the different neighborhoods vary widely in composition and character. Moshi is an urban area segregated residentially by racial origin, by ethnic group, and by religion.

The European residents of the town are concentrated in a ward characterized by spacious, often sumptuous, homes, lavishly maintained gardens, and

---

4. See the discussions in Tordoff, *Government and Politics in Tanzania,* pp. 166–69, and Bienen, *Tanzania: Party Transformation,* pp. 356–59. For the statement by the TANU publicity secretary announcing the introduction of cells, see Wilbert Klerruu, "Whys and Wherefores of the TANU Cell System," *The Nationalist,* 20 September 1965; see also, Tanganyika African National Union, *Utaratibu na Maongozi ya Chama cha TANU* (Dar es Salaam: Mwananchi Publishing Co., 1966?).

5. Unfortunately, it is not uncommon for studies of local government to consider party cells inconsequential in government and politics at the local level—for example, Dryden, *Local Administration in Tanzania,* especially Chapters 7 and 8.

6. Fortunately, comparative data on cell leaders in Tanzania is now available. The studies in other areas of the country in general found patterns of behavior to be very similar to those reported here. See J. H. Proctor, ed., *The Cell System of the Tanganyika African National Union* (Dar es Salaam: Tanzania Publishing House, 1971); and Jean F. O'Barr and Joel Samoff, eds., *Cell Leaders in Tanzania: Agents of Order and Change* (Nairobi: EAPH, 1974).

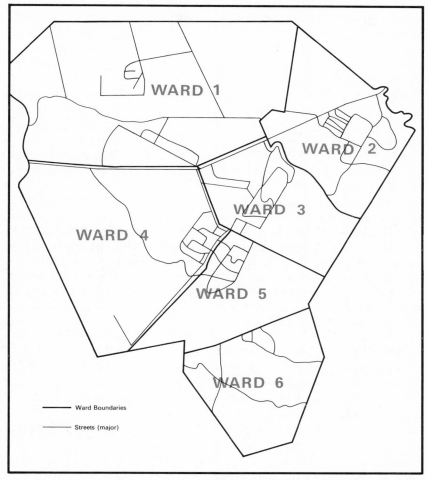

WARD 1

WARD 2

WARD 3

WARD 4

WARD 5

WARD 6

Ward Boundaries

Streets (major)

University of Wisconsin Cartographic Laboratory

Moshi Town Wards

tree-shaded lawns. The Asian population, though more dispersed than the European, is largely concentrated in the central business section of town, much of it living in multiapartment units or in flats over downtown shops. Correspondingly, the African population is concentrated in the other four wards, though Africans are in the majority in all but the central business ward. (See Table 8.1.)[7]

7. The census data used in this and succeeding tables are drawn from the Tanzania 1967 Census (Tanzania, *1967 Population Census,* vols. 1–4), which includes

The Politicians

Table 8.1.   Moshi Town: Ethnic Origin, by Ward

Wards:	1	2	3	4	5	6	Moshi
African	67.2%[a]	98.6%	47.8%	91.9%	89.4%	98.0%	88.6%
Asian	17.0	0.1	46.7	4.3	7.7	–	7.6
Arab	0.4	–	0.2	0.0[b]	1.2	0.1	0.3
European	11.8	–	0.3	0.1	0.1	–	0.9
Not ascertained	3.7	1.3	5.0	3.7	1.6	2.0	2.6
	100.1%	100.0%	100.0%	100.0%	100.0%	100.1%	100.0%
	(543)	(1,960)	(640)	(2,134)	(1,363)	(1,123)	(7,763)

Source: Tanzania 1967 Census (totals refer to heads of household).

[a] That is, 67.2% of the heads of household in Ward 1 reported they were African.

[b] That is, less than 0.05%.

Although Chagga comprise almost two-fifths of the town population as a whole, the proportion of Chagga in the different wards ranges from 6.7 to 54.4 percent.[8] Of course, the proportion of Chagga is smaller in those two wards where Europeans and Asians are concentrated. In Ward 6, an agricultural area in the plains south of the town recently incorporated into the town proper, the proportion of Chagga is substantially lower than in the older urban wards. (See Table 8.2.)

The wards differ by religion as well. Settlement patterns reflect the paths of religious influence. Islam was largely spread to Moshi by coastal traders who traveled up the Pangani (or Ruvu) Valley from the south, and the largest Muslim concentrations are in the two southeast wards, 5 and 6. Christianity came largely from the east (entry via Mombasa) and from the north (the hillside mission stations), and the northern and eastern wards, 1 and 2, have large Christian populations. Modern factors have reinforced this pattern: location of mosques and churches, types and locations of schools, immigration of coastal (largely Muslim) peoples to work on sisal plantations south of town. The population in Ward 4 is rapidly expanding, especially

small discrepancies in totals among the tables. To preserve the anonymity of informants, reference to wards will be by number.

8. The treatment of tribe is not fully satisfactory in the Tanzania 1967 Census. First, as has been noted, distortions may be introduced because only heads of household were asked their tribe. Second, census statisticians, in order to maximize comparability, largely limited themselves to the tribes listed in the Tanzania 1957 census, thus, perhaps, eliminating or coalescing by fiat groups whose linguistic affinities and common identification might otherwise lead them to be defined as tribes. Third, because of this a priori decision about what the tribes were, it is impossible to consider the shifting salience of ethnicity: the circumstances under which an individual in Kilimanjaro might identify himself as a man-from-Machame and those in which he would call himself a Chagga. Fourth, there was no attempt to deal with mixed tribal origins, an especially unfortunate decision for the study of urban areas. The totals presented here, however, are sufficiently accurate for the purposes of this discussion.

Moshi Cell Leaders

Table 8.2.   Moshi Town: Ethnic Group, by Ward

Wards:	1	2	3	4	5	6	Moshi
Chagga	13.9%[a]	44.9%	6.7%	54.4%	36.9%	19.9%	37.2%
Neighboring[b]	5.1	14.4	8.9	7.7	14.4	26.2	13.3
(Pare)	(3.3)	(10.4)	(6.6)	(6.6)	(10.5)	(22.9)	(10.4)
Other African	45.6	35.3	29.9	28.5	33.6	47.5	34.9
Not applicable[c]	30.4	1.2	48.8	5.2	9.5	0.4	9.7
Not ascertained	2.0	1.1	1.9	2.6	0.9	2.0	1.8
	100.0%	100.0%	100.0%	100.0%	100.0%	100.0%	100.0%
	(545)	(1,964)	(640)	(2,127)	(1,368)	(1,116)	(7,760)

Where Chagga in Moshi Live:	N	Percent
Ward 1	76	2.6%[d]
2	882	30.5
3	43	1.5
4	1,158	40.1
5	505	17.5
6	222	7.7
Moshi	2,886	99.9%

Source: Tanzania 1967 Census (totals refer to heads of household).

[a] That is, 13.9% of the heads of household in Ward 1 reported their tribe as Chagga.

[b] Includes: Arusha, Masai, Meru, Pare, and Taveta-Teita.

[c] Non-Africans.

[d] That is, 2.6% of the heads of household in Moshi who report their tribe as Chagga live in Ward 1.

as many of the prosperous coffee farmers have built homes there, and this perhaps explains the large Christian population in that ward. The Asian concentration in Ward 3 is reflected in the identification by nearly a quarter of the population of that ward with other world religions (for example, Hindu). The large number of Asian Muslims explains the high proportion of Muslims in that ward. (See Table 8.3.)

Ward 1, then, is almost entirely a residential ward, where most of the Europeans in town, as well as many of the more affluent Asians and Africans, live.[9] The Asian community in Ward 1—civil servants and prosperous local businessmen—is rather stable, but because housing for senior government officials is located in that ward, many of the Africans in Ward 1 are civil servants, subject to frequent transfer, and many of the Europeans are on short-term contracts. Tanzania's Police Training School is located in Ward 1. Also included within the boundaries of this ward is a small agricultural community. This area formerly was more densely populated, but the farmers are rapidly

9. This was the situation in 1969. It is unlikely that the nationalization of high-value property in Tanzania in 1971 substantially altered these residential patterns.

The Politicians

Table 8.3. Moshi Town: Religion, by Ward

Wards:	1	2	3	4	5	6	Moshi
Christian	59.1%[a]	66.8%	23.9%	66.9%	39.5%	36.0%	53.5%
Muslim	23.6	29.8	43.3	25.8	53.3	59.1	37.7
Other world religion[b]	8.5	0.1	23.6	0.6	4.8	−	3.6
Local belief	1.5	1.2	0.9	1.4	1.2	2.2	1.4
Other	0.2	0.4	0.5	0.3	0.1	0.1	0.3
Not ascertained	7.2	1.7	7.8	5.1	1.1	2.6	3.5
	100.1%	100.0%	100.0%	100.1%	100.0%	100.0%	100.0%
	(543)	(1,960)	(640)	(2,135)	(1,363)	(1,123)	(7,764)

Source: Tanzania 1967 Census (totals refer to heads of household).

[a] That is, 59.1% of the heads of household in Ward 1 reported they were Christian.

[b] For example, Hindu.

being forced farther out by the planned expansion of urban housing. This area, with little in common with the rest of the ward, functions almost as a TANU subbranch of its own.

Ward 2 is a relatively newer section of town, made up mostly of working-class Africans. The Town Council fire station and sanitation and street maintenance depots, as well as the most frequently used town football field, are located in this ward. Most houses are of reinforced mud construction, though there are an increasing number of larger, more substantial houses as well. A small market and a large Council-owned beer club are located in this ward. Ward 2 has its own TANU branch office, built by local residents, and a paid party secretary. The large number of temporary industrial employees and unskilled Town Council laborers who live in this ward make it somewhat more transient in character than the central urban wards.

Ward 3 is the primary business area of Moshi. Most major shops are owned and run by Asians, many of whom live above, or very near, their shops, The Town Hall, many of the regional and district administrative offices, the coffee cooperative headquarters, and regional, district, and branch party headquarters are all located in this ward. Ward 3 also includes the factory where all Tanzanian arabica coffee is cured, and a small settlement where many of the lower-level factory employees live, as well as the railway station and housing for railway employees. Nonetheless, the branch chairman in 1969 saw his job as representing and leading an entirely Asian ward.

Wards 4 and 5 include the oldest and most densely populated sections of town. But Ward 4, in which is located the central town market, also includes the newest section of town. In the newer area there are many large, fashionably decorated houses of cement block, of which a large proportion were built to provide rental income by coffee farmers who live on the mountain. Ward 5 is largely a lower-class African ward, where most houses are made of mud and wood. A large Council-owned beer club and most of Moshi's industrial establishments are located in Ward 5.

Moshi Cell Leaders

Ward 6 is a predominantly agricultural area only recently incorporated into the town. Because Ward 6 is physically distant from the built-up, urban area of the town, and because the residents and leaders of Ward 6 are only beginning to think of themselves as part of Moshi town, the cell leaders of Ward 6 were not surveyed.

The Survey

Developing a random sample survey of Moshi cell leaders proved a difficult and frustrating task.[10] A complete list of Moshi cell leaders did not exist, and the partial lists that could be found were inaccurate. Branch chairmen assisted in drawing up lists of the cell leaders in their branches, but at times even they were unsure whether a given individual was in fact a cell leader or still lived in his cell. Several people thought to be cell leaders by their branch chairman turned out to have moved or to have ceased serving as cell leader for some other reason. And one former cell leader (who was a high government official) thought that whoever had moved into his former house was the current cell leader. (He had left his cell leader flag flying there, hadn't he?)

Because of the differences among the wards, after corrected lists of cell leaders were constructed, a sample comprising 20 percent of the cell leaders in each ward was randomly selected. Individuals in Moshi who had already been interviewed as political leaders were excluded from the cell leader lists, both to limit the survey to ordinary cell leaders and to avoid giving undue weight to a few individuals' opinions. Many of the political leaders of Moshi indicated they had been elected cell leaders after having been selected for their leadership positions. That suggests that where a political notable lives in a cell, and where he has not estranged himself from the local residents, he is likely to be chosen cell leader, and that cell leadership may follow, not precede, selection to other leadership positions. Since the concern here is with the functioning and effect of the cell system as an institution grafted on to existing political structures, it is perfectly reasonable to exclude political leaders who also happen to be cell leaders. The latter have already been discussed; it is the former who are of interest here.

Local political notables introduced the interviewer to the cell leaders to facilitate cooperation and allay suspicion. The cell leaders selected were then interviewed at their homes, using an adapted, more closed-ended, version of the question schedule used for the Moshi political leadership. Twenty-nine such interviews, representing a random sample constituting 20 percent of the ordinary cell leaders in Wards 1–5, were conducted in 1969. Only one cell leader originally selected proved unwilling to cooperate.

It should be stressed that the data gathered from this survey can be

10. This section is intended to describe briefly the survey of Moshi Cell leaders; for a more detailed discussion of the survey and the complete question schedule used, see Appendix 2.

generalized to the cell leaders of Moshi town only with due caution. The sample of cell leaders interviewed was constructed to ensure that each of the branches, which varied widely in political behavior and attitudes, was represented, with the effect that the peculiarities of each branch may be overrepresented in the final results. Local political leaders, many of whom also served as cell leaders, were expressly excluded. The police barracks and the police training school, both enclaves of nonlocal people in Moshi, and both in the process of forming TANU branches of their own in 1969, together with the coffee-curing company village, all not yet major participants in the local political process, were not included. Ward 6, only loosely connected to the town, also was not included. Because the survey was dependent on the assistance of branch chairmen to construct cell leader lists, some very inactive cell leaders, either forgotten or expressly overlooked by their branch chairmen, may have been excluded. Thus, the sample of Moshi cell leaders can be taken to represent the ordinary, and among the ordinary perhaps the more active, cell leaders of the regular population of Moshi town.

Who They Are

In general, cell leaders in Moshi in 1969 were similar to the neighbors who elected them. Three-fifths (62 percent) were born in Kilimanjaro Region, and three-quarters (76 percent) had lived in their current residences for more than ten years (almost half had lived in their current residences for more than twenty years). Two-fifths (41 percent) of the cell leaders were Chagga, and 17 percent came from neighboring tribes. (Because only Asian cell leaders had been selected from Ward 3, Asians, constituting 17 percent of the sample, were overrepresented in comparison with their proportion of the total town population.) Almost half of the cell leaders (48 percent) were Christian, and 41 percent were Muslim. Most of the cell leaders, like most of the town residents, rented their homes. The cell leaders in general had less education than the district and regional level leadership: 31 percent had less than four years of schooling, and 65 percent had seven years or less. Cell leaders were not concentrated in a single occupation: 48 percent had salaried employment, 31 percent were self-employed, and 14 percent gained their principal income from farming. Almost all (90 percent) of the cell leaders interviewed were male, but that finding simply reflects the large number of males in the urban area (130 males to 100 females) and the fact that the continuing impact of tradition in Tanzania restricts access to most leadership positions to men. Cell leaders in Moshi in 1969 were not former traditional leaders. There were no traditional leaders with accepted claim to tribal authority regularly resident in the urban area, and Moshi as a town is so young that few people held office there for very long. Nor were Moshi cell leaders especially modern urban residents or ideological radicals. As will be noted, the most modern elements had little use for cell leaders and in any case were largely clustered into a single ward, and the very few individuals in Moshi who publicly expressed an ideology, other than repeating party doctrine, were either too young or too eccentric to be respected and trusted by their neighbors.

All of this suggests that, in Moshi at least, where there are functioning cells (and it should be noted that in 1969 there were several sections in town where cells did not function at all), local residents have elected as cell leaders people whom they regard as fundamentally like themselves. The cell leaders elected, because they are like their constituents, can be expected to be, on the one hand, people the residents of the cell will approach with little fear or hesitation and, on the other hand, individuals whom the district level leadership of the party can assume to be representative of the residents of their cells.

But not all cell leaders elected, excluding those areas in which there are no functioning cells,[11] actually perform any services, and in fact cell leaders tend to mirror their constituents' attitudes toward the cell system. Few Asians in Moshi see TANU as their party in the way that most Africans do, and consequently cell leaders in predominantly Asian cells report they have little to do. Likewise, few residents of the more affluent residential sections of town see any need for the type of reconciliation in local disputes and intercession with the bureaucracy that cell leaders perform in other parts of town, and consequently cell leaders in those sections also report they have little to do. These attitudes are reflected even at the level of the branch leadership, so that how active a cell leader actually is depends both on the nature of his cell and on the demands, encouragement, and support from his branch chairman.

What They Do

Ordinary cell leaders in Moshi were not political activists.[12] Four-fifths (83 percent) reported that no one in their families had been involved in political activity, and three-fourths (76 percent) report they themselves had not been politically active before independence or in the early postcolonial period. None of the cell leaders surveyed had been politically active for more than ten years (unlike the town councillors), and 83 percent had held no political positions before elction as cell leader; one-third said they had been active in politics for less than two years. Tenure as cell leader varied widely: one-third of the cell leaders surveyed had served as cell leaders for more than three years, while almost as many (27 percent) had been cell leaders for less than two years. Reported TANU membership is especially striking. Fully 38 percent had joined TANU after 1964 (one, when elected cell leader, decided he ought to join),

---

11. Short of a survey of the entire town population, which was not attempted, there was no easily available method for assessing the coverage of the cell system. Local leaders believed that some areas of the town were better covered than others; some areas could be identified that had no cell leaders. The population per cell leader in Moshi, with an average household size of 3.5 people, varied from 129 in Ward 5 to 340 in Ward 3.

12. It should be stressed again that individuals who held current active leadership positions (councillors, party chairmen and secretaries) were excluded from the cell leader survey.

The Politicians

Table 8.4.   Cell Leaders and Elected Town Councillors: Local Contacts

	Cell leader sample	Elected town councillors
Very many (11+ per day)	0%[a]	21%
Many (6–10 per day)	0	16
Average (1–5 per day, or at least 25 per month)	10	32
Few (2–7 per week, or at least 8 per month)	7	11
Very few (2–7 per month)	31	11
Only occasionally (1 per month or fewer)	38	11
None	14	0
	100%	102%
	(N=29)	(N=19)

Source: Moshi Political Leadership Survey (Question 13) and Moshi Cell Leader Survey (Questions 6–13).

[a] That is, none of the cell leaders reported that very many (11 or more per day) people came to see them for advice or assistance.

and one was not a TANU member at all in 1969. In an important sense, cell leaders may be major local figures and at the same time may not associate that position, either in their own minds or for their neighbors, with party membership or activity.

In general, cell leaders see their job as dealing with the disputes and conflicts that arise in their cells. They perform the linkage and intermediary sorts of roles in the fluid, transient, multiethnic, and multireligious urban setting that traditional leaders perform in areas where clan and tribe are still the basic social units and where traditional leaders have not been replaced by more modern sorts of roles.[13]

When asked what they think is the most important problem in their cells, more than half of the cell leaders (55 percent) listed the kinds of problems that might be grouped together as social dislocation: household and marital quarrels, disputes between landlord and tenants, drunkenness and unruly behavior, and petty theft and minor assault. Another 17 percent mentioned unemployment. When asked what they can do about these problems, only 28 percent said they could do nothing at all (a far smaller percentage than the proportion of other political leaders who described themselves as unable to deal with what they consider to be major problems). More than half (52 percent) said they took action that did not involve TANU. From another perspective, while 90 percent said the problems they mentioned could be resolved locally, only 17 percent said the problems they mentioned could be resolved politically. Thus, unlike the elected town councillors, cell leaders define as important those sorts of local,

13. Norman N. Miller stresses the continuing role for traditional leaders in new bureaucratic institutions in one area of rural Tanzania, in "The Political Survival of Traditional Leadership," but also notes the role of the local party organization in local dispute settlements, in "The Rural African Party: Political Participation in Tanzania."

Moshi Cell Leaders

Table 8.5. Scope and Nature of Problems Brought to Cell Leaders

	Cell leaders
Problems brought are:	
Local, individual[a]	66%[b]
Local, group	3
Local, both individual and group	17
Not asked (said no one came to see him)	14
	100%
	(N=29)

Source: Moshi Cell Leader Survey (Questions 7, 10, 12).

[a] "Local" refers to scope or arena, while "individual" and "group" refer to type: for example, domestic quarrels were coded as local, individual, while disputes between a group of parents and a school headteacher were coded as local, group; objective determination. Note that no cell leaders reported receiving problems that were national in scope.

[b] That is, 66% of the cell leaders surveyed reported that problems brought to them were individual in nature and local in scope.

immediate disputes and conflicts that trouble residents of their cells, and they think they can deal with them effectively, largely as reconcilers and arbitrators, without involving the political machinery.

By the local leadership's own analysis, fewer people seek out their cell leaders for assistance in their problems than seek out their councillors (see Table 8.4). The councillors of course represent more people than do cell leaders, and can be expected by local residents to be more influential. But it is also the case that local residents seek help from their cell leaders primarily for local quarrels and disputes—conflicts more likely to be brought to leaders whom the people know personally and in whom they have confidence. Almost two-thirds (66 percent) of the cell leaders surveyed said that the problems people brought to them were local in scope and individual in nature, and another 17 percent said that both individual and group problems, but all local in scope, were brought to them (see Table 8.5). That is, most cell leaders said that the problems people brought to them concerned a very limited local arena and rarely had an impact on anyone other than those who raised the problems. For example, a tenant who had lost his job may ask his cell leader to intercede with his landlord to request an extension on rent payments. Or a parent may seek the cell leader's help in reconciling her daughter and her daughter's husband. Problems dealt with by cell leaders occasionally do extend beyond the local area. In 1969, for example, one prominent cell leader, aided by elders living in the cell, spent several days dealing with a complex problem of marital discord, rights to the children, and ownership of bridewealth, in which one side of the family had to come to Moshi from Tabora to participate in the discussions. Nor are all problems concerned with individual disputes. Cell leaders are often asked to mediate between a group of parents and the headteacher of the local primary school.

Table 8.6. Cell Leaders: Dealing with Problems Brought to Them

	Cell leaders
Respondent is:[a]	
General source of assistance, advice	21%[b]
Pacifier, reconciler, arbitrator	55
Representative to the government[c]	7
Representative to TANU (including TANU and government)	3
Not asked (respondent said no one came to see him)	14
	100%
	(N=29)

Source: Moshi Cell Leader Survey (Questions 7–13).

[a] Coded from all problems brought to respondent, according to respondent's own description of his behavior, into mutually exclusive categories, beginning from the bottom.

[b] That is, 21% of the cell leaders surveyed reported they provided general assistance and advice to people who came to them with problems.

[c] Carries messages toward: for example, transmit a complaint brought by a cell resident to the ward councillor.

One of the most striking findings of this survey is that almost half of the cell leaders (41 percent) reported they were able to solve the problems brought to them by themselves, while not one of the elected town councillors said that. In dealing with the problems brought to them, three-fourths of the cell leaders said they served as a general source of assistance and advice, or as a pacifier, reconciler, or arbitrator. (See Table 8.6.) This supports the finding that cell leaders are primarily concerned with low-level local disputes and that they can use the authority that is associated with the cell leader role, together with their familiarity with local residents and their problems, to deal effectively with the problems brought to them. The cell leaders' definition of their own jobs further confirms this finding. Some 41 percent of the cell leaders surveyed said that they thought the primary job of the cell leader was to reconcile, arbitrate, and adjudicate (see Table 8.7).[14]

While they are engaged in dealing with these local disputes, many cell leaders also link the residents of their cells with the party, both because they are identified as TANU officials and the party supervises their selection and because most cell leaders said that they referred to the TANU office the problems they were unable to handle themselves. In fact, a majority (59 percent) of the cell leaders saw this—reconciliation in local disputes—as the major function of of the local TANU organization.[15] This perception of the cell leaders, that the

14. Norman N. Miller's survey in a rural area of Tanzania in 1965 found that only 7.8 percent of the individuals surveyed (only a small percentage of those surveyed were themselves cell leaders) mentioned this as the primary purpose of the party cell. See the Codebook: Basic Questionnaire Data, p. 22, prepared in connection with his "Village Leadership and Modernization in Tanzania" (Ph.D. diss., Indiana University, 1967).

15. Most cell leaders and ordinary citizens in Moshi regard the TANU office, and thus

Moshi Cell Leaders

Table 8.7.   Cell Leaders: The Job of Cell Leader

	Cell leaders[a]
Reconciliation, arbitration, adjudication	41%[b]
Receive complaints and pass them upwards	10
Receive complaints and send people to proper place	3
Receive complaints and deal with them himself	7
Explain policies of TANU, Tanzania	10
Lead, exhort, encourage, enthuse people in cell	17
Generalized assistance to people in cell	10
	98%
	(N=29)

Source: Moshi Cell Leader Survey (Questions 4, 23, 24).

[a] Major job, as defined by the respondent himself, coded into mutually exclusive categories.

[b] That is, 41% of the cell leaders surveyed saw their job as one of reconciling, arbitrating, and adjudicating in local conflicts.

primary task of TANU is to settle local disputes, is supported by the existence of a TANU Elders Council. When ordinary cell leaders visit the TANU office, they most often see the Elders, or the branch secretary who generally refers them to the Elders, and they are less aware of other TANU activities.

The Moshi Elders Council was a somewhat unique institution in Tanzania in 1968–69, but late in 1969 the government and party decided to establish Arbitration Tribunals, essentially similar to the Moshi Elders Council, throughout the country. The Council in Moshi, consisting of the chairman and vice-chairman of the elders at the district (town) level, sat daily in the TANU office to deal with local disputes and conflicts. They served as a board of appeal for decisions by cell leaders, they took the cases the cell leaders were unable to deal with, and they often heard cases brought directly by the parties to a dispute or referred by party or government officials. Without clear statutory authority and unable to impose sanctions,[16] they heard cases, kept records, and tried to reconcile the individuals involved. They were often successful in reuniting husband and wife, in settling inheritance and bridewealth disputes, in reconciling landlord and tenant and employer and employee, and even in finding agreement between debtor and creditor. In some disputes the parties simply agreed publicly to accept the Elders' findings, while in others a formal

the local party organization, as an undifferentiated unit, even though the TANU office houses branch, district (both urban and rural), and regional party offices, as well as the TANU Youth League, the Elders, the Women's Union, and the Tanganyika Africa Parents Association.

16. Although under Tanzanian law their findings might be considered decisions according to customary law and thus legally enforceable, the Council in Moshi, local government and party officials, and ordinary citizens all understood the Elders Council to have no legal authority.

signed agreement was created. Dissatisfied parties could then carry their cases to the primary court, but most primary court magistrates in Moshi were reluctant to hear cases of this sort if the parties had not already tried the Elders Council, and most acknowledged the agreements signed before the Elders as legally binding. Perhaps a major reason for the success of the Elders Council in Moshi was that both members also served as town headmen,[17] and thus carried the prestige and authority of the Town Council officials, and the chairman was also the local Muslim sheikh. Thus, the Elders Council combined the respect accorded elders with party, government, and even religious authority and prestige to deal with a wide array of local conflicts. In this way, as well, institutionalized mechanisms for conflict resolution that began at the level of the cell leader were incorporated into Tanzania's judicial machinery.

The prevalence of this view of the cell leader's job—reconciliation in local disputes—helps explain the infrequency of meetings called by the cell leader for all of the residents of the cell. Only 14 percent of the cell leaders had held a meeting within the previous month, and 28 percent said they never held meetings. If the major task is to assist individuals, why call everyone together? And although a few cell leaders did mention calling meetings to discuss theft or drunkenness within the cell, most meetings called were in response to instructions from higher party authorities, primarily to deal with elections.

The ordinary cell leaders in Moshi in 1969, then, were primarily concerned with local dispute settlement and providing general assistance to the residents of their cells. Because their first recourse, when they were unable to handle problems themselves, was to turn to the TANU office, they provided a link between the urban population and party and government. The most active of the cell leaders become advocates for their constituents within party and government structures. Most cell leaders feel competent to handle the problems brought to them, and most cell leaders think they are successful in doing so. And in dealing with these problems cell leaders assist the police, the local judiciary, and local government officials in performing their jobs. Less often are cell leaders concerned with downward communication: explaining party policy and mobilizing people to participate in government programs. Although the national leadership asserts that cell leaders are critical in communicating policy to up-country Tanzania, and although occasionally lower-level leaders exhort party cadres to explain national policy to the mass of the population, in 1969 few cell leaders in Moshi had the training or inclination to bear very much detailed downward communication. Few had a clear understanding of the Arusha Declaration, and fewer still were equipped or inclined to spend much time explaining it to others. After the 1969 party elections, national, regional, and district party and government leaders participated in political seminars, some lasting as long as three months. When the newly elected Moshi

17. As explained previously, this term is a carry over from the colonial period; the three Moshi town headmen might better be described as ward executive officers.

TANU Chairman returned from his three-month seminar, he met with the cell leaders in each ward, primarily to introduce himself and hear their problems, a common practice for officials assuming a new post. He spoke also of organizing seminars for cell leaders, but, as will be noted shortly, even with the seminars the obstacles to developing a set of dynamic and resourceful cell leaders will remain significant.

It should be stressed again that cell leaders in the most affluent sections of town, and in the sections of town where the concentration of the European and Asian population is high, felt they had little to do, were rarely sought out by the residents of their cells, and performed few services.

Another important factor in the performance of cell leaders, impossible to quantify because of the small number of cases in Moshi town, is the attitude and behavior of the branch chairmen. Where the branch chairman feels that cell leaders have little function, as was the case in the predominantly Asian ward in Moshi, cell leaders do little. The cell leaders were the most active in the two wards where the branch chairmen were self-employed and thus could always be easily found in their neighborhoods, and where the branch chairmen, who knew most of their cell leaders well, encouraged and supported their cell leaders. In the ward where the chairman's job kept him away from the neighborhood during working hours, and where the chairman was considered by many ward residents to be a somewhat irresponsible alcoholic, there were several blocks without any cell leaders, and many cell leaders said they did little. But it is an important comment on the vitality and viability of the cell system in Tanzania that in three wards with unenthusiastic and largely inactive leadership, small communities—residents of the police training school, the police barracks, and the village for coffee curing plant employees—which had a work-related stimulus to be active politically, had selected cell leaders, and had begun to form TANU branches of their own.

Conclusions

We have found that in Moshi urban residents elect as cell leaders people essentially like themselves. In 1968–69 ordinary cell leaders in Moshi were similar to their constituents in ethnic origin and tribe, in religion, and in level of income and type of occupation. The cell leaders were usually not traditional authority figures, nor were they often younger, better educated, or more modern than the residents of their cells. Ordinary cell leaders as a group had a relatively brief history of political activity, and few were active politically, at least outside their own branches, while they served as cell leaders. Cell leaders did not constitute a political, social or economic elite in Moshi. With few exceptions, this finding that cell leaders were not a local elite is supported by the other studies of cell leaders elsewhere in Tanzania.[18]

Two basic types of cell leader role had developed in Moshi by 1969. In

18. See, especially, the concluding chapter in O'Barr and Samoff, *Cell Leaders in*

wards where there were concentrations of affluent and/or European and Asian population, and to a lesser extent in wards where there was a largely lackadaisical or apathetic branch chairman, cell leaders performed few services for their constituents. In other areas of the town, however, cell leaders had active roles in local conflict resolution and generally assisted their constituents with their problems. The implication of this finding is striking. For the mass of the urban population, only relatively recently removed from a rural agricultural society, faced with the stresses and demands of urban life, of salaried employment (and, more likely, unemployment), and of imposing bureaucracies, without the security of traditional networks of obligations and support, cell leaders can help provide some of the links that bind the society together. Cell leaders assume at least some, and often a great deal, of the responsibility for dealing with the myriad little problems of human interaction in the multiethnic and multireligious urban community that might be dealt with more comfortably in the traditional society but become seemingly insoluble crises in the urban setting. The local ethnic organizations that are so common elsewhere in Africa and once flourished in Tanzania have, faced with concerted and persistent opposition from party and government, by and large disappeared into relative insignificance in Moshi.[19] That is not to say that there do not remain associations based largely on ethnic ties that bring together segments of the urban populace and perform for them a range of welfare functions. It is rather to argue that in Moshi in 1969 such organizations did not have the prominence and political power of similar organizations elsewhere and that for many Moshi residents, TANU, and especially the cell leaders, provided the welfare services that such organizations provide elsewhere. Where people in Moshi are more accustomed to dealing with the stresses and insecurities of urban life, as in the more affluent and upper civil service residential areas, or where people deal with these problems within their own communities in traditional ways, as in the Asian sections of town, cell leaders are less needed to perform these functions.

With a few exceptions, these patterns seem general throughout Tanzania. Rapid social change has generated a range of interpersonal and intercommunal conflicts. These conflicts are in an important sense new conflicts, in that they stem from a changing situation and in that existing conflict-resolving and tension-reducing institutions had not had to deal with them. Where existing institutions have been maintained despite the pressures for change, as, for example,

---

Tanzania, which summarizes the findings of the different case studies; see also, Proctor, The Cell System of the Tanganyika African National Union.

19. For comments on the strength of ethnic organizations in other urban areas in Africa, see, among others, William John Hanna and Judith Lynne Hanna, "The Political Structure of Urban-Centered African Communities," Chapter 7 in The City in Modern Africa, ed. Horace Miner (New York: Praeger, 1967); and M. Banton, "Adaptation and Integration in the Social System of Temne Immigrants in Freetown," Africa 26, no. 4 (1956): 354–67.

among the Asian communities in urban Tanzania, those existing structures have been utilized to deal with these new conflicts. But where existing institutions are themselves changing fundamentally, a new institution, the cell system, has become the site for dealing with these new conflicts.

In functioning in this way, in concentrating on general assistance and dispute settlement, cell leaders, as TANU officials, provide a link between the urban population, at least in those wards where cell leaders are active, and the party. In addition, by channeling problems into the Elders Council, cell leaders provide an extension of Tanzania's judicial machinery that reaches down onto the individual's front porch. Thus, the conflicts engendered by rapid social change, to a large extent fueled, if not initiated, by TANU, are often resolved within the framework of the party. In that way, the conflict resolution process, by developing norms that encourage ordinary Tanzanians to turn to the party rather than to other institutions for assistance, becomes a major vehicle for the integration of Tanzania's diverse communities. That cell leaders are more concerned with representing their constituents, and themselves, to the party and government than with explaining policy and mobilizing people reinforces the integrative elements of their roles.

There are several limitations on this kind of activity by the cell leaders. It has already been noted that in some sections of town they are rarely sought out by local residents. It has also been noted that the encouragement and support of the branch chairman are a key determinant of what cell leaders are able and willing to do. The combination of the transience of much of the urban population and the stringent leadership requirements of the Arusha Declaration provides a third limitation on the ability of cell leaders to function effectively. Although precise figures are impossible to obtain, it is clear that a large segment of Moshi's African population is transient. People from surrounding areas come to town to work for several years and then return home or move on elsewhere; as people find and change jobs they often change neighborhoods; and as families grow, rented quarters become inadequate. To function effectively as a cell leader, an individual must have lived in his neighborhood for some time and be known to its residents, but as leaders in Tanzania, cell leaders are not permitted to own homes to secure rental income. Thus, the stable residents in a cell are the landlords, who are barred from election as cell leaders, and the frequent moves among renters makes it difficult, in some neighborhoods at least, for cell leaders to develop the trust and respect necessary to their jobs.

All of this suggests that cell leaders play a key role in ameliorating the stresses of urban life, and in providing for the urban populace a visible link—one in which they can have some faith—with the party. To the extent that they are effective in performing these functions, they can integrate disparate communities into a single political system. But it also suggests that ordinary urban cell leaders (and it should be stressed again that all of this discussion refers to ordinary cell leaders in an urban setting) are insufficiently equipped and motivated to provide a dynamic local leadership able to relate national policies to the Moshi setting and to mobilize people to implement development schemes. The rewards for cell leaders, even symbolic, thus far are few. And where the cell leader is expected to function as something of a local elder, there is little to endear younger and more educated residents to their neighbors or to encourage them to seek the cell leader job.

It makes sense, then, to consider the cell leaders facilitators but not initiators of change. It also makes sense, however, to consider cell leaders as much local agents of order as facilitators of change. They are clearly significant elements in the development of viable institutions of local government. This is not to suggest that these postures are necessarily contradictory. It is rather to argue that there is a necessary interplay between order and change, and that Tanzania must establish a new order and promote change simultaneously. That these goals will occasionally conflict is clear. That some individuals are best suited to the one and inadequate to the challenge of the other is equally clear. And it is the cell leaders who are in the key position in this dynamic tension between change and order at the local level in Tanzania.

This leaves, then, something of a paradox. The place assigned to cell leaders in the national strategy for developing Tanzania calls for just the sort of individuals unlikely to emerge in the cell leader positions as they have come to be defined locally. And yet if it is not the cell leaders who are to carry the party ideology to the mass of the Tanzanian population and who are to carry the ideas, demands, and complaints of the ordinary citizens to its leaders, who are in short to be the backbone of a viable party at the local level, then who is it to be?

9

Politicians in Kilimanjaro

Having spent some time surveying the local political horizon through the eyes of the Moshi leadership, we can now supplement those observations with the perspectives of other leaders interviewed. Recall that the list of leaders consulted in this study was an expansive one: all individuals who, by virtue of formal position held, or by reputation, or by observation, seemed to be important actors in the local political system were interviewed.[1] In addition to those town leaders already discussed, political leaders at district, regional, and national levels were interviewed. This wide net included some elected individuals, some appointed, some party, some nonparty, and some with single, some with multiple roles. Their views, together with the findings of the issue studies, render more precise some of the more salient elements of political conflict in Kilimanjaro.

The aim here, then, is three-fold: first, to expand several points that have emerged in the study of Kilimanjaro political leaders; second, to discuss more generally several major themes of politics in Kilimanjaro; and, finally, to sketch out briefly the factional alignments that characterized political conflict in Kilimanjaro in 1968-69.

Some Observations

The Moshi political leadership is a relatively isolated one, with a narrow range of extraurban contacts. When they discussed the sorts of problems their

1. To avoid confusion over terminology: the term *political leaders* refers to that set of individuals assessed by virtue of formal position held, reputation, or observation, or any combination of the three to be significant actors in the local political arena; *politicians* refers to those political leaders who have contested office and to those who hold office at the pleasure of either the party or the President or both. In this discussion, *elite* refers simply to those relatively few people whose education, occupation, or wealth clearly set them apart from the mass of the population, and *elite status* refers simply to the prestige, perquisites, and presumed influence of elites. For an early anthology of research on this subject, see "African Elites," *International Social Science Bulletin* 8, no. 3 (1956), an entire issue devoted to African elites. For a more recent, brief, and caustic comment on the state of the discipline in the study of African elites by one of the leading

constituents brought to them, both the town councillors and the cell leaders reported that no one came to see them about problems that were national in scope. While no political leader reported receiving many such problems, the fact that none of the Moshi leaders received them is striking. Other indicators as well support this assessment of the limited scope of town leaders. While 80 percent of the urban leadership reported they rarely traveled outside of the town, almost half of the other district level leaders traveled extensively throughout Kilimanjaro. Of the political leaders who did not hold formal leadership positions, half reported they traveled regularly throughout Kilimanjaro and to Dar es Salaam, and all of the regional and national level leaders maintained regular contacts in the capital. In general, the appointed leaders traveled more widely and more often than did elected officials. To travel widely or frequently is of course not necessarily equivalent to representing constituents or linking them to other sectors of the polity. But this finding does suggest that when urban residents have problems that call for action at the regional or national level, or when they are interested in securing favorable decisions from officials not in Moshi, their councillors are able to be of little direct help to them. Support for this observation is also found in the leaders' descriptions of whom they would see to influence a national decision: most of the locally elected leaders said they would talk to other local people. In short, the locally elected leaders in Moshi in 1969 were a distinctly local leadership. Neither they nor their constituents thought much of their ability to provide representation in broader decisional arenas.

The study of issues and individuals thus far has suggested that there is no small elite with a monopoly of power in the local setting, able to influence outcomes in a wide range of issues. The observations of the political leaders themselves support this view. Leaders were asked to name people they considered to be "influential" or "powerful" locally; where further explanation was necessary, leaders were asked to name individuals who were usually able to convince other people and to secure favorable decisions on issues in which they were involved.[2] From a group of fewer than seventy-eight people,[3] some seventy-six individuals were named. By a minimum standard of influence—mention by at least 10 percent of those asked (eight or more mentions)—ten people could be described as influential, and no single individual was named by more than one-fourth of those asked. That is, although leadership and elite studies might lead us to expect relatively high agreement by most of those asked that a few indi-

practitioners, see William John Hanna, "Methodology, Technology, and the Study of African Elites," *African Studies Review* 13, no. 1 (April, 1970): 95–103.

2. See Appendix 1 for the complete wording of the questions used.

3. Cell leaders were not asked this question; a few leaders declined to respond, or would mention only positions and not individuals' names.

viduals were influential, in Moshi only a quarter of the leaders could agree on any one person, and fewer than 20 percent could agree on anyone else.

Likewise, there was little agreement among the leaders on whom to see to influence local or national decisions. For local influence, three-fifths of the district level leaders said they would see a local TANU officer, while one-fifth said they would see a local government official. To influence a national decision that affected the local area, local leaders tended to say they would see other local leaders, while among the regional and national-level leaders, some said they would take the matter up in Dar es Salaam, and none reported that he would see a local official.

There is thus little agreement among the Kilimanjaro political leadership on who is influential and little agreement on who could be helpful in influencing local and national decisions. This evidence supports the finding that there is no small cohesive elite with broad influence and power in Moshi and that the local populace has (or, rather, some of it has), and sees it has, several alternative, viable channels through which it can attempt to secure the decisions and outputs in which it is interested.

But to find competing elites is not the same as to find mass democracy. To what extent have political elites in Moshi been able to restrict access to key roles to a narrow stratum of the populace? And to what extent are the present political elites able to ensure their continued predominance in the local political system?

One of the major concerns of the Tanzanian leadership since Independence has been to attempt to ensure that the new leaders of Tanzania, those who replaced the departing colonial officials and those who assumed office in the new regime, did not use their access to political power to amass wealth, to guarantee continued access to political power, or to subvert national policy in order to develop and protect their own personal interests and fortunes. The manipulation of power to get rich and stay in power is of course not unique to Tanzania.[4]

In 1967 TANU announced a set of stringent prohibitions on the accumulation of wealth by both party and government leaders (see Table 9.1). In very broad terms, the problem is one of maximizing the utilization of scarce resources for national development without diverting substantial portions of those resources into the pockets of the nation-builders and without enabling

---

4. For a detailed exposition of the extent to which " '. . . a few African political and bureaucratic elite . . . are slowly merging with the commercial elite to form an apex at the top of the sociopolitical and economic elite' " (p. 259) in an economy still largely controlled by noncitizens, see *Who Controls Industry in Kenya?* (Nairobi: EAPH, 1968). For conflicting views on the significance of corruption, see the collection of papers edited by Arnold J. Heidenheimer, *Political Corruption* (New York: Holt, Rinehart and Winston, 1970). For an overview of elites, power, and wealth in West Africa, see P. C. Lloyd, *Africa in Social Change* (Baltimore: Penguin, 1967), Chapter 5.

The Politicians

Table 9.1.   Tanzania's Leadership Code

1. Every TANU and Government leader must be either a peasant or a worker, and should in no way be associated with the practices of capitalism or feudalism.[a]
2. No TANU or Government leader should hold shares in any company.
3. No TANU or Government leader should hold directorships in any privately owned enterprise.
4. No TANU or Government leader should receive two or more salaries.
5. No TANU or Government leader should own houses which he rents to others.
6. For the purposes of this Resolution the term "leader" should comprise the following: Members of the TANU National Executive Committee; Ministers; Members of Parliament; senior officials of organizations affiliated to TANU; senior officials of parastatal organizations; all those appointed or elected under any clause of the TANU Constitution; councillors; and civil servants in the high and middle cadres. (In this context "leader" means a man, or a man and his wife; a woman, or a woman and her husband.)[b]

Source: *The Arusha Declaration,* resolution adopted by the TANU National Executive Committee, Arusha, Tanzania, January 1967, Part Five (a). Published in Nyerere, *Ujamaa —Essays on Socialism,* p. 36.

[a] This has been interpreted to mean, among other things, that leaders should not hire permanent labor to work their farms.

[b] Leaders were given one year to divest themselves of holdings prohibited by this resolution or to resign their leadership positions. Since then each leader must file an annual statement of wealth, showing all income for him and his spouse for the previous year, for scrutiny by local and national party officers. Because children and parents are not mentioned in clause (6), some leaders have retained control of prohibited income by transferring formal ownership to their children or their parents.

those who manage the allocation of those resources to institutionalize their elite status. In personal terms, the problem is one of persuading or coercing leaders not to demand the luxurious life of the colonial officials they replaced and not to view leadership as a means to achieve wealth. In very human terms, the problem is one of convincing leaders not to act in what they see as their own self-interest.[5] One approach, embodied in Tanzania's leadership code, is to recognize that, despite governmental and party efforts to limit it, the easy life may be a necessary perquisite for many, if not most, successful leaders, and to concentrate, by restricting the accumulation of wealth, on ensuring that elite status is not a commodity automatically passed on to succeeding generations. A second approach, embodied in the TANU Guidelines,[6] is to strengthen

5. It is not suggested here that the manipulation of political power for personal interests by key leaders may not contribute substantially to rationalizing development efforts at the local level and to enlarging the scale of the nation. The development of local political machines will be discussed in Chapter 11.

6. Tanganyika African National Union, *TANU's Guidelines to Safeguard, Consolidate and Further the Tanzanian and African Revolution* (Dar es Salaam, 1971); see especially paragraphs 13–16.

Politicians in Kilimanjaro

the norm that leaders must be responsible and accountable to ordinary citizens.

Although this study has not been directed primarily toward questions of leadership recruitment and elite status, the data gathered do permit several observations on the ability of Kilimanjaro political leaders to manipulate political power for their own personal interests and to pass advantages thus secured on to their children.

Access to education and prominent occupations was severely curtailed for Tanzanians during the colonial period, and the fathers of most Kilimanjaro leaders surveyed in 1969 were farmers or otherwise self-employed. Yet decisions made during the colonial period, both by the colonial government and by the European missionaries, largely determined the composition of the new elite. Much of the early nationalist leadership was composed of mission-educated individuals, and education became the key determinant of who would replace the retiring colonial officers.[7] That this was true in Kilimanjaro is reflected in the fact that appointed leaders came from more educated families and were themselves more highly educated than other leaders and the population at large. In terms of education and occupation, then, Kilimanjaro leaders have already acquired elite status in Tanzania, where more than 90 percent of the population still lives in a subsistence agricultural economy.

Although most leaders surveyed reported little political activity in their families, the current leadership, with the exception of the cell leaders, has as a group held political positions for a long time. Some 40 percent of the regional and national level leaders held leadership positions during the early stages of TANU activity, and 60 percent have held political positions for more than ten years—since Independence. Thus, the current political leadership in Kilimanjaro is characterized not only by elite status in occupation and education, but also, with few exceptions, by early entry into political activity. Long political activity has in Tanzania, as in much of Africa (and the world), been associated with a rapid increase in wealth. Participants in the early phases of the struggle for independence were far from united in their agreement on specific goals beyond independence. In demanding independence TANU led a national movement that welcomed anyone who opposed the colonial government, largely regardless of individual political orientation.[8] Only several years after the end of colonial rule did President Nyerere and TANU begin to define the specific content of Tanzanian socialism and outline its implications for its leadership. It is not surprising, then, to find that some of the current leaders, who fought the colonial government to secure the good life for themselves, find it difficult to

7. On the educational determinants of elite status in Africa, see LeVine, *Political Leadership in Africa*, P. C. Lloyd, ed., *The New Elites of Tropical Africa* (New York: Oxford University Press, 1966), and Remi Clignet and Philip Foster, *The Fortunate Few* (Evanston, Ill.: Northwestern University Press, 1966).

8. Bienen, *Tanzania: Party Transformation,* makes this point; see Chapters 1 and 2.

accept and identify with the austerity now demanded of Tanzania's leaders. For these reasons, the leadership code of the Arusha Declaration notwithstanding, many of Kilimanjaro's leaders have used political office to move from humble backgrounds to lives of substantial comfort and affluence. Many, at least before the Arusha Declaration, had begun to use their wealth and access to power to accumulate property and shares in businesses to protect their status and pass it on to their children.

The impact of the leadership code seems to have been slow but steady in Kilimanjaro. Leaders divested themselves of prohibited sources of income only when it became clear, in some cases not until more than two years after the announcement of the Arusha Declaration, that they would lose their leadership positions if they did not. Some Kilimanjaro leaders, like several prominent national figures, ultimately resigned rather than comply. As has been noted, some local leaders continue to avoid the leadership restrictions by transferring formal control of prohibited income to children or parents. And some leaders are able to utilize state power to develop sources of income to provide for a comfortable retirement. One Regional Commissioner who served briefly in Kilimanjaro, for example, began planting near the capital the type of plantain seedling particular to the region of his former post, apparently using government transport and labor in the process. When his appointment as commissioner was revoked, he was able to begin immediately a profitable business of supplying to the inhabitants of his former region living in Dar es Salaam the type of plantain they preferred.

But while the leadership code may thus far have had some success in limiting leaders' incomes,[9] leaders have been able to ensure access to education to their children, thus guaranteeing that they too will be in a favored position in Tanzania, where education remains the major key to advancement. Education becomes an even more significant determinant of recruitment patterns as political ability and loyalty become insufficient criteria, by themselves, for selection to leadership positions.[10] Although quantification is difficult because many leaders had very young children, virtually all of the children of leaders in Kilimanjaro who had reached school age were in school, compared to the national average of fewer than half of school-aged children actually in school.[11] More

9. It is of course far too early to make any definitive assessment of the efficacy of the leadership code. Slow compliance is explained in substantial measure by the policy decision to enforce the restrictions slowly and selectively and to attempt to persuade rather than coerce recalcitrants.

10. Lloyd argues that children of the current elite in West Africa are outnumbered in the educational system by the "new entrants from the masses," *Africa in Social Change,* pp. 136–42. The evidence from Tanzania seems to suggest that, although there has been widely expanded access to primary education, because of the narrowly restricted access to higher education the new elite will continue to be drawn largely (but of course not entirely) from the children of the current elite for some time to come.

11. In 1969 47 percent of the Standard I age group found Standard I places. See *Tanzania's Second Five-Year Plan for Economic and Social Development,* vol. 1, p. 149.

than half of the leaders who had children twelve years old or older reported that the average length of education of their children was nine years or longer, while in 1967 Tanzania's total secondary school enrollment was under 3 percent of the appropriate age group. The mechanisms by which leaders ensure that their children progress in school (it is relatively easy to ensure that they complete primary school in Kilimanjaro) vary. Some are able to intercede with Education Ministry officials to obtain a second chance for their children at the secondary school examination or to secure secondary school places, poor examination results notwithstanding. Some provide a household environment conducive to and supportive of rapid educational progress. And many simply have sufficient money to be able to send their children to private schools when they are unable to secure places in the public school system. As one prominent leader put it:

> I would like to be a good socialist, but I have not been able to up to now because of my family and children. Someday I will be a good socialist.

Many leaders admit quite candidly that the pressure to ensure that their children, and often those of relatives as well, get an education prevails over their commitment to Tanzanian socialism and the Arusha Declaration. It is not that only the children of the current elite advance through the educational system, but that most of their children, and few of anyone else's, do gain access to higher education. Under the current circumstances, where education is so critical to advancement, it is difficult to imagine procedures which would effectively deny to the children of the current elite this comparative advantage. Thus, Tanzania's attempts to control elite formation, embodied in part in the leadership code of the Arusha Declaration, can be only partially successful as long as current elites can ensure educational advantage for their children.

It is important to mention briefly here the development of another kind of economic elite in Kilimanjaro, one not hampered by the leadership code. Several individuals, probably still numbering under a dozen in Kilimanjaro, have successfully utilized business opportunities to build sizable economic empires. One, for example, began as a poorly paid assistant in a tanning operation, became a skins trader, later bought and expanded the tannery, became a major beer, soft drink, and tobacco distributor, and organized, with a few associates, import, transportation, and other companies. The interrelationships of his enterprises are so intricate that tax records do not reveal their full extent, and he himself claimed to be unsure of all of the businesses in which he was involved and their worth. In 1969 he was raising seventeen children, and all who had reached secondary school age were either in or had completed secondary school or postprimary vocational training. Until now he has been able to secure what he wants without direct intervention into the political system, though it would be surprising if appropriately placed contributions and assistance were not a factor in his ability to secure requisite licenses and permits. Although he has been able to find new businesses to replace those nationalized or taken over by the government, and although he professes to be unconcerned about further nationalizations and takeovers, clearly as the Tanzanian government continues to expand its control over the economy he will find increasingly less room to maneuver.

There are two basic tensions generated by the success of these Kilimanjaro entrepreneurs, both as yet unresolved. Until very recently both national and local leaders have praised their individual enterprise as one of the foundations of Tanzanian development, and many young people in Kilimanjaro look to them as models to emulate. And yet they are rapidly entrenching themselves in a position of economic advantage clearly inconsistent with the egalitarian and communal tenets of Tanzanian socialism.[12] Likewise, as they promote development in Kilimanjaro, as the scale of their economic empires increases and at the same time comes into greater conflict with national development policy, the conflict between national policy and the local entrepreneurs increasingly coincides with the extant feelings of Kilimanjaro residents that they are being penalized by the central government because they have successfully developed. In other words, as they promote local development—and everyone seems to agree that they do indeed promote development—they facilitate the creation of an economic elite and nurture the existing feelings of alienation toward the Tanzanian government, neither of which is tolerable if current national policy is to prevail. From the central government's point of view the dilemma is that the expansion of the control of the economy in Kilimanjaro has thus far been carried out by increasing the activities of, and correspondingly, the burdens on, the Kilimanjaro coffee cooperative union.[13] The resulting paradox is that takeovers of private business by the cooperative implemented too precipitously overburden the cooperative: service to consumers is affected by the take-over. What had previously seemed to the coffee farmers to be an eminently successful institution began to look less and less reliable. Yet takeovers delayed too long permit the entrenchment of an economic elite difficult to replace. The problems encountered in relying on cooperatives and state-directed operations in Tanzania and elsewhere in Africa might seem to suggest it is difficult, if not impossible, under present circumstances to do without these local entrepreneurs. But Tanzania's antipathy to the entrenchment of a local economic elite seems thus far to have outweighed the disadvantages of available alternatives.[14]

12. J. Gus Liebenow found a similar tension in his study of southeastern Tanzania, *Colonial Rule and Political Development in Tanzania: The Case of the Makonde* (Evanston, Ill.: Northwestern University Press, 1971), pp. 328–29.

13. The trend in Kilimanjaro in 1969 was to transfer control from private enterprise to the KNCU, with the result that it had begun to expand into a broad range of activities, from marketing coffee, to organizing cattle-herders associations, to making loans, to selling hoes and grains.

14. In 1971 some large property holdings were nationalized. It is as yet difficult to

Politicians in Kilimanjaro

What this evidence suggests, then, is that it may not be reasonable to speak of clearly defined classes, class interests, and class conflicts in Kilimanjaro in 1969 as Lloyd does for West African urban areas,[15] but it is possible to observe the often successful attempts of individuals who have achieved elite status to pass that status on to their children. It is also possible to observe a growing congruence of the interests of diverse elements in Kilimanjaro society in opposing, delaying, and preventing the implementation of significant national policy. That growing congruence, coupled with the belief among many Kilimanjaro residents that their individual mobility in an increasingly stratified society is closely tied to the advancement of the Chagga as a whole, renders more distinct the outlines of a nascent conflict between national goals and programs and a coalition of opponents located in Kilimanjaro.

Structural Interpenetration

A major key to understanding politics in up-country Tanzania is the fact that ostensibly different political structures are related by the overlaps of key positions and by key leaders who hold several positions. Not only do government officers hold party positions and party officials, government offices, but also leaders of religious and ethnic communities hold political office as well. In addition, individuals frequently hold positions at several different levels: branch and district, district and region, and branch, district, and region together.

Two individuals filling multiple roles who are key in up-country Tanzania are, of course, the Regional and Area (District) Commissioners. Appointed by the President, and thus not directly responsible either to a local electorate or to the party, they serve both as heads of government and as party secretaries at the regional and district levels.[16] With access to government *and* party machinery, they can, though they do not always, bring strong pressure to bear to influence local decisions. For example, to accelerate action on problems of famine and malnutrition that plagued several areas of Kilimanjaro District in 1969, the Area Commissioner worked, simultaneously, through the District Executive Officer, district (and even regional) officials of the relevant Ministries,

---

assess the impact of those nationalizations on African as opposed to Asian entrepreneurs (who were the most directly affected) in Kilimanjaro.

15. For Lloyd's discussion of "incipient class conflict" in West African urban areas, see *Africa in Social Change,* pp. 306–20.

16. For the replacement of civil service with political appointees as commissioners, see Tordoff, *Government and Politics in Tanzania,* pp. 96–105. For comments on the diffuse role of the commissioners, see Bienen, *Tanzania: Party Transformation,* especially pp. 119–52 and 310–33. Note that both of these sources, written shortly after the politicization of the commissioner positions, are concerned more with expected behavior than with an analysis of actual performance up-country over time in Tanzania. As was noted previously, the commissioner system is currently being extended down to the ward level in Tanzania. The implementation of a decentralization plan in 1972 is likely to strengthen further the Regional Commissioners.

and district party leaders; though not a locally elected official, several times he appealed directly to the local population for support. In addition, he requested assistance from officials in Dar es Salaam. Yet, his inability to secure rapid action in this instance—he was thwarted largely by a cumbersome bureaucracy both locally and in Dar es Salaam—indicates the constraints on his ability to secure desired outputs, despite the weight he brought to bear on numerous pressure points in the local political system.

In a similar way, the party executive secretaries, who are posted from the center but who serve also as nominated members of the local councils, the district chairmen, who serve also as chairmen of the local councils, and the chief executive officers (the District Executive Officer and the Town Clerk), who in Kilimanjaro in 1969 served also on the party district executive committees, all link party and government, and all can have access to both party and government power. This structural interpenetration, instituted to promote coordination and ensure party control, often has the effect of merging party and government at the local level.

Not that the overlapping positions are limited to the local level—indeed, the linkages between the local population in Kilimanjaro and major decision-makers in Dar es Salaam are very diffuse. The Regional Commissioner serves both as an ex-officio Member of Parliament and as a member of the TANU National Executive Committee. The Regional Commissioner, the Regional Chairman, and the Member for Kilimanjaro—all serve on the National Executive Committee. All of these regional leaders, as well as Members of Parliament for constituencies in the region, serve on the party regional executive committee and are major participants in the Regional Development Committee.

It should be noted that not all of these individuals with key, multiple, positions resolve the inherent conflict between their roles in the same way. Some see clear boundaries between party and government authority and behavior and consider themselves to be more on one side or the other of the lines they draw, while others are unable or unwilling to differentiate distinctly between their roles and do not regularly subject either one to the other.[17]

This interpenetration does serve to promote a degree of coordination among policy-makers and administrators that the bureaucracy and other formal governmental institutions cannot provide. In development planning, for example, communication between ministerial offices and local government officials, and between development planners and party officials, is intermittent

17. For an incisive comment on the use of role conflict analysis in the study of African politics, see Alvin Magid, "Methodological Considerations in the Study of African Political and Administrative Behavior: The Case of Role Conflict Analysis," *African Studies Review* 13, no. 1 (April 1970): 75-94. Magid stresses that role conflict may be more presumed by observers than present in leaders' behavior: leaders may in fact not perceive conflicting expectations of their behavior, and those who are aware of conflicting expectations may not experience difficulty in reconciling them.

at best. But the fact that party leaders serve on the local government councils (and development committees) and local government officials sit in party committees does permit some duplication of effort to be avoided and some coordination of programs to take place. In a similar way, these overlaps serve to forge links between the competing factions and groups in the local political system.

Where overlaps are few and positions are functionally specific, factional conflicts manifest themselves in institutional settings. But where overlaps are many and positions very diffuse, individual leaders often find themselves at the crossroads of several conflicting demands. Local leaders, for example, must deal with the competing pulls of their local constituencies and their party leadership. Branch leaders who serve on the local councils are not infrequently caught in the vise of the incompatible pressures of their branch and district constituencies. Religious and ethnic community leaders who serve in governmental or party positions or both must simultaneously look to the needs of their own communities and to the resources and authority of government and party. And the individuals who are on the fringes of the local factional alignments must deal with the cross-pressures of their multiple allegiances. While some leaders do not perceive ostensibly inconsistent demands as conflicting, and while others react to conflicts with ambivalence, perceiving no need to reconcile them, the overall impact of the personalization of these conflicts in Kilimanjaro is a moderation in their intensity and a fluid mediation between extremes.

Tanzania's leaders, in fashioning their political system, have constantly tried to balance local responsibility and participation with a centrally directed development effort, or, in other terms, to manage the tension between those officers selected locally and those posted from the center.[18] For much of the local populace, these extensive overlaps, then, combined with the diffuse nature of official responsibilities, provide alternative channels through which to attempt to influence allocations—almost all of the major leaders are likely to be involved in the deliberations on most issues at some point or another. It is true that an individual who seeks some specific action by the Area Commissioner and who is refused may turn to the TANU office simply to find the Area Commissioner there in his capacity as party secretary. But it is also true that he can appeal to other party leaders to intercede with the Area Commissioner as party secretary to influence his decision as Area Commissioner. Without exception all local leaders agree that because positions overlap and authority is diffuse, individuals with problems seek assistance from the official who, in their estimation, offers the greatest chance of success. That is, where clan ties, or personal familiarity, or business or professional acquaintance, or recommendation from friends suggest that some official can be helpful, an

18. For a discussion of this tension, see Bienen, *Tanzania: Party Transformation,* pp. 153–57.

individual will seek him out, even though the problem involved may not fall directly within his competence. It is not uncommon to find an MP interceding for a constituent with the Regional Commissioner or Town Clerk, and then to find the Regional Commissioner or Town Clerk interceding for a local resident with the same MP. For the ordinary citizens, then, these overlaps provide a set of alternative advocates whose assistance can be sought. At the local level in Tanzania's one-party system ordinary citizens have much the same possibility of choosing among alternative advocates for their concerns that ordinary citizens have in multiparty systems.

From another perspective, however, this interpenetration has the opposite effect. While the institutions that aggregate interests are numerous and diverse, interest articulation is largely confined within formal party structures.[19] That is, while a wide range of groups—traditional societies, athletic clubs, religious and ethnic community organizations, informal groupings of bar owners, and the like —merges diverse demands into recognizable alternative courses of action, communication of demands and proposed courses of action to decision-makers at the center is confined within party structures. That many of the basic interest groups —trade union, women, elders, youth, cooperatives, parents—are in fact party auxiliaries reinforces this pattern. Demands for improving the life style and income of women, for example, may be dealt with in church groups, in women's associations, in traditional song groups, in bar owners' and beer brewers' gatherings, and in party branch meetings. A specific course of action proposed—that women's groups receive assistance and preferred treatment in opening shops and bars—is articulated through the local party structure to the various decision-making bodies and administrators. Where a recommendation by a church representative to the Liquor Licensing Board that women be assisted would be rejected as out of place and illegitimate, the same presentation by a party official is readily accepted and carries great weight.

Mobilization of Bias

The ways in which prevailing community sentiments and values render it difficult or even impossible for some issues and some points of view to enter decision-making structures have already been discussed. A proposal to form a party in opposition to TANU, for example, though occasionally mentioned in Kilimanjaro, could not easily be raised publicly. Likewise, proposals to eliminate private landholdings and to reduce the share of national educational resources allocated to Kilimanjaro, though certainly consistent with national policy, are largely excluded from the decision-making process by the local mobilization of bias.

The study of Kilimanjaro politicians suggests that the prevailing community

19. For the basic discussion of interest aggregation and articulation, see Gabriel A. Almond and G. Bingham Powell, Jr., *Comparative Politics: A Developmental Approach* (Boston: Little, Brown, 1966), Chapters 2–5.

sentiments and values exclude, or at least set substantial obstacles before, individuals as well as issues. A leader who seeks authority and power on the basis of an anti-TANU position is of course prevented from rising within party structures and is prevented by community acceptance of the illegitimacy of opposition from organizing, at least overtly, an opposition party. Less hypothetically, leaders who attempt to secure office by championing the abolition of private property or the diversion of national educational resources away from Kilimanjaro find only a few listeners and almost no supporters, despite the fact that these proposals clearly form basic elements of current national policy. Ideologues, and especially ideologues who are radical in the Tanzanian context, are simply not found in Kilimanjaro politics. Of course the process by which the mobilization of bias excludes issues and individuals from the center of political activity is a long and complex one. It is not that in 1969 individuals who proposed certain party policies were excluded. Rather, as the current leaders were educated and socialized they were little exposed to such ideas; these proposals are seen to be a clear threat both to the pattern of individual landholding that at least the Chagga see as basic to their social organization and also to the ready access to education that the people of Kilimanjaro see as the fundamental gateway to the good life. During the 1969 party elections, for example, at the Regional Conference one candidate for Regional Chairman was asked to explain *ujamaa* (socialist) villages. In his response he backed himself into the position of asserting that Chagga villages were the antithesis of *ujamaa* villages. His position might have had some support among party leaders in Dar es Salaam, but it brought hoots of derision at the election meeting and helped convince party delegates that he would not be a good advocate for Kilimanjaro and thus contributed to his defeat. Since Independence the successful Kilimanjaro politicians have been those who served as buffers against the threat of Dar es Salaam's intrusion into Kilimanjaro and not those who welcomed increased central control over and direction of local endeavors.

One of the results of this mobilization of bias is that local politics in Kilimanjaro have a very pragmatic cast. Support for leaders revolves around what they can do for their constituents. Traditional ties, detailed and attractive ideology, and even personality are secondary factors, while a prospective leader's education, place of residence and birth, and previous political service are all evaluated through the prism of what the candidate can be expected to do for his constituents. To argue that there are no successful radicals among Kilimanjaro politicians is not to argue that national party policy is not accepted and enunciated, but simply to suggest that to speak in favor of party doctrine is little more than a basic requirement for receiving serious consideration and does not in itself provide significant support.

Religion and Ethnicity

Allegations of religious influence in politics are not uncommon in Kilimanjaro. It was widely believed in 1969, especially among the supporters of the unsuccessful candidate, that the success of the winner in a race for a prominent party office resulted from the promotion of his candidacy by local clergymen of one of the major religious groups, both from the pulpit and in their daily contacts with their parishioners. Likewise, all of the major participants in a substantial rejection of top officeholders in the coffee cooperative union agreed that religion played a major role. And the leaders of the major religious communities each referred to one of the major political leaders as "their" leader.

The situation in regard to ethnicity is similar. Complaints by members of one Chagga subgroup that they were disadvantaged in the location of a government project because the local councillor was a member of a rival Chagga subgroup are common.[20] During the 1969 party elections opposition to electing a non-Chagga Regional Chairman was openly verbalized. Some of the local opposition to a major party representative at the national level, as well, centered on the fact that he was not Chagga.

Yet none of the major political leaders posted from the center was a Chagga, and town party members readily replaced one non-Chagga with another as Town Chairman in an electoral contest in which none of the candidates was a Chagga. Thus, clearly, in dealing with the impact of religion and ethnicity on Kilimanjaro politics, it is essential to pay careful attention to the shifting salience of ethnicity and religion, a factor all too often overlooked in studies of African communities.[21] How individuals group and identify themselves is largely determined by the patterns of conflict that develop. Individuals who recognize a common ethnicity, or religion, in one set of circumstances might well see those very people previously identified as coethnics or coreligionists as enemies in other circumstances.[22]

20. As has been noted several times, it can be very misleading to think of all of the people of Kilimanjaro who are usually called Chagga as a single ethnic group. The Chagga-language-speaking area is comprised of peoples who speak several different, and often mutually unintelligible, languages. To call them all Chagga is to overlook the significance of the differences among them—the shifting salience of ethnicity—that is precisely the point at issue here. For the purposes of this discussion, *Chagga* refers to the entire set of people who consider themselves Chagga, and *Chagga subgroup* refers to the smaller groups of inhabitants of Kilimanjaro who speak a common language and who recognize a common identity. A classic discussion of ethnicity in the politics of recently independent states is, of course, Clifford Geertz's "The Integrative Revolution: Primordial Sentiments and Civic Problems in the New States," in his *Old Societies and New States: The Quest for Modernity in Asia and Africa* (Glencoe, Ill.: Free Press, 1963). But the term *primordial* is an unfortunate one, since it stresses the historic origins and psychological depth of such ties at the expense of attention to the specific situational determinants of their exercise.

21. See, for example, Hanna, "Influence and Influentials in Two Urban-Centered African Communities." Hanna discusses "co-ethnics" in a "polyethnic" community without dealing with the problem that coethnicity may be situationally determined: in the eastern Nigerian town Hanna studied, an individual's coethnic might be a fellow villager in one circumstance and anyone from eastern Nigeria in another, and in the Ugandan town Hanna studied, under certain conditions a Hindu's coethnic may be another Hindu, while in other circumstances his coethnic might well be any other Asian.

22. Several authors have made this point. See, among others, Charles W. Anderson,

Politicians in Kilimanjaro

The shifting salience of ethnicity and religion is quite clear in the history of the peoples of Kilimanjaro. During the early period of missionary expansion Kilimanjaro was divided into thirty or more small chiefdoms and into two major religions.[23] That is, when the lines of conflict were drawn between the small states, the major religions, each without competition in its own area, could bridge the gaps between the warring parties and thus were integrative by enabling peoples to broaden the scale of their basic allegiance. More recently, when the lines of conflict between the (former) small Chagga states have begun to diminish in significance before the conflict between the two major religious groups, the recognition of Chagganess, spurred by conflict between the hillside (Chagga) and plains (non-Chagga) peoples and between Kilimanjaro and the rest of Tanzania, has served to moderate religious competition and is thus integrative by enabling people to recognize a broader community.

In the current behavior of the peoples of Kilimanjaro the shifting salience of ethnicity and religion is also quite clear. While people from different Chagga subgroups compete vigorously in local politics, they recognize their common identity with no difficulty when faced with the prospect of electing a non-Chagga as party Regional Chairman or when confronted by anti-Chagga sentiment in Dar es Salaam. And while Lutherans and Roman Catholics may consider each other archenemies in the struggles over the location of new schools, they have little trouble recognizing their common Christianity when dealing with what they perceive to be excessive Muslim influence in party leadership. Perhaps the most striking recognition by local leaders of the situational determination of ethnicity came when applications were being solicited from Kilimanjaro residents to move to new lands in western Tanzania in 1969. Since some of the funds to support the move came from a Chagga Land Fund originally established to compensate the Chagga for land alienated to European settlers, only Chagga were to be permitted to go. But who was legitimately a Chagga? The question came up at a meeting of the Regional Development Committee in regard to an individual who had been born and raised in Kilimanjaro but whose father was not Chagga. After some discussion there was widespread agreement on the proposal by the District Chairman (the elected leader of the Chagga district in Tanzania) that all those who had lived their lives in Kilimanjaro and considered themselves Chagga faced the same land shortage as everyone else and should therefore be officially considered Chagga for the purpose of permitting them to move to the new lands.

Fred R. von der Mehden, and Crawford Young, *Issues of Political Development* (Englewood Cliffs, N.J.: Prentice-Hall, 1967), Part One; M. Banton, "Adaptation and Integration in the Social System of Temne Immigrants in Freetown"; Howard Wolpe, "Port Harcourt: A Community of Strangers" (Ph.D. diss., Massachusetts Institute of Technology, 1967), and "Port Harcourt: Ibo Politics in Microcosm," *JMAS* 7, no. 3 (1969): 469–93; and Martin Staniland, "The Rhetoric of Centre-Periphery Relations," *JMAS* 8, no. 4 (1970): 617–36.

23. Islam never became firmly entrenched on the Kilimanjaro hillsides.

The Politicians

In Moshi town ethnicity and religion seem to play a much less significant role in local politics. Although ethnic and religious residential segregation are evident, there was no outcry over the election of a non-Chagga Muslim as Town Chairman. Several factors differentiate the urban area from its rural hinterland in this regard. First, although the town is segregated, there is still substantial heterogeneity in living patterns. Where the congruity of place of residence, ethnicity, and religion on the hillsides usually strengthens their collective impact, the urban heterogeneity—neighbors may differ in both ethnicity and religion—seems usually to moderate the conflicts. Moshi is a trading and administrative center, and the presence of many nonlocal civil servants, travel, work contacts, and intermarriage reinforce this heterogeneous pattern. Second, that so many of the urban Muslims are in fact Chagga or neighboring peoples diminishes the alien cast characteristic of Muslims in other Tanzanian urban areas where they have coastal and Zanzibari origins. Third, the psychological focus of the Chagga, at least as they themselves describe it, is on the mountain and away from the town. Many of the most prestigious and affluent district leaders do not build homes in the former European quarter of town, but rather take pride in their return to their homes, often quite sumptuous, in the rural area each evening or at the end of the week. That in general Kilimanjaro leaders do not see in Moshi the Muslim domination of urban politics common in other Tanzanian urban areas,[24] that the urban Muslim and non-Chagga populations do not regard themselves as subjected to continuing Christian, Chagga rule, and that in general Chagga leaders are more concerned with the rural district than with the town, all reduce the extent to which the possibly conflicting groups perceive each other as threatening and diminishes the intensity of those conflicts that do arise.

Conclusions

To draw together the study of issues and politicians in Kilimanjaro, it is appropriate to begin to suggest the outlines of the major factional alignments in the local political system. Of course, any such sketch must be tentative, since the patterns of political conflict have been fluid and since there have been, and continue to be, important changes among the major participants; the alignments described here, those that characterized political conflict in 1969, have already begun to be altered since the 1970 parliamentary and local government elections. Thus, though the specific individuals may change, this analysis is useful in that it sheds light on the major patterns of interaction and organization among the political leaders of Kilimanjaro.

All of the evidence available supports the rejection of the view that allo-

24. See, for example, Hyden's comments on Muslims in the local TANU organization in Buhaya in *Political Development in Rural Tanzania,* pp. 133–34. See also Bienen's comments on Muslim and Swahili influence on TANU and Tanzanian urban politics in *Tanzania: Party Transformation,* pp. 45–49; 187–88. Bienen very perceptively stresses that individuals identified as Swahilis in a political context are not necessarily either coastal or even Muslim.

cations in Kilimanjaro are dominated by a small, cohesive power elite. The evidence does suggest, however, that there are a number of informal networks, factional alignments, whose competition and coalition largely determine which interests are served by decisions in the local political setting. In the late 1960s there were three major factional alignments in Kilimanjaro, and several minor ones, none of which was sufficiently strong to prevail regularly without the support of the others.

Political change is very rapid in Tanzania. As was noted in Chapter 1, there have been three major turnovers in the Kilimanjaro political leadership since the early days of the British colonial period, and there are indications that another major change is taking place. The life span of the current networks of political allegiance is relatively brief (Tanzania has been independent for scarcely ten years), and an analytic approach stressing equilibrium could not adequately encompass the successive turnovers and rejuvenations in the political leadership. The leadership factions in Kilimanjaro are further disrupted by the frequent transfer of high-level government and party personnel. Yet it is possible to delineate these factions, whose outlines will be discussed briefly here.

In 1969 one major network revolved around the Regional Commissioner, and included the Area Commissioner, the District Executive Officer, and most upper level government officials. This faction, which essentially represented central government power in Kilimanjaro, usually included as well the District Chairman, who was dependent on the commissioners and on the District Executive Officer and his subordinates for support in his competition with the Regional Chairman. It is important to note here that the Kilimanjaro District Chairman functioned almost as the Member of Parliament for his constituency, since the MP, his brother, a party elder statesman, had been incapacitated by illness in Dar es Salaam for several years. The District Chairman visited Dar es Salaam regularly two or three times a month to keep his brother informed and to see central government and party officials.

A second grouping revolved around the Regional Chairman and included the head of the women's organization, much of the Lutheran leadership (the Chairman was an official of the Lutheran Church), and much of the traditionalist (former chiefs and clan heads and respected elders) element from the mountain. Although there was usually fierce competition between the Regional and District Chairmen, on some issues they did ally.

A third major grouping revolved around the Kilimanjaro Member of the National Executive Committee, and largely represented the interests of the plains (as opposed to the hillsides), the urban area, and the Muslims.

There were also several somewhat weaker and less tightly organized networks. One revolved around the Member of Parliament for the far eastern side of the mountain, and represented the interests of the residents of that part of the district, who have long claimed that they have been disadvantaged vis-à-vis the rest of the district. This MP, the only Roman Catholic among the major leaders despite the Catholic plurality in the district, was also seen by local leaders and by the Catholic hierarchy to represent Catholic interests. A second grouping linked the MP for Kilimanjaro Central and a National Member of Parliament who resided in Moshi[25] and represented much of central Kilimanjaro, which includes several large sisal plantations and a sugar plantation located in the plains, as well as the urban area and especially its Asian population. This grouping was somewhat transitory because the Kilimanjaro MP, a Junior Minister, spent most of her time away from Kilimanjaro and because the National MP, an Asian with no real constituency either locally or in Dar es Salaam, was often reluctant to exercise forceful leadership on his own. Very often this faction allied with the grouping around the Regional Commissioner; the Kilimanjaro MP depended more on local government officials than on party officers to keep her informed on developments in her constituency. At least until the 1969 party elections a third small network functioned in Moshi town and usually supported the factions led by the Regional Commissioner and the MP for Kilimanjaro Central. Common background and experiences facilitated coordination among the top town leaders. Until the middle of 1969 the top town leadership—the Town Chairman and vice-chairman and the Town Clerk and deputy town clerk—were all raised as Christians with a missionary education in a largely Muslim area, had all served in government posts, and were all except the deputy town clerk members of the urban district party working and executive committees. A fourth small network, the remnants of the previous generation of party leaders (who had been largely replaced in party offices in the early 1960s) retained some control of major offices in the coffee cooperative union, but all were removed from office by a coalition of all of the other major factions in 1969.

These factions differed in their sources of authority, in their access to power, and even in their ideological outlooks. The grouping around the Regional Commissioner drew its authority from Presidential and governmental appointment and had control of government machinery, including the forces of coercion. The grouping around the Regional Chairman traced its authority to the local party electorate,[26] and relied on persuasion and popular support in its competition with other factions. The grouping around the Kilimanjaro Member of the National Executive Committee drew its support from a combination of a Dar es Salaam base and the local Muslim and plains population, and relied heavily on access to key decision-makers in Dar es Salaam for leverage in the local factional struggles. In outlook, the Regional Commissioner's faction was in general primarily concerned with the management of development and

25. Under Articles 24 and 30 of the Interim Constitution of Tanzania, the National Assembly selects ten members from a list of nominees submitted by institutions designated by the President as national institutions. The National MP residing in Moshi, an Asian, was originally nominated by the Chambers of Commerce.

26. Party chairmen are elected by the delegates to party conferences at each level, and not by the population or the party membership at large.

administrative tasks, while the network supporting the Regional Chairman regarded itself as the representative of Chagga interests and the faction led by the MNEC considered itself the representative of the interests of the plains-dwellers and Muslims.

Because of the frequent changes among the party executive secretaries in Kilimanjaro in 1969,[27] they were not closely aligned with any of the major factions, and served to mediate among them. Ironically, party executive secretaries saw themselves as, and were, "above" local political competition.

A few examples may sharpen the images of these factional alignments and their interaction. At the elections for the top leadership of the Kilimanjaro Native Cooperative Union in 1969, the Regional Commissioner, reflecting pressure from Dar es Salaam to deal with management problems in the coffee cooperative, the District Chairman, motivated by a long-standing enmity toward the current KNCU president, and the Regional Chairman, who had replaced the KNCU president as Regional Chairman, all allied to defeat the incumbents. This alliance, which had been unsuccessful in previous attempts, succeeded in 1969 largely because it was able to enlist the support of disenchanted Rombo farmers and Catholics by supporting the Rombo MP for the presidency. A common goal forged an alliance among the major factions.

In competition over the location of new and expanded schools, for another example, the District Chairman regularly allied with local government officials to oppose the demands of the Regional Chairman. The District Executive Officer willingly approved travel allowance payments to the District Chairman and several councillors who supported him for frequent and seemingly purposeless visits to Council headquarters. And at election time, the District Executive Officer and Area Commissioner boosted the District Chairman's candidacy by introducing him at meetings as a man who had done so much for the district, thus suggesting that his intervention was indispensable in securing governmental allocations. The District Chairman in turn was a vociferous supporter of the Area Commissioner and District Executive Officer in his local contacts on the mountain: both faced the resentment of local inhabitants because they were seen as outsiders sent to govern the Chagga, and the District Executive Officer suffered from the additional stigma of being considered an individual from a tribe too backward to have authority over the Chagga. By cooperating with those thought to be the most malleable of the locals (those who showed some national orientation and whose own position was somewhat weak), the newcomers enhanced their ability to govern.

There are also, of course, exceptions to these patterns. For a brief period in 1969 a particularly disliked Regional Commissioner was unable to hold

27. During the course of 1969 there were three regional executive secretaries and three rural district executive secretaries; the urban district executive secretary spent most of 1969 at a training course in Dar es Salaam. Between the departure of one secretary and the arrival of his replacement, as well as during the absence of the urban district executive secretary, the office was vacant.

The Politicians

together his network of supporters and was regularly stymied in competition with other major leaders, his frequent use of dire threats notwithstanding.

One major conclusion that flows from this study of issues and politicians, then, is that leadership in Kilimanjaro is not characterized by a cohesive and unified power elite but that it consists of a set of interrelated and interdependent factions, none of which is strong enough by itself to prevail regularly.

A second major conclusion might be termed the paradox of local leadership. The national policy of planned development and substantial state direction of change requires competence, commitment, and effectiveness at both individual and institutional levels. And in fact the shortage of skills and resources that, as Bienen suggests, is an obstacle to the implementation of national policy throughout Tanzania is not a major difficulty in Kilimanjaro.

But the competent and effective individuals and institutions in Kilimanjaro are those that are responsive to local interests. Ordinary citizens and leaders alike agree that the most important characteristic of local leadership is the ability to resist central intrusion into local affairs. The competitive factions and the nascent economic elite are united in their commitment to protect local interests.

Thus, fiercely local leaders are expected to implement national goals that require both a redistribution of resources from affluent to less-affluent areas of the country and a prohibition on the accumulation of individual wealth by those already relatively wealthy. To implement these policies, local leaders must be effective. To be effective, they must be locally responsive. To be locally responsive, they must, to some extent, resist these policies. Hence, the paradox of local leadership. (And hence the utility, for an understanding of this problem throughout the country, of a study of one area in which the lines of conflict are already clearly drawn.) That in 1972 a Chagga was appointed Regional Commissioner in Kilimanjaro, despite the general policy that individuals not serve in their home areas, is evidence of the recognition at the center of the import of this paradox.

PART IV / *The Party*

10

The Local Party Organization

Introduction

A major goal of this book has been to examine the local party in Moshi: to study its goals, its structure, and its behavior. The issue-area studies provided one set of insights into the local party organization by asking which groups prevailed in the decisions concerning those key issues and in what ways the party was involved. The leadership studies provided another set of insights on the party by asking local leaders to describe the local political system and their perceived roles in it. Thus, while the discussion has thus far focused on issues and leaders, it has also concerned the party: what is the role of the local TANU organization in an up-country urban area. It is important to stress that, even though the larger setting was that of a single party state, it was not assumed that the local party organization monopolized (or even had any role in) local decision-making; nor was local power studied simply by assuming that TANU officials were the key leaders in the local political setting. The aim was to explore, from as broad and as encompassing a perspective as possible, the goals, structure, and behavior of the local party organization in order to provide some insight into the content, rather than simply the theory, of a functioning single party in Africa. The search for what the party does in Moshi has made it abundantly clear that for a wide range of political outcomes the direct role of the local TANU organization is very modest indeed.

This chapter and the next, then, will deal with TANU in Moshi. The primary attention here will be focused on the composition of the local party organization—its sections and affiliated institutions—and an analysis of its structure.

It is clear that the major thrust of the Tanzanian political system, especially as it has developed in Kilimanjaro and despite the constraints imposed by decisions made at the center, is to encourage and foster attention to local issues and problems. Politics in Kilimanjaro had a very local orientation during the period of British rule, and local concerns continued to occupy the center of the political stage in Kilimanjaro throughout the first decade after Independence. Supportive of this orientation is the disjointed and poorly articulated nature of inputs from the center. As a result of these and other factors, the local party organization largely concerns itself with communication and mediation in the local political setting.

The principal goal of this chapter, then, is descriptive: how the local party is composed, how it is structured, and what its basic orientation is. Since this study is concerned with the political system of Moshi town, the bulk of the comments in the chapter will refer to the urban party organization. But because party headquarters for both the rural district and the region are located in Moshi town—in fact in the same building—because some of the party auxiliaries do not have a separate functioning urban organization, and because it would be impossible to understand the behavior of the urban party organization without setting it in its rural and regional context, the discussion will as necessary include both rural Kilimanjaro District and Kilimanjaro Region.

Composition

The picture of the local party organization in Moshi that emerges from the discussion thus far is one of a congeries of formal interest groups and informal alliances, a set of relatively fluid networks in which different elements prevail in different circumstances. To fix on the fact that the urban party chairman is selected by the urban District Annual Conference,[1] for example, is to overlook the fact that he also serves as Chairman of the Moshi Town Council, that the District Executive Secretary is posted from party headquarters, and that the District Secretary is the Area Commissioner, appointed by the President. To stress the supremacy of the local party organization over the local council is to overlook the facts that two-thirds of the councillors are ultimately responsible to their popular electorate—only some of whom are party members—and that the remaining one-third of the councillors are appointed by the President and may be primarily responsible to organizations or bureaucracies not directly under party control.

The local party organization in Moshi, then, encompasses the elected and appointed officers, representatives from the party sections, and representatives from the party affiliates, as well as individuals selected at regional and national levels (see Table 10.1 for the composition of the District Executive Committee). The linkages among these individuals are characterized by diverse sources of authority and patterns of responsibility, cross-cutting and congruent hierarchical chains, and independent and interdependent roles. (See Table 10.2 for a schematic representation of the linkages among the members of the District

1. The officers and organs of TANU are defined in the Constitution of the Tanganyika African National Union, appended to the Iterim Constitution of Tanzania, 1965, as the First Schedule. *The Interim Constitution of Tanzania, 1965* is published as Act No. 43 of 1965 (Dar es Salaam: Government Printer, 1965); it can be found also in Tordoff, *Government and Politics in Tanzania,* Appendices, Part B. A slightly revised version was published in Swahili in 1967: Tanganyika African National Union, *Katiba ya TANU* [TANU Constitution] (Dar es Salaam: Government Printer, 1967).

The Local Party Organization

Table 10.1. Composition of the District Executive Committee

District Chairman
District Secretary (Area Commissioner)
All members of the Regional Executive Committee resident in the district
All members of Parliament representing constituencies in the district[a]
Members of the District Working Committee appointed by the District Chairman[b]
Ten delegates elected by the District Annual Conference
One delegate from each of the affiliated organizations[c]
One representative from each of the following sections in the district: Women's Section,
    TANU Youth League, Elders' Section
District Executive Secretary[d]

Source: The Constitution of the Tanganyika African National Union (First Schedule to the Interim Constitution of Tanzania, 1965), Article IV, C, 3, (1), and *Katiba ya TANU*, 1967.

[a] In Moshi this was taken to include the National Member of Parliament (who is elected by the Parliament and thus does not represent a local constituency) who resided in Moshi. The 1967 TANU Constitution explicitly includes such MP's.

[b] The District Working Committee was composed of the Chairman, the District Secretary, the District Executive Secretary, and up to four persons appointed by the Chairman. In 1969 the composition of the District Working Committee was altered to include representatives elected at the party District Annual Conference, and they are in turn included in the District Executive Committee.

[c] Conditions for affiliate membership in TANU are defined in Article III, Section B, of the TANU Constitution.

[d] Although not specifically designated in the TANU Constitution, the District Executive Secretary, posted from TANU Headquarters, carries on most of the day-to-day party business and serves as secretary of the District Executive Committee.

Executive Committee.) The procedure used to elect members of the District Executive Committee at the District Annual Conference virtually ensures regular turnover in its membership—election is by nomination. In the chaotic tumult of claims for recognition from all corners of the hall, names are proposed and seconded, and when the allotted vacancies have been filled, the election is declared completed. Chance plays a large part in determining which of the better-known party leaders are thus selected.[2]

2. No election procedure is specified in the TANU Constitution. This procedure—election by nomination—was utilized at the District Annual Conferences for the urban and rural Kilimanjaro Districts and at the Kilimanjaro Regional Annual Conference in 1969 to elect members to the Executive Committees and to elect delegates to the Conference at the next level and to the National Annual Conference. In the excitement of the elections at these three Conferences, the Chairmen recognized more than one delegate who had no one in mind to nominate. Ticket-balancing was impossible because it was impossible to be sure who had already been elected and difficult to obtain recognition by the Chairmen. At the rural Kilimanjaro District Annual Conference the Chairman was accused of having recognized only delegates from one area of the hall (and thus one area of the district); after some discussion the original election was annulled and the process begun anew.

Table 10.2.   Schematic Representation of Linkages within the District Executive Committee (Moshi)

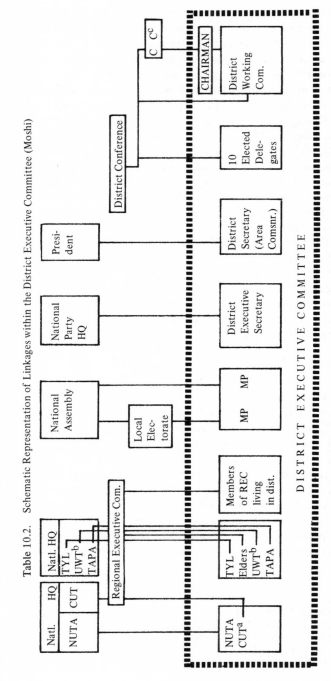

Note: This diagram is concerned with the composition of the District Executive Committee. Horizontal links at regional and national levels are not shown. The diagram groups Executive Committee members according to actual chains of authority for Moshi (they differ slightly from those specified in the TANU Constitution).

[a] In Moshi, this means the Kilimanjaro National Cooperative Union. There is no CUT organization at the district level.

[b] The UWT is both a party section and an affiliated organization.

[c] Prospective candidates for District Chairman must be approved by the Central Committee, which receives recommendations from Regional and Area Commissioners, among others.

The Local Party Organization

Formally represented within the local party organization are the women's, youth, and elders' sections of the party, as well as NUTA, the CUT (which in Moshi usually means the KNCU), and TAPA. Before proceeding to discuss each of these groups separately, it is important to make two general comments. First, in Moshi in 1968–69, these organizations, although formally part of the political party, functioned, when they functioned at all, as interest groups and only rarely participated in the more specifically political activities of the local party organization. That is, by and large they concerned themselves with servicing that specific subset of the population for whom they are organized, and only infrequently, with some important exceptions, did they become involved in broad programs of political education, mobilization of the general populace, and implementation of broad aspects of national policy. They were expected to remain aloof from electoral campaigns and to communicate with governmental bodies at the local level only through the party. For example, although one of the functions of NUTA is to promote the policies of TANU,[3] apparently the party leadership has determined that party branches are to be established in industrial situations to promote party policies.[4] In Moshi at least one factory had both TANU and NUTA branches, while in Dar es Salaam some factories had simultaneously TANU, NUTA, UWT, and TYL branches. Second, the primary reason for the restricted scope of these party sections and affiliates is the unwillingness of the party to permit the development of organizations that could provide strong, alternative, competing power bases.[5]

Party Sections

The TANU Youth League (TYL) in Kilimanjaro has been continually beset by difficulties in defining its purpose and in finding effective leadership. Local factors, as well, have inhibited the development of a self-conscious youth group. Because of the dense population and highly commercialized coffee cultivation in Kilimanjaro, youths require substantial sums of money to leave their parents and start out on their own. And because Kilimanjaro residents were among the most educated of Tanzanians at the time of Independence, many young people secured employment by replacing the departing Europeans, thus minimizing, until very recently at least, the emergence of a large group of unemployed school leavers. The lack of unused land suitable for settlement by a youth group (as has occurred elsewhere in Tanzania), a continued dependence

3. From the Act creating NUTA; see Tordoff, *Government and Politics in Tanzania*, p. 148.
4. For the party announcement of this policy, see the Secretary's report prepared for the 1969 TANU National Annual Conference: Tanganyika African National Union, *Taarifa ya Ofisi Kuu Kuhusu Hali na Kazi za Chama, Novemba 1967–Aprili 1969* (Dar es Salaam: Printpak Tanzania Limited, 1969), pp. 11–13.
5. A clear case in point is the party's unwillingness to permit autonomous activity by the trade unions.

on parents for income and land, and, at the same time, individual opportunities for employment have all been obstacles to the creation of a coordinated, energetic, and effective youth organization in Kilimanjaro.

This is not to suggest that no youths have been politically active. Many of the leaders of the antichief agitation and many of the early TANU activists were young. The TANU Youth League was active in the 1958 Legislative Council elections and was accused of overzealous activity on behalf of one candidate in the 1965 parliamentary elections.[6] Youth League members have assisted local government and party officials in maintaining law and order. But the problems in defining a clear purpose for the TYL and the leadership difficulties have prevented it from emerging as a strong, or independent, force in Kilimanjaro.

One obstacle, both to defining goals and finding effective leadership, is that although in theory members of the Youth League are to be not more than thirty-five years old, in fact several of the most prominent members of the TYL in Moshi in 1969 were fifty years old, or older, and were simultaneously active in the Elders Section.[7] The older members were unwilling to accept a substantially younger leadership, yet they themselves were unable to provide effective leadership for the bulk of the TYL membership. At the 1969 TYL District Annual Conference for Moshi town the older members were reluctant to recognize the legitimacy of the full participation of the representatives of the TYL school branches. In the contest for urban Chairman, the former Chairman, a petty merchant supported by most of the older members, and the Principal of Tanzania's Cooperative College, a forceful and eloquent educator supported by many of the teachers present, were defeated by a local auto salesman, supported largely by the school children. The older members took the election results as an indication of the lack of wisdom in permitting school children to participate actively in decision-making and seemed unwilling to work with the new Chairman. Without the support of these individuals, some of whom were branch officials and town councillors, the new Chairman, an affable young man with little previous political activity, was unwilling or unable to initiate activity, with the result that the leadership burden fell on the secretary posted from Dar es Salaam. Because of transfers and unfilled vacancies, the secretary was responsible for both the rural and urban Kilimanjaro

6. For a report on the challenge, dismissed by the Chief Justice of the High Court, to the election of S. N. Eliufoo, see the *Reporter* (East Africa), 25 March 1966, pp. 11–12.

7. The age limit is specified in the TANU Constitution, Article V, A, 2. In a booklet explaining to members the TYL reorganization, the TANU Youth League stipulates that members are to be from six to thirty-five years old, with current members who have passed thirty-five to continue as "advisers" (*mshauri*): *Muhtasari wa Mafundisho Kwa Vijana wa TANU* (Dar es Salaam: Dar es Salaam Printers, 1969?), p. 3. This distinction of member and adviser is not made in Kilimanjaro, nor does it seem to have any significance in most of Tanzania. Raising this very problem, national TYL leaders decided in 1971–72, apparently, to exclude "advisers" from active leadership positions.

districts. Overwhelmed by the mammoth reorganization necessary in the two districts and disenchanted with his work, he devoted little time to Youth League activities in town.

Projects begun under the previous TYL leadership had been largely unsuccessful. Youth League members pressured local officials for land and began a communal cotton plot, but active work in the field was short-lived, with the result that the cotton planted was never harvested.[8] The TYL was active in recruiting volunteers to join the move to western Tanzania, but those young people who went did not go as a TYL group.

A major restructuring of the TANU Youth League, directed from TYL national headquarters, was begun in 1969.[9] As of January 1969 TYL membership lists were discarded, and new membership applications, to be verified by both local and central TYL officials, were to be accepted. In announcing the new policy, Moshi TYL officials explained that it was necessary to eliminate the existing confusion over current membership lists and to ensure that all Youth League members were firm supporters of the Arusha Declaration, especially its requirement that an individual's income be produced by his or her own work.[10] It was suggested, though never clearly stated, that youths whose fathers were considered exploiters under the definitions of the Arusha Declaration would not be accepted as TYL members. The TYL secretary indicated that there had been approximately 2,000 Youth League members before January 1969, and that by September 1969 some 3,000 membership applications had been approved by TYL central headquarters, with an additional 20,000 pending.

As a concomitant to the new policy, almost all previously existing TYL branches in Kilimanjaro were eliminated, and the process of forming branches was begun anew. Where the jurisdiction of the former branches had largely been congruent with that of party branches, the new branches were opened almost exclusively in schools. In October of 1969, of 13 branches in Moshi town, only 1 was not a school branch, and of the total of 148 branches registered in rural and urban Kilimanjaro, all but 3 or 4 were in schools.

Youth League headquarters prescribed a wide range of activities for TYL branches, depending on members' ages, and ranging from parading to storytelling to learning how to handle weapons, all grouped under the rubrics

8. The District Secretary (Area Commissioner) commented caustically, ". . . youths who are not in school have a lot of words but no action," in the District Secretary's Six-Monthly Report for July–December 1968.

9. The change was announced in a letter by the TYL President, L. N. Sijaona, dated 18 October 1968. The new organizational pattern, concentrating on schools, is explained in *Muhtasari wa Mafundisho Kwa Vijana wa TANU.*

10. The TYL booklet states that since Independence there had been no clear purpose or plan for the TYL and that many members were simply card members—TYL membership card-holders unwilling to engage in any TYL activities. The conclusion was that the only way to develop an active membership was to begin anew. See *Muhtasari wa Mafundisho Kwa Vijana wa TANU,* pp. 1–2.

politics, culture, and defense. In 1969, TYL activity in Kilimanjaro schools was limited for the most part to parading and marching, though some TYL branches in secondary schools and colleges had a much wider range of activity. There were extensive celebrations of Youth Week, which included a gathering in Moshi of youths from throughout the region and competitions in everything from athletics to farming skills to traditional singing and dancing. A national TYL campaign against decadent influences of foreign cultures—soul music, short skirts and shorts, makeup, skin and hair bleaches, and wigs—was not well received in Kilimanjaro and had a short-lived impact. As a part of Tanzania's redefinition of its national goals, agricultural training and political education were introduced as required subjects in all schools.[11] Although in some schools TYL branches take the lead in these activities, they are required for all students and are taught by regular teachers according to syllabi provided by the Ministry of Education, and thus cannot be considered primarily Youth League activities.

Thus, the lack of a clear purpose and the difficulty of finding effective leaders, coupled with local factors that impede the development of a self-conscious youth group, have produced in Kilimanjaro a Youth League whose activities are intermittent and inconsistent. Youth League headquarters has recognized the problem of the lack of purpose and has begun a major reorganization of the TYL to attempt to deal with it. But the beginnings of the restructured TYL have been uneven at best, in Kilimanjaro, and the concentration on schools has done little to cope with the problems of leadership and of finding a suitable vehicle for the vast number of school-leavers. Perhaps it is this last that is most striking—with very restricted access to postprimary education, why orient the youth organization toward those already favored, those few in school? No satisfactory discussion of this decision has yet emerged, but two factors seem important in the concentration on the schools. First, since the conflict between the government and the university students in 1966, it is widely believed that the students pose a more serious threat to national policy and leadership than the school-leavers. And, second, because the leadership will be drawn largely from the more educated, their political education is the more important. But if TYL is to concentrate on the schools, which of the party sections and affiliates is to work with the school-leavers, not an insignificant group in Tanzanian society?

Women have long been prominent in Kilimanjaro politics. Almost as soon as TANU was established in the Northern Province, party minutes listed a Provincial Lady Chairman along with the Provincial Chairman. Several of the most active early TANU supporters in Moshi town were women; several of them later

---

11. The defects of the educational system adapted by Tanzania from its colonial heritage in the early 1960s and its tendency to develop an elite ill prepared for implementing national policy goals are discussed in a TANU policy booklet published in 1967, *Education for Self-Reliance,* reprinted in Resnick, *Tanzania: Revolution by Education,* pp. 49–70.

became councillors. The daughter of one of the most active women became the MP for Kilimanjaro Central and a Junior Minister in the Tanzanian government.

A branch of the Umoja wa Wanawake wa Tanganyika (Union of Tanganyika Women, UWT) was formed in Kilimanjaro in 1963, and when separate rural and urban districts (for UWT purposes) were created in August 1968, there were more than 6,000 members in rural Kilimanjaro and about 600 members in Moshi town, according to UWT records. Membership is a deceptive index of strength and activity, however, since few women, including many of the leaders, regularly pay their dues, which must be paid in addition to the basic TANU dues. Membership numbers are misleading also in that they include all membership cards ever sold and do not take into account women who have died, who have moved, or who have purchased new cards because they lost the old one or because they are unwilling to pay all the dues that would be required to validate the old one. During 1968-69, regular UWT participants were probably far fewer than, and certain UWT activities probably reached far more than, the recorded membership.

UWT activity in Moshi town has been concerned largely with business enterprises. Forming themselves into what they call cooperatives, groups of women have opened shops and bars. As was noted in the discussion of liquor licensing, even though these groups functioned as private shareholding companies rather than cooperatives, they received preferred treatment when applying for licenses and assistance from governmental agencies. Lack of business acumen and quarrels among the group members have led to a continuing series of complaints about poor leadership, unpaid dividends, and unprofitable operation. Often those profits that are realized are divided at the end of the year, rather than returned to the business. One major tea room operated by a women's group, for which it offered the Town Council less than half of the monthly rent offered by two private bidders, and which is guaranteed a substantial trade as the only tea room serving the town bus depot, has been troubled by internal conflict since it opened. Moreover, it has continued to pay its employees less than the minimum wage, claiming it could not pay them at all if it were forced to pay them more.

Along with its business activities, the UWT runs a small sewing class at the TANU building in town and cooperates with development assistants in running occasional sewing and cooking classes. The UWT in town also has a facilitating role: it calls together women's groups and assists government officials in running seminars on nutrition and child care. The UWT urban Chairman, a bright and energetic young school teacher, spent most of 1969 at a political education course in Dar es Salaam and indicated that she expected to take a much more active leadership role when she returned. In general, then, the UWT in town has been neither very active nor very strong, though some of its ward organizations were individually successful in running classes for women and operating businesses.

The rural Kilimanjaro District UWT organization had more diverse and extensive activities, though much of its energy in 1969 was also concentrated on encouraging and aiding women's groups in opening businesses. One reason for its more extensive activity was that the rural Chairman was employed as a rural development assistant and was thus able to combine her work throughout the district on development projects with her UWT leadership. In promoting the opening of a day-care center, for example, she was both a rural development assistant and the UWT Chairman. A second reason for greater activity in the rural district was that the local churches have traditionally organized women's associations for the women of the parish, and those organizations have become the local UWT branches. This pattern is very common in Kilimanjaro— the youth group of the parish becomes the local TYL branch (at least before TYL branches were limited to schools), the women's group becomes the UWT branch, and the parents' association becomes the TAPA branch. The group members are the same, changing only their label, and not always that, when they move from fund raising for the church to organizing the celebrations for a party holiday. When a local women's group meets in the parish church to learn sewing skills, whether they are called the UWT or church women's group depends on who is talking about them. This relates to a third reason for greater activity in the rural district. Women are encouraged in the Christian churches to engage in activities outside the home, to develop a private income, and to meet with other women to talk about their problems, while the activities of the larger number of Muslim women in the town are still circumscribed by traditional attitudes toward the seclusion and protection of women.

Although the 1967 version of the TANU Constitution places the UWT in the anomalous position of being at the same time both an integral section of the party and a TANU affiliate,[12] the UWT in Kilimanjaro has its primary responsibility to the regional party leadership rather than to the UWT national headquarters. The party Regional Executive Secretary serves as regional secretary for the UWT (and the TYL as well), and party files in Kilimanjaro are replete with admonitions by central party headquarters to local party officers to improve and strengthen the UWT, indicating clearly the subordination of the UWT to local party leadership.

During the 1969 party elections, only one candidate had submitted nomination papers for the post of UWT Regional Chairman, and she was declared elected without opposition at the Regional UWT Annual Conference. The TANU Regional Working Committee, however, felt that this newly elected Chairman, a very early party activist in Kilimanjaro who had developed many enemies throughout the region, did not have the full support of the membership. The election was annulled and a new Conference scheduled; the official explanation was that the original election had not been properly publicized

12. See *Katiba ya TANU*, Paragraphs 7 (8) and 10 (i) (g). This means that in theory at least the women have two votes in the District and Regional Executive Committees.

throughout the region. According to the party leadership, that decision of the party Regional Working Committee could not be appealed to UWT national headquarters, and in the event it was not. At the second Conference, the woman who had previously been elected unopposed withdrew her candidacy, saying she would run for the vice-chairmanship and then seek a national UWT office. Subsequently she was both defeated in her bid for the vice-chairmanship and unsuccessful in seeking national office. The rural district Chairman, who had previously served as a national UWT vice-president, was elected regional UWT Chairman. Although some local leaders argued that as regional and district UWT Chairman and a rural development assistant she held too many offices, there was little pressure on her to give up her district post. Some leaders suggested she was laying the groundwork for a second bid for a parliamentary seat (she had been defeated in her bid in 1965), and in fact she ran and won in 1970.

Another example of this relationship—that the local UWT organization is directly responsible to the local party leadership—developed when one of the urban UWT branches asked the Town Council to construct a tearoom at one of the town markets and then rent it to the UWT branch. The TANU Branch Chairman and the Regional Executive Secretary, both very disturbed that they had not been informed, explained to the councillors that it was party policy that such requests should go from the UWT branch to the party leadership and only then to the Council. Thus, the chain of command links the UWT to the local party organization first, and only second to the national UWT headquarters.

The UWT in Kilimanjaro does serve as an advocate of women's causes. When one urban UWT branch applied to the Town Council for permission to open a bar in the town community center, its application was rejected on the grounds that selling alcohol was an inappropriate activity for the town community center and that the proposed bar would conflict with other activities, especially classes in sewing and cooking, that took place there. A UWT leader appealed directly to a Minister, who was a personal friend. Shortly thereafter an officer from the Ministry attended a meeting of the Council executive (finance) committee—a meeting that was technically illegal because of the short notice on which it was called—and the original decision was reversed, because, it was announced, the councillors had been unaware that the women's group had already been granted a liquor license and it would be unfair to deny them the bar when they already had their liquor license. In another case, when small-scale merchants in the town market were required to take out full merchant's licenses, the urban UWT leadership vigorously pressed the case of the women (a few men were also included) at all levels: with the Town Clerk, the Area Commissioner, the Regional Commissioner, and various party leaders. After an acrid meeting in which the Town Clerk was called to the TANU office to defend the Council decision before the assembled women, and after two Council subcommittees looked into the equity of the decision, the women were finally compelled to comply.

UWT activity in Kilimanjaro, then, has been spasmodic. In the urban area it reaches a few women with its classes and other educational activities, it reaches more women in its business activities, and when it advocates a particular cause or facilitates a particular program it may reach many women indeed. And although many of these activities may have little directly to do with the implementation of national policies and Tanzanian socialism, they do have the effect of drawing the women out of the seclusion of their homes, encouraging them to work together for their mutual benefit, and demonstrating to them that through concerted action they can have impact on governmental outputs.

The functioning of the TANU Elders, the third party section, has already been discussed. The Elders are informally organized, where they are organized at all, in the urban branches, and the pattern seems to be similar for the rural branches. (In rural areas the role of local elders, who may or may not have been organized as TANU Elders, in dispute settlement and conflict resolution may create some friction between them and local cell leaders; the data gathered for this study, however, concentrated on the urban area.) The urban district Elders Chairman, who, as has been noted, also served as the regional Muslim sheikh and a town headman, presided over a semiformal court that heard cases and attempted to mediate, arbitrate, and reconcile. It seems likely that the formal creation of local arbitration tribunals, begun in 1969, will strengthen and enhance the authority and prestige of the Moshi Elders. As of 1969 there had not developed an Elders organization at the regional level in Kilimanjaro, and the urban district Elders Chairman sat as the Elders' representative at regional level meetings. As a matter of fact, when a new Elders Constitution was introduced in 1969 calling for the establishment of separate Elders membership fee and dues, few Moshi Elders were willing to pay the additional fee to get the new cards. Why pay another fee, most argued, when they could participate as effectively and get the same services without paying the additional fee.

A number of Moshi Elders formed a farmers' cooperative and cultivated a communal plot in town. Their organization has been plagued with continuing administrative problems, and the sale of their harvest has often been barely adequate to cover their costs. Although formally a separate organization, the Elders farmers' cooperative was led by the principal members of the urban party Elders Section, met in the TANU office, and used the services of a TANU branch secretary to take minutes and keep records.

These activities only hint at the special role played by the TANU Elders. As in many societies where tradition accords elders a special respect and deference, elders in Tanzania, both those formally organized in the TANU Elders Sections and those not part of the party structure, are often called upon for their interpretation of traditions and precedents, for their advice on important matters, and for their assistance in settling disputes. This role is institutionalized in the Tanzanian judicial system, where lay assessors, most often elders, assist primary court magistrates, and in special cases higher magistrates and judges, in hearing cases, evaluating evidence, and deciding on judgment.

Although the TANU leadership has always been characterized by youth-fulness, the TANU Elders have since TANU's inception had a special role in party activities. While of course some Elders do participate in the day-to-day decision-making, the Elders as a group, considered somewhat removed from the hard debate over policy alternatives and program strategies, are utilized to give legitimacy to, and enhance the weight and importance of, policy decisions by sharing the status accorded them as elders. President Nyerere, for example, summoned the Elders to hear his explanation of the decision to allow Tanganyika citizenship to non-Africans. Later they were convened to hear the explanation of his resignation from the government in 1962. In 1966 President Nyerere summoned the Elders to hear his explanation of the conflict between the government and the students at University College and his defense of the decision to send home most of the students.

In a similar way, not only do the Elders in Moshi function as a semiformal arbitration tribunal, but also by virtue of their status as elders they are in a position to criticize the behavior of party officials. On many occasions they have summoned a party official to inform him that his behavior, especially drunk-enness, was unacceptable and undermined respect for the party. When one Regional Commissioner was abusive of TANU Youth League members, and even of party officials, the Elders called him in to chastise him for his behavior.

Thus, although it is not well organized in Moshi, the Elders Section does have a special role in the local party. The Elders' semiformal arbitration tribunal is a widely used and highly respected institution for dispute settlement and conflict resolution, and their status as elders permits them to assess critically the behavior of even senior party officials. In performing both of these tasks they not only assist ordinary citizens with their everyday problems, but they also provide them with a direct channel of access to the local party and with a trustworthy friend in court. It should be stressed here that much of the success of the Moshi TANU Elders in these endeavors is due more to the energy and activities of the Elders Chairman (also the sheikh, also the town headman) than to any organizational pattern or constitutional charge.

There is a continuing tension, then, between the attempts to establish the TANU sections as at least partially autonomous organizations and the need to maintain tight party control over their activities. Organized now largely in schools, the Youth League has the most autonomous existence, at least to the degree that most of its members are not yet old enough to be admitted to full party membership. Most of the women and elders in Kilimanjaro, however, see little reason to pay an additional fee to belong to an organization that they differentiate little from the party itself. That is, for women who see TANU and the UWT as one and the same thing, there is no point in paying to belong to both.[13]

In more general terms, the question is: if TANU encompasses everything, why have strong party sections? This question relates to the difficulty of defining the nature of an independent single-party system. When the struggle was against the colonial government, the enemy was clear and easily identifiable, and the party sections could each deal with some of the organizational and tactical problems to strengthen the national independence movement. Now, when the enemy has been defined as ignorance, poverty, and disease, and when it is TANU policies that determine the allocation of scarce resources, the enemy is much harder to see clearly. A tension develops between a need to use the UWT, for example, to lead the women, and a need to ensure that in defending the women the UWT does not lead the battle against the TANU government. How can an organization be developed that is strong enough to have an impact on the women's behavior and sufficiently identified with women to be accepted as a legitimate leader, and yet at the same time does not set women's interests first and foremost? This paradox will be taken up again in relation to the organizations affiliated to the party.

Party Affiliates

The establishment of close government and party control over the trade union movement through the creation of the National Union of Tanganyika Workers (NUTA) in 1964, shortly following the army mutiny in which some trade union leaders were implicated, capped a decade of alternating cooperation and hostility between the party and the trade unions.[14] Although some 7.5 percent of Tanzania's mainland employees work in Kilimanjaro Region, which ranks fifth among the regions in total number of employees and fourth

13. In fact, the TANU Constitution, in defining the party sections, stipulates that all TANU women and elders belong to the appropriate sections: Article V, A.

14. For the development of conflict between the trade unions and the party in Tanzania, see William H. Friedland, "Co-operation, Conflict, and Conscription: TANU-TFL Relations, 1955–1964," Chapter 3 in Jeffrey Butler and A. A. Castagno, eds., *Boston University Papers on Africa. Transition in African Politics* (New York: Praeger, 1967); and Tordoff, *Government and Politics in Tanzania,* Chapter 5. For the history of trade unions in Tanzania, see William H. Friedland, *Vuta Kamba: The Development of Trade Unions in Tanganyika* (Stanford, Cal.: Hoover Institution Press, 1969). Discussions of the important question of consumptionist vs. productionist activities of African trade unions can be found in Elliot J. Berg and Jeffrey Butler, "Trade Unions," in *Political Parties and National Integration in Tropical Africa,* ed. James S. Coleman and Carl Rosberg, Jr. (Berkeley, Cal.: University of California Press, 1964); and Ioan Davies, *African Trade Unions* (Baltimore: Penguin, 1966). For the investigation of NUTA and the government reactions to the investigating commission's report, see Tanzania, *Report of the Presidential Commission on the National Union of Tanganyika Workers* (Dar es Salaam: Government Printer, 1967); and Tanzania, *Proposals of the Tanzania Government on the Recommendations of the Presidential Commission of Enquiry into the National Union of Tanganyika Workers (NUTA)* (Dar es Salaam: Government Printer, 1967).

in total wage bill, NUTA is little active in Kilimanjaro and in general is neither liked nor trusted by Kilimanjaro residents.

In part this is because NUTA officials often find themselves in the position of representing, and defending, the employers (often the government) to the employees. NUTA is charged not only with representing workers, but also with leading the government's struggle to prevent the development of a small group of privileged salaried workers whose high salaries and benefits consume a disproportionate share of national resources in an agricultural economy. When an official from NUTA central headquarters met with Moshi Town Council employees in 1969, his opening cry of "Freedom!"—a common salutation in meetings of a political nature in Tanzania which usually brings the response of "Freedom and Work!" or "Freedom and Peace!" from the audience—was greeted by the assembled workers with a shout of "Freedom and Hunger!" After explaining to the workers that long-promised improvements in wages and conditions would be delayed still further by the financial difficulties of the local councils, the NUTA official, together with local NUTA and Town Council officers present, was accused by the workers in harsh and strident language of failing to represent their interests. The responses of the NUTA officials, which drew repeated and loud expressions of disagreement and discontent from the workers, were in terms of explaining why wages could not be raised, benefits could not be increased, and individual requests could not be granted. Never did the NUTA leaders assume the posture of representing the employees to their employer (the Town Council). In many cases they simply supported the responses of the Town Council officials present.

Perhaps more important in explaining the discontent with NUTA in Kilimanjaro was the widespread belief that NUTA officials supported, and even participated in, various corrupt and illegal employment practices. As was mentioned in Chapter 4, jobs could be had in some local factories only through payment of a bribe to the personnel officer, and it was not uncommon to find employees working on terms and conditions proscribed by law. Nor was it uncommon to hear of employees fired for protest against these illegal terms of employment.

The primary result of this distrust of and dislike for NUTA was that employees often brought their problems directly to the TANU office instead of taking them to their NUTA representatives. Not only did individuals seek party assistance, but even the TANU branch formed in a local factory wrote to the Regional Secretary (the Regional Commissioner) complaining, among other things, that "the Workers' Committee . . . does not fulfill its responsibility, especially its Chairman. . . ."[15] TANU officials in Kilimanjaro, who have

15. Letter from the Chairman, TANU Branch, Kibo Match Corporation, Ltd., to Regional Secretary, Kilimanjaro Region, dated 21 February 1969. The letter was especially interesting in that its major complaint was that production, and employment, were being reduced by adverse market conditions manipulated by capitalist entrepreneurs from another country, thus linking suffering by the employees with decreased

often criticized NUTA for lack of attention to workers' problems, usually dealt directly with the problems brought to them rather than referring them to NUTA.

In Kilimanjaro, then, this combination of the need to prevent the concentration of scarce resources in the hands of the few salaried workers, the lack of trade union autonomy, and the apathetic, if not corrupt, behavior of local NUTA officials mean that NUTA neither really represents the workers in protecting their wages, hours, and working conditions nor has shown itself to be effective in utilizing its branch organizations to increase production. Nor has it served as an additional source of support for TANU and its policies or as an additional channel through which Tanzania's leaders can reach the employed sector of the population to involve it in development policies and programs. NUTA, perceived as an unreliable ally or even an enemy by the workers, undermines support for TANU and restricts its access to the workers. Because NUTA concentrates on the minimal tasks it is required to perform—formal representation of workers in contract negotiations, some dispute settlement in cases that have come to public notice, and some attempts to deal with dislocations caused by the fall in sisal production—it comes to be seen as a superfluous adjunct to the Labour Office. To the extent that it is distrusted and disliked by workers, it restricts party access to them and cannot provide a positive channel through which the party can communicate policies that call for self-restraint and sacrifices by the workers. It undermines support for the party to the extent that workers conclude that this organization affiliated to and clearly controlled by TANU is unresponsive to their demands and is more concerned with protecting employers than employees.

The second major institution affiliated to TANU is the Cooperative Union of Tanganyika (CUT). The CUT is a union of cooperatives, and, unlike NUTA, the CUT does not maintain regional and district offices.[16] Where CUT representation in TANU committees is called for, it is normally the KNCU (and occasionally the two other major cooperative unions in the region) that is represented. The other cooperatives active in Kilimanjaro, including in 1969 thirteen consumers' cooperatives, twenty-three saving and loan cooperatives, and eleven other cooperatives, among them the economically very strong association of

---

production. The author of the letter reported that as far as he knew no action had been taken by October 1969.

16. While workers in Kilimanjaro belong directly to NUTA, the ordinary coffee farmer is two steps removed from the CUT: he belongs to his local cooperative primary society, which belongs to the KNCU, which in turn belongs to the CUT. For an analysis of the structure of the cooperative movement in Tanzania, see Tanzania, *Report of the Presidential Special Committee of Enquiry into Co-operative Movement and Marketing Boards* (Dar es Salaam: Government Printer, 1966); and Tanzania, *Proposals of the Tanzania Government on the Recommendation of the Special Presidential Committee of Enquiry into the Co-operative Movement and Marketing Boards* (Dar es Salaam: Government Printer, 1966).

estate coffee producers, were not formally included within the local TANU organization.

The political role of the KNCU is a long and rich one, and it was discussed in Chapter 1 and earlier in this chapter. With a membership of some 70,000 in 1969, the KNCU occupies a central position in the daily lives of the vast majority of Kilimanjaro residents, so that the leadership changes discussed earlier are clearly a reflection of the fundamental political alignments in the region. The KNCU merits a study all its own; it is important here, however, to make two general observations about its impact on the local party organization.

First, after the rejection of the former leadership in the 1969 KNCU elections, the KNCU was directed by what could only be an interim administration. The Manager, seconded from a Dar es Salaam post, saw his task as one of remedying basic defects and establishing a strong administrative structure and appeared anxious to return to his former position in the Ministry. Because the new Manager was associated with the replacement of the former Manager, a widely liked and respected individual, and because he was suspected of being in league with the ousted president, a relative, many of the local farmers and primary society leaders as well were anxious to see him return to his post. The new president took an important position in Dar es Salaam and commented afterward that he did not think he could continue as KNCU President while living in the capital. In 1970 he was defeated in his bid for reelection to Parliament. Other KNCU leaders agreed that it would not be possible to have the organization's president live in Dar es Salaam. Thus, the current KNCU administration came into office primarily as a lever through which to pry the former officeholders out of office. But since its major support developed from votes cast against the old leaders rather than for the new, each of the major elements of the alliance that elected it can be expected to attempt to install its own preferred officeholders; it is not impossible that those evicted in 1969 will attempt to return to office.

Second, as the Tanzanian government has moved to expand its control over the economy it has increasingly relied on the KNCU as its basic agent in Kilimanjaro. As of 1969 the KNCU had assumed monopoly control over the wholesaling of all crops except cotton, had been assigned a monopoly on the sale of tin and cement, and had begun to assist in the development of dairy farming in Kilimanjaro. At the same time, TANU leaders have concluded that, unlike other areas of Tanzania where communal farming schemes have been used to introduce socialist principles, in Kilimanjaro the cooperatives must serve as the main vehicle for introducing and developing socialism. That is, because the shortage of land and the tightly held attitudes on individual landholding preclude any significant local development of communal farming schemes, the cooperative societies are to be utilized for educating the public about the principles of Tanzanian socialism.[17] Even though the Presidential Special

---

17. "Socialism—like democracy—is an attitude of mind," begins a TANU pamphlet, *Ujamaa—The Basis of African Socialism,* first published in 1962. For a succinct statement

Committee of Enquiry into the cooperative movement recommended against forming cooperatives solely for political purposes, numerous cooperatives, ranging from artisans to bar owners, have been begun in Kilimanjaro with little attention to their economic utility and viability, several with markedly little success.[18] The combination of these two trends suggests the development of a strong, self-supporting, and somewhat autonomous cooperative movement. But it can hardly be expected that cooperative societies sufficiently strong and independent to provide services to their members and to act as a vehicle for voluntary acceptance of socialist norms will refrain from occasionally opposing and attacking TANU and its leaders in order to be responsive to their members' interests. Although possible conflict between strong cooperatives and the local TANU organization may for a time be contained within the TANU structure by the assurance of CUT representation on decision-making bodies, it is difficult not to imagine a repetition of the trade union scenario: conflict with the party, followed by the institution of firmer party control over the cooperative movement. An example of this pattern, in regard to communal village settlement schemes in southern Tanzania, took place in 1969, when, apparently over President Nyerere's objections, the TANU National Executive Committee decided to impose direct TANU control over the administration of the villages, replacing the semiautonomous association created to manage them.

There is nothing in the ideology of the Tanzanian single-party system that precludes the development of strong, somewhat autonomous, trade union, cooperative, women's, and other groups. In fact, it may be the interplay among such groups that nurtures the ability of the single-party structure to recognize undesirable policies and to correct or eliminate unviable programs. The conduct of contested elections clearly indicates that competition and conflict, at least within the broad bounds defined by the party leadership, are not inimical to the strong, centralized governmental structure that Tanzania's leaders have developed in their attempts to foster and direct development. But the current leadership, or at least a strong, persuasive segment of it, seems unwilling to tolerate the development of powerful institutions that might serve, at least in some localities, as a counterweight to the party, especially where such institutions threaten the local power basis of national leaders.

---

of Tanzanian socialism, see Julius K. Nyerere, *Freedom and Socialism/Uhuru na Ujamaa* (Dar es Salaam: Oxford University Press, 1968), Introduction. For a fuller review, see the series of TANU papers (including the one mentioned above) collected in Nyerere, *Ujamaa—Essays on Socialism.*

18. See the *Report . . . Co-operative Movement and Marketing Boards,* Paragraph 51 and Part Ten. The government accepted the criticism that premature registration of unviable cooperatives had led to problems in some areas, but reiterated its intent "to employ the economic arm of co-operation to achieve the political aim of socialism. . . ." See the *Proposals of the Tanzania Government . . . Co-operative Movement and Marketing Boards,* p. 17.

The Local Party Organization

The third organization affiliated to TANU, the Tanganyika African Parents Association (TAPA), has never developed as a separate entity with a clear purpose and effective leadership. Just after Independence TAPA's purpose was defined as the organization and management of schools, in order to assist in the rapid expansion of the very limited educational establishment left by the departing colonial administration. But in Kilimanjaro, where parents did not need to be convinced of the value of educating their children, and where the local parents, aided and encouraged by the missions, were already building schools as fast as they could, TAPA had little to do. The one TAPA school in Moshi town so misused a building lent to it by the Town Council that councillors refused to continue to make it available to TAPA. The TAPA record in Kilimanjaro also includes recurring allegations of misuse of funds by TAPA officials.

By 1967–68 it was decided that the establishment of new schools should be carefully coordinated under Ministry supervision. At the same time it was clear that many, if not most, TAPA schools were poorly run with untrained staff in substandard buildings. The TAPA schools then in existence were placed under the jurisdiction of the local councils, and TAPA was expected to function in some sort of overseer role for all schools. In Kilimanjaro new TAPA officers were elected, but because TAPA's purpose had not been clearly defined, they were unsure of their duties, and as a result did little.

Currently TAPA is to be represented on all school committees (committees of parents and teachers) in order to explain national education policy. At the same time, parents are to bring their problems to TAPA, rather than to Ministry officials or the local council, and TAPA will act on behalf of the parents to seek remedy for their complaints. This new plan has yet to be fully implemented in Kilimanjaro, and it is thus too soon to assess TAPA's effectiveness under its new charge. Yet it seems clear that Kilimanjaro parents are so accustomed to taking problems directly to Ministry and council officials or their local churches (which run the schools) and have so little faith in the independence and power of the school committees that unless TAPA can produce clear and prompt action, it will continue to be little used.

Before the most recent changes in TAPA's role, only parents who needed TAPA schools for their children became members; some 1,300 members were enrolled in all of Kilimanjaro District. TAPA activity in 1969 focused almost exclusively on attempting to explain its purpose, to increase its membership, and to raise money. But with little to offer Kilimanjaro parents, TAPA leaders met with little success.

A Paradox

Several observations emerge from this analysis of the TANU sections and affiliated organizations. First, despite its seeming comprehensiveness and inclusiveness, the local party organization does not encompass the entire range of an individual's activities. Not only are the day-to-day family interactions and the holding and use of land (and even the operation of such important institutions as the schools) little affected by TANU, but also several of the institutions important to Kilimanjaro residents retain identities and operating patterns that are distinct from, and occasionally in conflict with, TANU. The local churches, which are perhaps the institutions with the most significant impact on the daily lives of many residents of rural Kilimanjaro, are of course not incorporated within the local party. Women's groups, youth groups, parents associations, and the like, which are in many areas organized by the local clergymen and meet in the churches, function at times as the UWT, TYL, and TAPA branches for the neighborhood, but at other times they retain a distinct, local, nonparty identity. The KNCU, whose control over coffee marketing, and thus to a significant extent over production, affects the daily lives of almost all residents of Kilimanjaro—for even the urban businessmen depend on the coffee crop for their livelihood—fits imperfectly at best into the local party organization. In fact, to develop the additional services now required of it and to promote a socialist orientation through its operations, it may seek greater, rather than less, autonomy from party direction and control. And even where TANU sections and affiliates do seem to encompass broad segments of an individual's life pattern, the lack of organizational definition and poor leadership may mean that these institutions have little regular, sustained impact on much of the population.

Second, although the ostensible purpose of incorporating all of these organizations within the party structure is to promote coordination and prevent conflict among them, lack of coordination and the existence of conflict are still evident. Rarely does a KNCU meeting take place when complaints are not heard that farmers on their way to sell their coffee are harassed by party secretaries to pay their dues.[19] The TANU office absorbs many of the trade union functions of NUTA. Although the TANU leadership, where the UWT is represented, commits itself to reducing the consumption of alcohol, the women's organization stresses opening bars as part of its program to assist women.

Third, the humanpower weakness apparent in government and party at the national level in Tanzania is clear in the local party organization as well. Organizations are inactive for lack of effective leadership. Programs begun are left unfinished. Often the effective leaders posted from the center are needed elsewhere in the country and are transferred on short notice. And on

---

19. This practice continues despite government acceptance of the committee of enquiry's finding that cooperative societies may refuse to permit such collections on their premises. See the *Report . . . into Co-operative Movement and Marketing Boards,* Paragraph 300, p. 77, and the *Proposals . . . the Co-operative Movement and Marketing Boards,* p. 19. Where the primary society does not refuse permission, or where the party secretary stations himself near but not on the society's premises, such collections are, of course, perfectly legal.

occasion even when central leaders recognize the inadequacy of a particular local leader, they are at a loss to find a capable replacement.

Fourth, despite the seeming breadth of coverage of the party sections and affiliates, some segments of the local populace are represented only poorly, at best, in local decision-making. Although a major theme of this study has been that the diffuse nature and overlapping positions of the local party organization provide Moshi residents with alternative advocates, it is clear that some groups—the workers, for example—are often effectively excluded. To the extent that the urban party office is unable to respond adequately to the demands placed on it by the urban unemployed and school-leavers, they, too, are effectively excluded. Those not well represented by the party are forced to turn to alternative institutions, especially the churches in Kilimanjaro, to press their demands.

Finally, these comments return us to the paradox that the implication of the incompatibility of program goals and humanpower weaknesses is that programs and policies can be implemented only through strong, functionally specific, institutions. And yet the party is unwilling to yield those institutions the independence that seems to be the necessary concomitant of strength. If TANU cannot itself meet all of an individual's needs—protecting his status as a worker, for example—then it must rely on some other institution to do that job; but it cannot expect that institution—NUTA in this case—to do its job effectively if in order to minimize possible conflict between TANU and NUTA, NUTA is effectively emasculated. To suggest that TANU's fears of competition from its auxiliaries are groundless, or, conversely, to suggest that TANU disregard its humanpower problems and disregard its policy goals in order to attempt to be all things to all Tanzanians, would be gratuitous. Tanzania's political system has exhibited an elasticity and its leadership a willingness to experiment that have thus far enabled contradictions of this sort to be dealt with without severely impeding orderly development. To highlight this particular paradox here is simply to stress the dilemma of attempting to utilize fragile institutions and inadequately prepared leaders to manage the reconciliation of conflicting goals and to build practical utopias.

Structure

There is a tripartite structure to TANU's leadership at the regional and district levels, and a similar pattern is currently being extended to branch level. The Chairman is elected by the delegates to the party Annual Conference at each level.[20] The Commissioner is the party Secretary at each level: the Regional Commissioner serves as the regional party Secretary, and the Area

20. Although termed Annual Conference, the meetings are normally convened every second year. In the urban district all cell leaders are entitled to attend the Conference, while each of the more numerous branches of the rural district sends delegates. More than 800 delegates were entitled to attend the Kilimanjaro Regional Annual Conference in 1969.

Commissioner serves as the district party Secretary. The Executive Secretary at each level is a party employee. The Regional and District Executive Secretaries are posted from Dar es Salaam and are subject to transfer throughout the country, while most branch (executive) secretaries are employed from within the district. It should be noted in passing that it is not uncommon for individuals to cross these lines, frequently moving from party to government service. Early Provincial Chairmen and Secretaries became Regional and Area Commissioners, while several Regional Executive Secretaries have been appointed Area Commissioners.[21]

This tripartite leadership provides structural links between the party and the government. The District Chairman is automatically the chairman of the district or urban council, thus holding both local government and party posts. At the same time, as council chairman, he must look to the Area Commissioner, his party secretary, for assistance in implementing council decisions. Likewise, the Area Commissioner, who must utilize party assistance to implement central government directives, must also depend on the party machinery under the supervision of the District Executive Secretary.

The point here is simply that the tripartite party leadership, together with the structural overlaps and the political networks that characterize the local political system discussed in Chapter 9, though they may create a tangled maze on a bureaucratic chart, serve to link significant institutions within the local community. This was particularly clear in Kilimanjaro in the rejection of the former KNCU leadership: the different networks allied in opposition to the old leadership and in so doing reinforced the KNCU's position in the mainstream of political competition in Kilimanjaro. During the course of 1969, conflict in Kilimanjaro between the Regional Chairman and the Regional Commissioner, in part over the latter's handling, as party Regional Secretary, of an incident with an urban Asian businessman, served, as the conflict rippled through the town, to link the Asian business community, often a reluctant party supporter, with the Regional Chairman and Regional Executive Secretary. It is also clear, however, that however much this tripartite leadership structure may serve as a counterweight to the centrifugal tendencies inherent in Kilimanjaro politics, the continued strength of the churches testifies to the incompleteness of the party's dominance of the local political system.

A second dimension of the linkage effect of the tripartite local party leadership relates to the ties it provides between the center and up-country in

21. According to Bienen, by 1964 of ten individuals who had been Provincial Secretaries in 1961, six had become Regional Commissioners and three had become Area Commissioners, while of nineteen Provincial Chairmen in 1961, seven had become either Regional or Area Commissioners; see Bienen, *Tanzania: Party Transformation,* Table 6, p. 134. During the course of 1969 the Regional Executive Secretary in Kilimanjaro was appointed an Area Commissioner (after having served briefly as Regional Executive Secretary in two other regions) and the current Area Commissioner had been a Regional Executive Secretary.

The Local Party Organization

Tanzania. TANU at the center has continued to rely on local grievances and on local party organizations to provide its main source of strength and support, but at the same time the local party organization is dependent on the center for its continued operation. For example, although basic local party expenditures are paid from entrance and membership fees, sales of party posters, calendars, and pamphlets, and miscellaneous collections, the largest party expenditures in the local area—the salaries of party employees—are paid from centrally supplied funds. At the center, the party depends not on its local party organizations but on the government for the bulk of its revenue. In 1968, for example, all of the regions in mainland Tanzania forwarded to central party headquarters a total of only Shs. 217,000.80, while the direct government subsidy to the party for that year amounted to Shs. 4,370,000. The support from Kilimanjaro Region to central headquarters for 1968 was Shs. 6,000.[22] In fact, although the government subsidy to the party increased, party income showed a substantial decline from the 1966/1967 to the 1967/1968 fiscal years. Income for the three party districts of Kilimanjaro Region (Kilimanjaro rural, Moshi urban, Pare) decreased by almost half in that period, while the government subsidy to the party as a whole increased by some 41 percent, from Shs. 3,000,000 in 1966/67 to Shs. 4,240,000 in 1967/1968.[23] Thus the share of local party operations financed from subsidies from the center exceeded the share financed from local collections.

Although the central and the local party are linked by this need for mutual support, there is a continuing tension between the locally and centrally selected party officials. In his comprehensive study of TANU, viewed largely from the center, Bienen argues that, since the commissioners are the interpreters of the center at the local level and carry the weight of governmental authority and force, they normally prevail over the local chairman.[24] The case is much less clear, and regular, in Kilimanjaro than Bienen suggests. While it is true that the political networks centered on the Regional Commissioner and the Regional Chairman are frequently in conflict, basic conflicts are usually resolved in the Regional Executive Committee, where neither can be sure of

22. Reliable statistics for party income and expenditures are difficult to obtain. The figures cited here were taken from **TANU**, *Taarifa ya Ofisi Kuu . . . Novemba 1967–Aprili 1969*, pp. 37–41.

23. Tanganyika African National Union, *Minzania ya Mapato na Matumizi ya Ofisi Kuu na Mikoa, Mwaka wa 1966/67 na 1967/1968* (Dar es Salaam: TANU headquarters, 1969).

24. The tension between central and local and the inability of the central party headquarters to control fully the behavior of the local party organizations are main themes of Bienen's work, *Tanzania: Party Transformation;* for the statement of the relative positions of the commissioners and chairmen, see p. 157. Bienen stresses that commissioners prevail through a process of compromise and consensus and do not rule through fiat, p. 456. He suggests as well that Dar es Salaam inputs are more likely to be influential locally on personnel matters and factional conflicts than on development goals.

prevailing regularly. In 1969, for example, the Regional Chairman often prevailed over a particularly disliked individual who served briefly as Regional Commissioner, but the Chairman was much less successful with both that Commissioner's predecessor and his successor. In dealing with these conflicts among the political networks, the TANU Regional Executive Secretary self-consciously attempted to hold himself aloof and to establish himself as a mediator and arbitrator among them.

What is suggested here is that formal organizational patterns and hierarchical chains of authority are only one determinant of fundamental decisions within the local party organization. Other factors can, and do, permit the weaker networks to overcome the resources available to the commissioners.

Another important factor is tenure in office. A local chairman who has held office for a long time and who has developed allies within the party is in a strong position vis-à-vis a recently posted commissioner who has not yet had time to develop his own position and allies locally. Of course, the reverse may also be the case, when it is the commissioner who has had a long tenure in office and the chairman is newly elected.

A third factor that conditions the development of a local power base is the individual personality of the principal leaders. The abrasiveness and ready willingness to resort to the use of coercion of one Regional Commissioner in Kilimanjaro, coupled with his aloofness from the local populace and his occasional inebriated appearances in public, severely crippled his ability to win local support and allies. On the other hand, the personal charm of his predecessor, his willingness to socialize with the local populace, and especially his leadership in developing local football teams and competitions, helped overcome some of the natural hostility to an outsider in Kilimanjaro.

A fourth factor is the ability of local leaders to project themselves as defenders of local interests. The forcefulness of the Area Commissioner in attempting to cut through the bureaucratic red tape that delayed central government assistance to areas of the district suffering from famine and malnutrition and his perseverance in traveling to the new Chagga settlements in western Tanzania to deal with troubles that developed there enhanced his already substantial access to government authority and power as commissioner. In the process he overshadowed the District Chairman.

Access to a Dar es Salaam power base is also an important factor in the local political competition in Kilimanjaro. The Regional Commissioner, who combines his direct access to the Ministry of Local Government and, on occasion, the President, with seats both in Parliament and in the National Executive Committee, is normally in a stronger position than local leaders who sit in only one of those: the MPs, the Regional Chairman, and the Member of the National Executive Committee. Evaluations of the prospective candidates by the Regional (and Area) Commissioner also are important inputs when the party Central Committee screens candidates for local elections. But the other leaders themselves may have strong, or weak, ties in Dar es Salaam. The

The Local Party Organization

Kilimanjaro Regional Chairman, at best a lukewarm supporter of national policy, was accused of using tribal and religious ties in his bid for reelection. Although he was able to thwart an investigation by party headquarters requested by the Regional Executive Secretary, it is clear that his voice has lost much of its persuasive force in Dar es Salaam. On the other hand, the District Chairman, whose brother was an MP, an early party activist, and the leader in the antiparamountcy fight, visited Dar es Salaam regularly and maintained close ties there whose support he could draw on in local competitions.

Two recent changes both strengthen and weaken the chairman's position. Until 1969 the membership of the Working Committee at each level (effectively the set of party leaders who actually carry on party business) was largely selected by the chairman, so that the basic day-to-day decisions were made by a committee dominated by the chairman and his appointees. Since all members of the Working Committee are automatically members (though nonvoting) of the Executive Committee at that level, the chairman was assured of several faithful allies in that forum. The changes introduced in 1969 require that some members of the Working Committee be selected by the party Annual Conference at the appropriate level, thus reducing the chairman's ability to select his own allies. At the same time, amid complaints that leaders, both party and government, were in office in a particular locality too short a time to accomplish their tasks successfully, the chairman's term of office was extended from two to five years, thus ensuring a long time when the chairman will be secure from defeat, and, as well, perhaps guaranteeing that the chairman's tenure will be longer than that of the commissioner.

Two more general points are important here. One is that Tanzania's leaders will continue to react to criticisms that decisions do not adequately reflect local participation and preferences and that development strategies are being subverted by inefficient and uncooperative local officials and institutions by experimenting with new organizational patterns. Terms and conditions of office will be altered, overlaps will be increased or eliminated, and the composition and authority of decision-making bodies will be varied. This suggests, second, that structural forms will continue to be only one of the determinants of power within the local political system and that the strength of the local roots of the local political networks will be an important determinant of political outputs.

It is important to note here another trend in Tanzania that has a significant impact on the local party organization. As has often been stressed, one of the party's most frustrating problems has been to find able, honest, and dynamic leaders. In recent years at least four party officials have been dismissed in Kilimanjaro for misuse of party funds. At the same time, it has become clear that some party activists who were welcomed as allies during the struggle for independence have become liabilities as Tanzanian socialism has become more clearly defined. In the Arusha Declaration the TANU National Executive Committee noted that the time had passed when all Tanzanians were

The Party

welcome members of the party, and its charge that only those individuals who fully supported party policy be accepted as members was repeated in the report to the 1969 TANU Annual Conference:

> Since the Party was founded we have put great emphasis on getting as many members as possible. This was the right policy during the independence struggle. But now the National Executive feels that the time has come when we should put more emphasis on the beliefs of our Party and its policies of socialism.
>
> That part of the TANU Constitution which relates to the admission of a member should be adhered to, and if it is discovered that a man does not appear to accept the faith, the objects, and the rules and regulations of the Party, then he should not be accepted as a member.[25]

From November 1968 to December 1969 the appointments of four Regional Commissioners and fourteen Area Commissioners were revoked.[26] A substantial number of would-be candidates for regional and district party chairmanships were disallowed at the national level. Nine Members of Parliament were dismissed from the party, and thus from Parliament, in 1968.[27] Clearly a weeding-out process has begun, directed from the center. Although it is too soon to gauge its significance for, and the reactions of, local party organizations in Tanzania, its impact on them will be substantial.

Summary

This extended description of the composition and structure of the local party organization in Kilimanjaro has made it clear that a wide range of complementary and contradictory trends and institutions are encompassed by the local party organization. The overlaps of structure and personnel that link sections and affiliates within the party, that tie party and government, and that provide bridges to other institutions in the community are complex and often not clearly defined. Because of the multiple channels through which it must percolate, communication from the center is intermittent and discontinuous. The humanpower weaknesses that plague the party and the government

25. *Arusha Declaration,* Part Four. The charge to the 1969 Annual Conference is in TANU, *Taarifa ya Ofisi Kuu . . . Novemba 1967–Aprili 1969,* p. 13.

26. As announced in the *Tanzania Gazette.* Reasons for these revocations are not given; at least one Area Commissioner was an older man who retired, at his own request, from active political life. Another major shuffle of officeholders took place in 1972.

27. Except for two accused of attempting to subvert TANU and the government (one was in exile, the other in preventive detention), specific reasons were not given for these expulsions; several of those expelled had been consistent critics of the government and party. Since only party members may serve in Parliament (Paragraph 27, Interim Constitution of Tanzania, 1965), those expelled from the party automatically lost their seats in Parliament. For a discussion of the expulsions, see Thoden van Velzen and Sterkenburg, "The Party Supreme," pp. 73–74.

at the center are present up-country as well and further weaken the links that tie the local party organizations throughout Tanzania, and the center continues to be unable to impose clear, firm, direct control on the behavior of its up-country units.[28] The continued dependence of TANU on its local party organizations, coupled with its inability to impose firm control on them, and the practical impossibility of opposing basic party policy at the local level combine to foster a continuing local orientation to politics in Tanzania—a concern with local grievances and with who among the local leaders can best represent his area in the competition for the allocation of national resources.

Like TANU at the center the local party organization is a cluster of political networks and factions, at times in alliance, at times in competition. In this way, the local party organization is a framework within which many of the basic conflicts over the allocation of resources at the local level take place. The TANU officers posted from the center, while they do attempt to ensure that the competitions take place within the limits prescribed by national policy, devote much of their effort to acting as go-betweens among the competing factions. In performing in this way, the local party organization provides important communication and mediation functions, both among the factions at the local level and between Kilimanjaro and the center. At the same time, it is clear that some of the conflict over substantial local allocations takes place largely outside the local party organization.

---

28. Bienen stresses this point in *Tanzania: Party Transformation*, Chapter 14, especially pp. 451–52.

11

TANU in Moshi

Introduction

The outlines of party, and of power, in Moshi are by now quite clear.
This chapter, then, is concerned with combining the analyses of structures,
of issues, and of behavior to develop a fuller understanding of what TANU
means in Moshi. At one level, the goal is just that: to explore how the local
party functions, how it is directed, and whom it serves. At another level,
the goal is to summarize and group these findings both to construct a more
comprehensive base for developing broader generalizations and also to refine,
to clarify, and to challenge some of the sweeping generalizations characteristic of the literature on African politics.

To deal with the complex and multifaceted nature of the local party
organization in Kilimanjaro, the approach of this chapter will be to examine
TANU from several different vantage points. Because TANU is different
things to different people in different circumstances, and because TANU's
functioning is characterized by extensive spatial and temporal variations, it
is useful to examine the party in Kilimanjaro from both a local and a national
perspective, and from a concern with development and national integration,
in order to encompass as fully as possible what TANU is all about in Moshi.

A major task of the Tanzanian leadership is the reconciliation of the
goals of economic growth (often called development)—rational planning,
increased productivity, expansion of income—with the goals of politics—
independence, participation, control, harmony—in Tanzania. Much of the
dilemma of policy choice derives from the frequent contradiction of these
two goals. The major mechanism for this reconciliation is the single party,
TANU, structured nationally as an assembly of more-or-less autonomous
local party organizations. The local TANU organization in Kilimanjaro is
one of the constituents of this national assembly, but it, too, is a coalition
of subunits and represents a regularized factionalism. One important TANU
role in Kilimanjaro is to educate. A second is to provide support for TANU
and the government and legitimacy for TANU and government policies.
A third is to facilitate communication, both horizontally within Kilimanjaro
and vertically between Kilimanjaro and the center. A fourth is to mediate

among the factions in Kilimanjaro. In providing support, legitimizing outputs, facilitating communication, and mediating, TANU also stimulates participation. In this way, the local TANU organization becomes a framework within which much of the major local conflict takes place; and while it is only one of the institutions that serves to aggregate interests, interest articulation is essentially monopolized within party channels.

While noting all of these TANU roles, it is important to note as well that the local TANU organization in Kilimanjaro does not have a monopoly on resource allocation locally, nor are its functions principally distributive or regulative. And, unlike what has apparently been the experience of single parties in other African single party states, TANU has thus far not become in Moshi and Kilimanjaro a tool through which the elite is able to institutionalize its status and to deny access to new elites. In fact, to a large extent, the opposite seems to be taking place. TANU provides an openness and a lever through which the old elites can be evicted and new elites substituted. This observation should not be phrased in terms of social class, however, since the data concern elites and not the behavior of large segments of the population. That TANU is stimulating a significant circulation of elites in Kilimanjaro is clear. It is also clear, however, that some segments of the population fare better than others in that circulation; from these data it is difficult to determine whether or not some segments of the population are excluded entirely.

Finally, it should be stressed that one of the most significant (and at the same time one of the most troublesome for analytic purposes) features of TANU is the commitment of its leaders to continually refine, reorder, and reorganize structures and personnel to achieve their goals.

National Perspective

Viewed from the center, the local TANU organization is expected to lead, to mobilize—to be an agent of change.[1] In the revolution in mass attitudes and behavior necessary to develop Tanzania, TANU is expected to be a prime motivator. In Kilimanjaro, however, only a few party officers can be described as largely oriented toward social change. Further, the studies of several key issue-areas clearly indicate that TANU does not have a monopoly on resource allocation in Kilimanjaro and therefore cannot always (or even frequently)

---

1. See the Introduction to Nyerere, *Freedom and Socialism,* especially p. 30; see also Nyerere's "Independence Message to TANU," reprinted in Julius K. Nyerere, *Freedom and Unity* (Dar es Salaam: Oxford University Press, 1967), pp. 138-41. The Arusha Declaration asserts: "It is the responsibility of TANU to see that the country produces enough food and enough cash crops for export." (The Arusha Declaration, along with other papers on Tanzanian socialism is reprinted in Nyerere, *Freedom and Socialism,* as well as in Nyerere, *Ujamaa—Essays on Socialism*; this quotation can be found on p. 247 of the former.) In his study of TANU and development in Tanzania, Bienen concluded that "TANU sees itself as the propagator of social change"; see *Tanzania: Party Transformation,* p. 334.

control the direction of change in key issues. A tacit coalition among the churches, much of the local populace, and several important leaders renders TANU unable to stem the rapid expansion of education in Kilimanjaro. Yet, that expansion of education makes it difficult to divert resources from Kilimanjaro to other areas of Tanzania, thus reinforcing the inequalities in development between Kilimanjaro and other areas, and nurturing the problems engendered by the annual output of a large number of school-leavers who cannot be absorbed in salaried nonagricultural employment. In this issue-area, the local TANU organization has in fact become a spokesman for local interests at the center, rather than the implementer of national policy at the local level.

Likewise, despite the publicly enunciated goal of managing, and restraining, the sale and consumption of liquor, TANU has been unable to control the rapid expansion of the liquor trade in Kilimanjaro. To a large extent, TANU's behavior has been responsive both to local pressure and to the involvement of several of its key leaders in the liquor trade: to avoid becoming directly involved in this issue as much as possible. While the publicly enunciated goal of restraining liquor consumption may indeed mask private goals oriented toward expansion rather than restriction, the evidence is clear that the local party organization has not been able to ensure the implementation of a goal enunciated publicly at both national and local levels.

Similarly, TANU, as TANU, has been largely unable to bring about significant change in the major patterns of social organization in Kilimanjaro by itself: it does not have the skills, manpower, and resources required, nor does it control the skills, manpower, and resources, themselves limited, of the government.[2] It has not attempted to alter the pattern of individual landholding that many party leaders argue is a major obstacle to the rationalization of agricultural production and a major impediment to the development of the communal rural socialism envisaged in party policy. Nor has it attempted to prevent the accumulations of large landholdings, or the aggregation of massive business interests, by the very individuals local party leaders recognize as becoming an entrenched and resourceful opposition to party and government policy.

TANU has been able, however, to play an important role in facilitating change introduced by other institutions. By legitimizing specific governmental outputs, for example, it has enabled an easier acceptance of the displacement of Kilimanjaro residents to other areas of Tanzania.

There are two important problems involved in attempting to use upcountry party structures to foster change. One is that development, as defined by the national leadership, may depend on the ability of the party and government to do the very things that alienate it from the urbanized and educated segments of its population without provoking them to intransigent resistance and rebellion. The commitment to equality and to a reversal of the trend toward

2. Bienen, *Tanzania: Party Transformation,* stresses this point; see especially Chapter 14.

concentrating national resources in the areas of the country already most favored means that party and government must demand sacrifices, must restrain demands for better living conditions, higher salaries, and the like, and must focus on rural and less developed areas, all of which serve to make the educated and urbanized segments of the population feel they have been neglected and deprived.

Thus the role of an urban TANU organization is paradoxical in that it must work to restrain the demands of the urban populace and at the same time convince them that it is working to promote their interests. It must attempt to persuade them that the apparent unresponsiveness of the government to their demands is a temporary situation and that in the long run there is a congruence of local interests and national goals. To exercise this restraining influence, without frequent recourse to coercion, the party must be responsive to local demands in order to develop an identification with and commitment to the party that will permit it to facilitate the acceptance of policies to which there is local opposition. In other words, in order to implement national policy at all, the local party must seem more responsive to local demands than to national directives. To the extent that servicing local individuals and groups (servicing, because the resources available to the local party are largely symbolic rather than utilitarian or coercive[3]) promotes a willingness to accept policy outputs, TANU is able to facilitate change. And to the extent that some groups, like the town workers, have at best limited access to such services, they are unresponsive to calls to support national policy. That TANU has been able to convert the provision of services into a willingness to accept governmental decisions in Moshi is evident from TANU's ability to calm the market women angered over demands that they pay high license fees and ultimately to persuade them to acquiesce in the new fees. Similarly, that the party did not insist that land in the new settlements in western Tanzania, to which Kilimanjaro residents were being moved, be farmed communally (with the result that the pattern of individual landholding common in Kilimanjaro was transplanted into the new areas) was an essential element in the party's ability to persuade a large number of people to make the move.

This particular paradox highlights the importance of the pedagogical and socialization roles of the local party. It must be an instrument to educate people about development and nation-building, and it must strive to persuade them that sacrifices in the short run are justified in terms of long-run gains. In a setting where most adults have had little, if any, formal schooling it must be a vehicle for communicating and nurturing the values of Tanzanian socialism. At the same time, it must deal with immediate needs and teach people how to have better lives with the resources available.

---

3. That is, as has been noted, the party has few material rewards to distribute, and, in general, is reluctant to resort to coercion.

The pedagogical and socialization roles of the local party also depend on its ability to secure acceptance among the local population. Distrusted and disliked, it cannot be effective. But to win acceptance often means that the party must mute its teaching. Rather than moving directly and forcefully toward communal settlement schemes in Kilimanjaro, where land is short and the attachment to individual landholdings is strong, the party attempts to explain and promote Tanzanian socialism by focusing on cooperatives. Rather than stressing the sacrifices demanded of the more affluent sections of the population, the party is often responsive to local demands for more schools, more hospitals, and more government services.

The second problem in attempting to use the local party to foster change is the combination of the reliance on the bureaucracy to manage socioeconomic change—since it is the only institution with the necessary skills—with a conception of bureaucratic management ill suited to developmental tasks. The rapidity with which available managerial skills have been concentrated in the bureaucracy has been amply demonstrated throughout Africa.[4] In Tanzania as well, after Independence skilled manpower was funneled into government service. As skills become concentrated in the bureaucracy, civil servants are assigned the major role in shaping and directing development.[5] But the bureaucracy, characterized, at least in theory, by impersonal decisions based on clear-cut norms and rules and a compartmentalized hierarchy shielded from public and political pressures, is an inefficient managerial tool in a state in which the government assumes a major role in shaping and directing the economy.[6] Its commitment to impersonal decisions and hierarchical chains makes the bureaucracy too slow-moving and cumbersome to develop new programs.[7] For example, a major obstacle to alleviating the famine and mal-

4. For a selection of views on the role of the bureaucracy in developmental administration, see Joseph LaPalombara, ed., *Bureaucracy and Political Development* (Princeton, N.J.: Princeton University Press, 1967).

5. Bienen stresses the reliance on planners, as opposed to politicians, in the planning process in Tanzania; see *Tanzania: Party Transformation,* especially Chapter 8.

6. Donald B. Rosenthal, in reference to India, argues that specific historical circumstances make Weber's legal-rational bureaucracy "a highly inefficient instrument for a modern welfare state of a new nation seeking rapid modernization." See "Deurbanization, Elite Displacement, and Political Change in India," *Comparative Politics* 2, no. 2 (January 1970): 169. That the bureaucracy in new nations may in fact be less impersonal, compartmentalized, hierarchical, and shielded than bureaucratic theory requires indicates the persistence of traditional, antibureaucratic, obligations and relationships and also supports the argument made here.

7. B. B. Schaffer offers support for this point in arguing that a bureaucracy is adaptive rather than innovative and more concerned with maintenance than with change; see "The Deadlock in Development Administration," in Leys, *Politics and Change in Developing Countries,* pp. 177-211. Schaffer concludes that where rapid change is sought, bureaucratic administration is an inappropriate means. For a similar conclusion, see Okello Oculi, "Applied Literature and Social Imagination in Africa," *EAJ* 7, no. 8 (August 1970): 17.

nutrition that plagued some areas of Kilimanjaro in 1969 was the inability of the bureaucratic structures charged with dealing with this problem to react quickly and to deal with the root causes as well as the immediate effects. The bureaucracy does not have the political resources, except for the occasional use of coercion, to implement new programs, especially where there is strong resistance to the social changes embodied in the new programs. Only when the party took an active role in recruiting Kilimanjaro residents to move to other areas of Tanzania did the repeated attempts of civil servants to encourage migration show some success. Nor does the bureaucracy have the access to and the support of the mass of the rural population, which, in the absence of the use of coercion or of substantial resources to distribute, offer the only viable means of attempting to attack the local resistance to change that is one brake on development.[8] It does not provide administrators with the necessary discretionary power to work toward general societal goals,[9] nor does it provide them direct and immediate feedback on reactions to and the success of ongoing programs.

One response to this problem in Tanzania has been to create a set of commissioners who link the bureaucracy and the civil service. Combining authority from the center with some control over the civil servants under their jurisdiction and with a key role in the local party organization, they are expected to be able to minimize the impediments of the bureaucracy and to make firm, bold decisions.[10] There are some indications of success in Kilimanjaro in this regard: in organizing and facilitating the movement of Kilimanjaro residents to other areas of Tanzania, and in encouraging the organization of cooperatives among urban craftsmen, for example. But the bureaucratic norms are already well established in Tanzania. Local civil servants in Kilimanjaro have proved to be much less responsive to the local commissioners than to their superiors at the Ministry level in Dar es Salaam, to the extent, as was noted above, that both the Kilimanjaro Regional and Area Commissioners, together with the local party leaders, were unable to accelerate the provision of relief to areas of the district suffering from famine and malnutrition.

8. Albert Meister, writing specifically about East Africa, follows René Dumont in stressing the need for a revolutionary core among the leadership elite willing and able to break down traditional attitudes that constrain development. See Meister, *East Africa: The Past in Chains, the Future in Pawn,* trans. Phyllis Nauts Ott (New York: Walker, 1968); and Dumont, *False Start in Africa,* trans. Phyllis Nauts Ott (London: Deutsch, 1966).

9. Michael J. Brenner makes this point in arguing the inappropriateness of the Weberian notion of bureaucracy in areas of economic management in reference to modern industrial states; see "Functional Representation and Interest Group Theory," *Comparative Politics* 2, no. 1 (October 1969): 122.

10. This, of course, runs counter to the recommendations of many of the commentators on bureaucracy and development. LaPalombara, for example, argues that "democratic development requires some separation of political and administrative roles." See *Bureaucracy and Political Development,* p. 24.

The Party

Another aspect of the problem, of course, is the need to ensure that the reliance on the bureaucracy to manage economic development does not nurture a class of managers committed to no ideology and responsible to no one outside the administrative structures or responsive only to the narrow elite from which they are increasingly drawn. Or, in other terms, it is essential that this reliance on the bureaucracy not foster among civil servants an orientation toward their own norms, status, and power that makes them resistant to, rather than managers of, the fundamental socioeconomic changes envisaged in party policy. The creation of commissioners attempts to deal with this problem by appointing the commissioners party secretaries. While the commissioners appointed have indeed been responsive to party goals, attempts to develop a political commitment among civil servants, who in general are expected to be party members and to adhere to leadership norms, have shown little success in Kilimanjaro.

Viewed from the center, then, TANU's role in Moshi in fostering change has been one of legitimizing and facilitating governmental outputs. In attempting to maintain the support among the urban population that enables it to perform this legitimizing function, it has had to walk a narrow tightrope between restraining the demands of the most favored sectors of the population and alienating those individuals and groups best situated to oppose and thwart party and governmental initiatives. In order to legitimize, the party must be responsive to local demands. At the same time it must utilize its legitimizing ability to support policies and programs that may be very unwelcome locally. It must develop patterns of interaction such that legitimizing governmental outputs does not undermine its ability to legitimize.

Local Perspective

TANU had early difficulties in penetrating Kilimanjaro. The thrust of colonial policy since the 1930s was to restrain the inclination of Kilimanjaro leaders to link local grievances with national opposition to colonial rule. Local issues absorbed political energies in Kilimanjaro, and not until the paramountcy was eliminated in 1960 did TANU begin to expand beyond the small base it had earlier developed. Its spread in the 1960s indicated the willingness and ability of Kilimanjaro leaders to use TANU to pursue their own local ends.

It is clear that TANU is not a monolithic organization in Kilimanjaro, even to the extent that it is almost confusing to speak of a single TANU organization, since the local party encompasses so many groups and individuals among whom competition is often more significant than cooperation.

In some cases, TANU is a framework for local conflict. Some, though far from all, key policy decisions are battled within the norms and structures of the local party. In providing a framework for local conflicts, TANU functions to mediate and to facilitate communication. It mediates in that the secretaries posted from the center define their job as one of mediating among the different TANU sections and affiliates and among the principal local party leaders. Conflicts over allocations are often expressed in terms of conflicts between personalities, many of which are resolved through the intervention of local party leaders. It facilitates communication within Kilimanjaro in that competing groups turn to the party for support and in so doing ensure that proposals, opposition, and alternatives are filtered through the network of factions that constitute the local party and thus throughout the district as a whole. Parenthetically it should be noted that the local party has a major role in mass communication in Moshi because word-of-mouth remains the basic medium of communication.[11] Located in the center of town and frequently visited by both party leaders and ordinary citizens, the party offices provide a continuous stream of information (and, on occasion, misinformation) about what is happening in town and in the country as a whole. Urban residents often turn to the party office, or to someone who has visited the party office, to seek information and to verify rumors. TANU also facilitates communication between Kilimanjaro and the center in that at times it is more responsive to local demands than other institutions with links in the center, interests are almost always articulated through one or another of the party channels, and party leaders have direct access to the principal decision-makers.

Because the TANU organization in Kilimanjaro is not monolithic and because it does not have a determining role in all key decisions, there are channels for avoiding it. The local churches, for example, have been able to wind their way into, out of, and around the party on the provision of primary education so that they seem to be working in harmony with the party when in fact they are in direct conflict with it. To the extent that basic issues are defined as technical, rather than political, and there is a strong inclination among those political leaders who represent the center to define key issues in that way, conflicts over allocations are focused on administrative officers and regulatory boards, with the party little involved. The bureaucratic norms—that decisions are technical and should be made only by experts—often override the political norms—a commitment to an integrated party-state apparatus in which emphasis is placed on the political consequences of technical decisions. As well, the paucity of skills and resources directly available to the local party renders it unable to assert itself in many local conflicts.

It is important to stress, however, that in the local political situation expected outcomes, rather than central directives or specific structural arrangements, determine the locus and type of conflict. That is, the anticipated reactions of particular individuals or structures condition the forums in which

11. Although in the past there have been local newspapers in Kilimanjaro, none was published during 1968-69. The average daily sale of all national newspapers, which occasionally contained local news, in Moshi in October 1969 was 1,512, for a town of nearly 30,000 population serving a district with a population of close to one-half million. Many more people, of course, had access to radios, but even more infrequently did national news broadcasts include local news.

conflict takes place. Because party structures extend into many aspects of urban life, and because local responses to policy and programs emanating from the center are usually articulated through party channels, TANU does form the umbrella under which much local conflict takes place.

TANU in Kilimanjaro is a coalition of factions. The rapidity of change in Tanzania and the frequency of transfer among party and government officers, coupled with the persistence of the basic geographic and religious cleavages within the district and with the basic incompatibility of the demands of the urban, salaried, educated and the rural, agricultural segments of the population, nurture continual realignments among the factions. There thus develops a regularized factionalism, a continuing search for allies, and an ongoing attempt to find a base for support. Associated with this regularized factionalism is a circulation of elites. Old leaders are replaced by new, with those currently predominant unsure that they will continue to prevail.

In organization, TANU in Kilimanjaro has stood somewhere between a party seeking mass membership and a party seeking to restrict its membership to a leadership vanguard. Almost anyone may join TANU, but until individuals are seeking some specific party action (either in general, like independence, or in particular, like a job), or until the party leadership mounts a campaign to encourage people to join, they see little purpose in doing so. TANU leaders in Kilimanjaro themselves differ on whether or not the party should seek mass membership, and no one has an accurate idea of how many members there are.[12]

The regularized factionalism, the circulation of elites, and the openness of party membership combine to ensure that the local party organization remains responsive to local demands and that it thus builds a base of support it can utilize in legitimizing policy and program outputs. But because it is responsive to local demands, the local TANU organization, or major elements within it, is often unable and unwilling to implement directives from the center.

The relationship between center and locality in Tanzania is thus both confused and paradoxical. In some situations, the center sets clear limits on what the locality can, or cannot, do. A clear example of this is the requirement that Town Council budgets be approved by the Ministry in Dar es Salaam. In addition, the appointees of the center (the commissioners, the party executive secretary, the civil servants), make, directly, many ostensibly local decisions and set boundaries on the extent of the local initiative. But at the same time, as was detailed in the discussion of the party organization, directives from the

12. Despite extensive efforts over almost eighteen months to arrive at reasonably accurate party membership figures for Kilimanjaro, I was never able to reconcile satisfactorily the widely divergent estimates of party leaders and the error-ridden party records. Studies that make important use of party membership figures in Tanzania, as, I suspect, in much of Africa, unless the scholars have been able to collect or verify the figures themselves, can therefore only be misleading.

center are modified, altered, and even reversed by the time they reach the locality. Limited resources and personnel, together with the continuing debate over the appropriate role for local participation, make the center heavily dependent on the locality for communicating policy and implementing programs. This in turn poses other problems for TANU as a developmental institution in Tanzania.

Development

Development is a term widely used in the literature of comparative politics, but only rarely is it defined very closely. Despite repeated attempts to formulate culturally neutral or objective definitions, all definitions of development explicitly or implicitly contain a set of value choices describing which alternatives are desirable and suggesting how they should be sought, value choices that may, or may not, be related to the definition of development by the leaders of the country being studied.

Rather than become entrapped in that semantic and ethnocentric blind, let us take development as it is commonly defined in Tanzania—elimination of poverty, ignorance, and disease; and the specific set of programs designed to achieve those goals within a commitment to an egalitarian pattern of social organization, to independence from external control, and to self-reliance as the primary means of development.[13] In this context it is important to stress that in general Tanzania's approach to development programs is noncoercive; a politics of accomodation prevails over a politics of rapid development. While some authors have argued that it is not possible to promote development without instituting programs that are fundamentally socially disruptive, that is not the primary concern here. The aim is to examine the local party in Kilimanjaro as a vehicle for fostering development as it is defined in Tanzania and within the framework in which it is approached in Tanzania.

As is the case in much of Africa, Tanzania's leaders are confronted by

---

13. Elimination of poverty, ignorance, and disease is the shorthand formulation used popularly throughout the country, and is contained in the TANU Creed, defined in the Arusha Declaration, Part I. The more explicit formulation, in terms of increase in the per capita income, self-sufficiency in trained manpower, and rise in life expectancy, all by 1980, can be found in the address of President Nyerere to the National Assembly announcing the (First) Five Year Development Plan, 12 May 1964, reprinted in Hadley E. Smith, ed., *Readings on Economic Development and Administration in Tanzania* (London: Oxford University Press [for the Institute of Public Administration, University College, Dar es Salaam], 1966), pp. 360-70. Of course, development is defined as diversely in Tanzania as elsewhere, but a thorough reading of party position papers and pamphlets, almost all written by President Nyerere, makes it clear that this definition, including the commitment to equality, elimination of dependence, and self-reliance, describes the specific elements of the general concern with the improvement of the quality of life enunciated as Tanzania's major goal. For a recent party statement on development, stressing the elimination of exploitation and the promotion of human dignity, see Tanganyika African National Union, *TANU's Guidelines*, "Our Economy and Development."

what they regard as a fundamental conflict between the economic and political goals of development.[14] Economic development is conceived in terms of rational management of the economy, planning, and the like, while the political goals have to do with participation, control, stability, and unity and independence. To a large extent, development planning has been regarded as a technical matter, to be kept out of the hands of politicians.[15] A major manifestation of this conflict is the commitment of Tanzania's leadership to a politics of accommodation: it is generally deemed preferable to shelve a particular program or decision that threatens party unity than to push ahead with it. There is a tendency to avoid issues that might foster deep divisions among the leadership and to handle possibly divisive crises slowly and with great caution.[16] A clear case in point is the decision taken in 1969 to transfer control of a series of village development schemes in southern Tanzania from the association created to manage them to the party itself. The growing challenge to local political leaders by some of the participants in the successful villages was deemed a greater danger than the risk that reducing the villages' autonomy would hamper the development effort. In Kilimanjaro the initiatives likely to cause the greatest conflict among local party leaders—even those deemed to be integral aspects of the development effort, such as the consolidation of landholdings and the prevention of the emergence of a group of wealthy local entrepreneurs—are treated in ideological and policy terms. While local leaders may make forceful statements about the incompatibility of development and capitalist enterprise, local entrepreneurs are not named and rarely, if ever, is specific action proposed. And when action is taken, almost always the initiative emanates from national rather than local leaders.

At the center of this conflict between economic and political goals upcountry is the local party organization. On the one hand it is the only institution in Tanzania whose contact with and support among the mass of the rural population enables it to attempt to liberate individuals from the traditional constraints that impede development. It can be a vehicle for mobilizing people to make abrupt changes in life style and social relationships, for facilitating the acceptance of new methods and technology in farming, and for com-

14. Nyerere discusses this problem in a position paper prepared for the TANU National Executive in 1966, *Principles and Development* (reprinted in Nyerere, *Freedom and Socialism,* pp. 187-206).

15. See Bienen, *Tanzania: Party Transformation*, Chapter 8, for comments on the First Five Year Plan, and p. 441 for comments on the Second Five Year Plan. Hyden also stresses the lack of political participation in the planning process in Tanzania; see "Planning in Tanzania: Lessons of Experience," pp. 13-15. Many authors have dealt with development and planning in Tanzania; Bienen's Bibliography provides a useful starting point.

16. Pratt makes this point; see "The Administration of Economic Planning in a Newly Independent State: the Tanzanian Experience, 1963-1966," pp. 38-59. Recent events, including the nationalization of housing and sweeping leadership changes, suggest a greater willingness to accept the disruptive consequences of fundamental change.

municating new sets of values. On the other hand, the local party needs to win the support of the local population in order to use that support to facilitate change and foster the acceptance of new programs. A major TANU function in Kilimanjaro, then, is to develop a set of structures and relationships with which local people can identify and over which local people feel they have some control and then to use those structures and relationships to foster development.[17]

One major innovation, originating from the center, is the attempt to co-ordinate and reconcile political and economic goals through the commissioners. Success in this regard in Kilimanjaro has been intermittent. Certainly until 1969 development policy and planning were the province of technical advisers and ministerial officers, with little input from either local governmental units or from the party. The individuals who were appointed Regional and Area Commissioner in Kilimanjaro in 1969 were much more successful than their predecessors in translating development programs into terms and alternatives comprehensible to local leaders and in communicating political priorities to the officers involved in implementing the programs. This was due both to the skills of the individuals involved and to the renewed commitment of national leaders to involve local leaders and the party in development planning. Nevertheless, planning and programs remained largely removed from local control: basic decisions continued to be made by technical advisers and ministerial officers with little, if any, consultation with local political leaders. At the same time there was no attempt to pursue initiatives that might severely threaten local party unity. That is, Tanzania's leaders seem willing to accept the private landholding and the rapidly expanding group of local entrepreneurs in Kilimanjaro in return for Kilimanjaro's contribution to the national economy and for political quiescence. In return, Kilimanjaro's leaders grudgingly acquiesce in what they consider to be a disproportionately small share of national resources in return for a national willingness not to force changes in fundamental patterns of social organization. This understanding is of course tacit and not explicit, but, although described here in simplistic terms, it seems to characterize the situation adequately.

A second structure developed to reconcile political and economic goals is the set of local development committees in which both civil servants and local

---

17. It should be noted that many of the major changes in farming technology with which the local party organizations in other areas of Tanzania are primarily concerned have already taken place in Kilimanjaro. The problem there is not one of encouraging people to recognize the value of fertilizers, pesticides, and the like, but one of further improving soil productivity and crop quality, and ultimately, of developing communal patterns of crop production and income distribution. It should also be noted that the discussion here concerns the impediments to development within the local setting. It concerns the extralocal factors (continued dependence on foreign capital and expertise, need to import high-cost manufactures, and the like) only to the extent that strong local institutions can assist in managing the local impact of broad-scale national policies.

political leaders participate. But as has been mentioned, the local development committees have largely functioned to legitimize decisions made by government officials, with little attention to the political concerns expressed by local leaders. Only where local leaders have been able to enlist the assistance of officials at the national level have they been able to rearrange the priorities established by civil servants.[18]

There has been continuing pressure in Tanzania to decentralize development decision-making. The creation of the Regional Development Fund was one attempt to increase local control over the allocation of development resources. In 1972 sweeping changes among officeholders were designed, it was announced, to further localize development planning and implementation. Many very capable officials were posted to the regions, and the regional administration itself was refurbished. In one sense, then, this decentralization is another effort to reconcile economic and political goals by increasing the capabilities and authority of up-country institutions. The dilemma, however, is that moving officials and programs from Dar es Salaam to the regional capitals is not necessarily the same as localizing control, since popular input is least direct at the regional level.

A third structure that has been developed is a variant on the machine model discussed by Zolberg and others.[19] Developed from the urban experience in America, the notion is that the local political party, working in the context of a transitional population where deference patterns have been weakened by socioeconomic change and where vertical ties can be maintained only through patterns of reciprocity, is able to utilize frequent electoral competition to secure power and then distribute material particularistic rewards to govern in a situation where other institutions are less viable. In the one-party state in Tanzania, however, the party is not concerned with securing votes. Although elections are contested, all candidates must be approved by the party and must support party policy. But the machine model is useful in understanding the reciprocal nature of the interaction between party and people in Kilimanjaro: the party provides services, which range from finding jobs, to reconciling conflicts, to interceding with landlords, to attempting to alter governmental outputs, in return for—since the party does not need votes—support for party and government policies. The objections of market women to the high license fee and of street vendors and artisans to their eviction from the public sidewalks

18. For example, a project to supply water to the drier, eastern section of the district showed little progress until one of the Kilimanjaro MPs took special interest in it and lobbied extensively for it in Dar es Salaam. From his perspective the water supply project was an obvious symbol of the service he was providing to his constituents.

19. See Zolberg, *Creating Political Order,* especially pp. 159-61. See also Scott, "Corruption. Machine Politics, and Political Change," pp. 1142-58. The literature on political machines in American cities is extensive; particularly perceptive is Mandelbaum, *Boss Tweed's New York.* Also relevant are the studies of patron-client relationships: for useful references see John Duncan Powell, "Peasant Society and Clientelistic Politics," *APSR* 64, no. 2 (June 1970): 411-25.

are cases in point, where local TANU leaders were able to utilize the support among the population earned through the provision of services to persuade those who were aggrieved to accept the governmental decisions. It is true that much of the mass acceptance of TANU stems from its role in leading the fight against colonial rule and from the personal prestige of President Nyerere, and, to a lesser extent, other important leaders. But that kind of acceptance, which has withered away in other African countries and even in some areas of Tanzania, has been preserved and reinforced in Kilimanjaro both through TANU's ability to distribute particularistic rewards—jobs, reduced rents, plots to farm, and the like—and through TANU's ability to service larger sections of the population by affecting governmental outputs. TANU has been able to demonstrate to local residents that they can have some control over the governmental decisions that affect them. In so doing it has encouraged widespread participation in the local political system as people seek remedy for their grievances. And it has been able to translate some of that participation into a willingness to accept unwelcome decisions.

Another aspect of this pattern is its potential for fostering integration in Moshi. Because of the broad range of activities in which it is involved, TANU brings together the major groups in Moshi. It is one of the few institutions that forces Asians and Africans, Christians and Muslims, rural and urban to interact continuously. At the same time, in functioning as a local machine, TANU provides services primarily to the unattached populations of the town. That is, it is most often those individuals who do not belong to one of the major groups, who have just recently moved into the urban area, or who belong to some minority group who seek services from the local party. In servicing them, TANU helps Pare see they have something in common with Chagga, workers with farmers, and the like. TANU is able to do this because, at least in the urban area, it is scrupulously nontribal and nonreligious in base and orientation.

Because TANU can thus provide legitimacy for governmental outputs, the regulative and distributive capacities of local government are in fact increased through TANU support. It is in this regard that the local party has been most successful in making an immediate contribution to the development effort. Also, in the rapidly changing environment of Moshi town, TANU provides a certain stability and continuity and at the same time communicates a set of values relating to the nature of the change that is desirable and how it should be brought about, all of which are a foundation for development.

The evidence indicates that, for the moment at least, TANU has not become a tool of perverse growth in Moshi: it has not been captured and dominated by an urbanized, educated, and salaried elite as a focus for opposition to national policy.[20] In fact, the local party organization has not been captured

---

20. See Giovanni Arrighi and John S. Saul, "Socialism and Economic Development in Tropical Africa," *JMAS* 6, no. 2 (August 1968): 141-69.

by any principal class, or group, or faction locally. In part this is because many of the principal party leaders are not elected locally, so that the local political arena has very permeable boundaries, permitting both inflows from the center (officials posted by Dar es Salaam to Moshi) and outflows to the center (alternate channels that permit avoiding the local party).

In part, too, this is due to the leadership provisions of the Arusha Declaration. Even though the restrictions on leaders' sources of income have not been fully enforced, they have had the effect of forcing out of the local party most of the major local landowners and entrepreneurs and of destroying the legitimacy of their claim to access to major decision-making centers.

In part TANU has not become a tool of perverse growth because it must do the very things that alienate it from the urban elite. Since the party, and its trade union auxiliary, for example, are busy attempting to restrain demands of salaried employees, the party often becomes their enemy. Likewise, since the party is trying to restrain the demands of the educated elite, they too often turn away from it.

To some extent, all of this reduces the ability of the party to promote participation and legitimize governmental outputs. And to some extent, rather than shielding the center from the host of demands it cannot satisfy, it forces some of those demands to be directed to the center. Similarly, to the extent that major segments of the local population feel alienated from the party, clearly it cannot appear responsive to their demands. But the important point is that the party must continually walk a tightrope, balancing attempts to win the support of the local population with attempts to do the very things that will alienate them. Strong local institutions, though at times they may themselves become an obstacle, are necessary for change to take place at all. Accommodation to local interests, though it too may seem an obstacle, is also necessary for change. The striking finding is not that the party has not been more successful as a major agent of social change, but that the party has been able to renew itself locally and has been able to remain sufficiently responsive to local demands to provide a base of continuity and stability from which the development effort can progress.

National Integration

It should be stressed, once again, that TANU in Tanzania is best described as a national assembly, bringing together a number of locally based party organizations. TANU at the center cannot exercise clear and direct control over its local units in matters about which both the center and the local unit care a great deal. In practice, the center cannot really order, nor can the local units directly refuse, and neither can disregard the constraints on the other, but there is a filtering process that often distorts what passes between them.[21]

---

21. Bienen stresses this fundamental characteristic of TANU as a party; see *Tanzania: Party Transformation,* especially Chapter 14.

The lack of resources at the party center and the fragility of party institutions produce an imperfect, intermittent direction of local party units. Thus, the national party must rely on semiautonomous local organizations for its strength and support.

This relationship between center and locality fosters continuing conflict between them, a conflict that is often congruent with the extant tensions between center and up-country in Tanzania's plural society. This conflict is manifested in local government: while local leaders demand greater autonomy, central leaders move toward restricting their scope of operations. As was noted previously, successful Kilimanjaro politicians have been those whose primary concern was to protect local interests against central control. It is also manifested in the behavior of Members of Parliament, Members of the TANU National Executive Committee, and other leaders who represent their constituencies at the center: while they seek to represent local interests, they are at the same time expected by national leaders to subordinate parochial attitudes and allegiances to the principles and needs of national policies and programs. And this conflict is manifested directly in the local party organization in the tension between locally and centrally selected officers.

But this is not to suggest that this tension between center and locality has been dysfunctional or destabilizing. To the contrary, the evidence from Kilimanjaro supports the conclusion that this tension has had a stabilizing effect and that it promotes, rather than inhibits, growth.[22] This tension has permitted the political system to be responsive to local demands and sensitive to local discontent. It has permitted some shielding of the center from a broad set of local demands that the center cannot meet.[23] And it has permitted an expansion of the polity not possible with the resources available to the center—direct contact with much of the rural population development of identification with and some commitment to the values and structures that characterize Tanzania as a nation, and the creation of structures to permit participation and communication.

Through this process of interaction between center and locality there has developed a continuing localization of politics in Tanzania. It is true that national leaders often express their dissatisfaction with their inability to ensure that local areas adopt what they consider to be appropriate and necessary developmental strategies. Yet in the first decade of independence, this localization,

22. Growth both in the sense of progress toward explicit and implicit development goals and in the sense of increasing the capabilities of existing structures, creating new institutions, and fostering structural differentiation and flexibility of response.

23. See Stephens, *The Political Transformation of Tanganyika,* for a discussion of the ways in which the mobilization process has led to an increase in demands that sorely challenge Tanzania's resources and capabilities. Unfortunately, Stephens' reliance on sets of unreliable and poorly chosen data and on a model of modernization that does not encompass some fundamental elements of the Tanzanian situation leads him to overlook sources of stability in the Tanzanian political system.

in the context of the very limited resources of the center and within the commitment to foster a sense of national unity as a prerequisite to development without coercion, has been a facilitating and not inhibiting factor. At the same time, this localization has promoted the integration of Tanzania's disparate ethnic and religious communities, at least at the level of enabling people to recognize a commonality of identity and interests and building institutions that require functional interaction, and has not so far manifested the disabling reinforcement of parochialisms that leaders and observers so fear.

These more general observations apply as well in Kilimanjaro. The regularized factionalism of the local party organization has permitted it both to incorporate the disparate elements of the Kilimanjaro population and to be responsive to the often strident demands of the local citizenry. This is not to minimize the magnitude of the divisiveness of the ethnic and religious cleavages that persist in Tanzania, but to argue that the local TANU organization plays a key role in developing patterns of interaction and sharing and thus fostering a recognition of commonality of identity and interests. To the extent that Chagga and Pare market women, and Muslim and Christian sidewalk tailors, to pursue those two examples once again, seek remedy for their grievances in the party, they recognize an affinity that, at least for the moment, and when that affinity is reinforced probably for much longer, overcomes the cleavages that divide them. Similarly, this is not to suggest that Kilimanjaro, as a relatively well developed and highly mobilized area in Tanzania, will not continue to press many demands inconsistent with national policy. It is rather to argue that the local TANU organization plays a key role—by being responsive to local demands even when that means delaying or avoiding the implementation of national policy to avoid severe conflicts —in developing a sense of identification with the norms and structures of the Tanzanian political system and thus promoting a willingness to press demands through it and accept outcomes from it.

It is important to set this discussion of the local party organization and national integration in Tanzania in the context of two more general observations. One concerns the concept of integration employed here. Integration is understood as a process (rather than a state-of-being) that takes place at a specified level in terms of a specified goal. Tanzania's leadership is attempting to encourage particular sorts of social change. To encourage that change requires compliance with national directives. Unwilling and unable to resort to massive coercion, the leadership looks to the party to initiate and manage that change. By definition, there is resistance to particular changes sought, else the changes involved would be trivial. In other words, there is an initiative by the center, resistance by (some elements of) the locality, and a resolution. What is key is whether or not the resolution in a particular case leads to increased ability to secure compliance in future, similar cases. In these terms, then, the argument here is that many of the conflicts engendered by the pressures for change are resolved within or through the party in such a way that its ability to introduce and manage further change is enhanced. At the same time, it is important to make a second observation: integration is a process that increases social control. When party behavior is integrative, as when it serves to legitimize or socialize, it facilitates the control of ordinary citizens by whoever is in power. National integration, in and of itself, is no more likely to lead to increased development or to more equitable distribution of resources than national disintegration. The consideration of national integration, therefore, must not be divorced from the consideration of who is in control and what goals are sought.

Summary

TANU does not govern in Kilimanjaro. The local party organization, a coalition of factions characterized almost as much by competition as by cooperation, spends most of its time expediting demands made on government and party and resolving a large number of small conflicts. It uses its continuing appeal from the independence struggle, together with its ability to distribute particularistic rewards and affect some local allocations, to legitimize governmental outputs and to extend the perimeters of the polity. In other words, TANU in Kilimanjaro legitimizes, it facilitates change, and it fosters both horizontal and vertical integration, but only rarely does it have direct control over local decisions or propose or initiate change.

TANU does not represent initiative at the local level. Likewise, little policy is made at the local level. In fact, most local party leaders have an imperfect and incomplete, at best, understanding of the content of basic national policy, and in general have great difficulty in relating national policy to the local setting.

Yet despite the paucity of skills and resources, and despite the fundamental underlying discord between the values of the relatively educated, prosperous, entrepreneurial coffee farmers of Kilimanjaro and the national policy of communal rural socialism, the local party in Kilimanjaro has proved a surprisingly resilient institution. It has played an important intermediary role between Kilimanjaro and the center, as well as among the local factional groupings. In so doing it has nurtured patterns of communication and interaction that facilitate development and national integration. TANU has been able, albeit haltingly, to institutionalize its accountability to an increasingly larger constituency, and in the process has begun building a set of institutions and relationships that can promote and facilitate major social change. It has, as well, developed an ideology that is conducive to change, has remained flexible and responsive to social forces resistant to change, and has not assumed a comprehensiveness, a finality, and an intensity that would make it distant from and inaccessible to the mass of the population and that would require fanatical adherence and perhaps coercion to pursue.[24]

24. Manfred Halpern makes these points in referring to the accountability and ideology

Lest this picture of TANU's success in Kilimanjaro seem too rosy, it should be stressed that major paradoxes remain unresolved. The conflict between political and economic development goals, the conflict between central direction and local autonomy, and the conflict between reliance on functionally specific institutions and the assertion of party supremacy all present major and continuing challenges to the Tanzanian political system. Institutions remain fragile and the shortage of skilled humanpower continues to be a great problem. The party has vastly extended participation in the national political system, no mean accomplishment in the Tanzanian, and African, setting; yet some groups do find themselves excluded from active participation. TANU has clearly accomplished successfully a renewal of its independence mandate, but then independence is scarcely a decade old in Tanzania. Perhaps what is most exciting about politics in Kilimanjaro, at least to one observer, is the selectivity and eclecticism of party officials in choosing appropriate models, and their flexibility in fashioning appropriate institutions to build a nation and manage its development.

---

of parties in the Middle East and North Africa; see *The Politics of Social Change in the Middle East and North Africa* (Princeton, N.J.: Princeton University Press, 1963), Chapter 14.

PART V / *Self-Reliance*

12

The Politics of Self-Reliance

Introduction

Case studies have two major strong points. On the one hand, they permit the exploration of general concepts and theories in precisely defined circumstances. The richness of their detail and the depth of their insight permit the examination of the many small links among ideas, institutions, and behavior, links often overlooked when the perspective is macroscopic. Much of the study thus far has been primarily concerned with this sort of examining, detailing, and linking. On the other hand, case studies are also starting points for general concepts and theories. Scholars carry with them a set of assumptions, understandings, and expectations, but even as those constructs are used to gather data they are found to be inadequate and insufficient. Major paradigms suggest specific observations, which in turn may yield findings inconsistent with the original paradigm. Whether the observation is refined, or the paradigm altered or rejected, the conflict between what is expected and what is found forces evaluation and assessment. That was indeed the case in this study.

As was argued earlier, no town in Tanzania should be considered typical. Moshi certainly is not. In fact, it was found that Moshi was historically a locus of opposition to central control in Tanganyika, and that, the widespread support for TANU notwithstanding, several factors seem to be forging an alliance among opponents to central direction. If Moshi is relatively unique in this resistance to central direction, then its uniqueness enhances its value as a focus for careful study. It is in the crucible of this local resistance that the temper of Tanzania's institutions and leadership will be most sorely tested. General propositions about the ability of party and state to initiate and manage social change are subject to rigorous evaluation in this setting.

The point here, therefore, is to draw on this case study to explore the political implications, at the local level, of a self-reliance strategy for development.

Much of the current writing on Africa concerns itself with Development. Especially since the rapid termination of direct colonial rule in most of Africa during the late 1950s and early 1960s, studies in comparative politics have

Self-Reliance

been forced to pay more attention to change, or lack of change, in the Third World. The study of Development now has its book series, its journals, and its academic entrepreneurs.

The language of Development studies refers to growth, takeoff, and independence. Yet the intellectual origins and the practical implications of the study of Development are rooted in the colonial situation, with the result that, its references to the promise of a better future notwithstanding, its primary impact is to explain and defend stagnation, inability to take off, and continued dependence.

As the problem is commonly posed, there is some inadequacy, or cluster of inadequacies, of African economies and societies that has prevented development. Thus the problem for the student of development is to identify those sources of backwardness within Africa and construct some appropriate remedy. The prescriptions that have flowed from such studies have involved the export of specific institutions (elections, parties) or functions (political socialization) from Europe to Africa, the manipulation by African elites (and their advisers) of symbols and attitudes, and the encouragement of reliance on foreign capital and expertise.

That this way of posing the problem and thus seeking solutions is so pervasive in the writing in Europe and the United States on Development reflects the nearly complete failure to recognize that the roots of the major obstacles to development lie in the colonial situation. To argue the importance of the patterns developed in the colonial situation is not to deny that in particular circumstances existing habits and attitudes may indeed be obstacles to change. Rather, it is to argue that the major obstacles to development lie not primarily in the values and customs of indigenous societies but in the set of international relationships, political and economic institutions, and national elites molded during the period of the colonial underdevelopment of Africa.[1] Analyses of development that do not address adequately the origins of underdevelopment and that do not recognize the interrelationship of the development of Europe (and the United States) with the underdevelopment of Africa can contribute significantly neither to understanding the problems involved nor to solving them.[2]

It has become increasingly clear, both to the leadership of Third World states and to some academic observers, that the termination of direct colonial rule and the pursuit of the advice proffered by western Development experts

1. A useful summary of the process of underdevelopment can be found in Walter Rodney, *How Europe Underdeveloped Africa* (London: Bogle-L'Ouverture, 1972), especially Chapters 1-4.

2. The purpose here is to explore the political implications of an alternative conception of, and strategy for, development. Critiques of the dominant themes of development studies can be found in most of the works cited in this chapter.

on How to Develop have maintained, if not increased, the economic dependence and political subordination of most of the Third World.[3]

More recently, the debate on Development has finally recognized the existence of alternatives to the strategies of development fashioned from western capitalist experience, though few western scholars consider such alternatives viable.

The argument over strategies has been characterized by Berg as a choice between gradual and structural transformation approaches.[4] Berg's conclusion, in fact, is that there is really little choice—because of shortages of investment capital and human resources, only the gradualist strategy is currently viable.[5] In a similar fashion, Wallerstein has recently proposed a choice among seize-the-initiative, by-invitation, and self-reliance strategies. He, too, is not very sanguine about the viability of the self-reliance approach.[6]

An increasing number of critics have argued that even in terms of economic growth, the continued reliance on foreign aid and expertise and the pursuit of the gradualist, hence dependent capitalist, approach can, for most Third World states, only make the situation worse.[7] What is important for our purposes here is that Tanzania is widely described as a country attempting to develop a strategy of development that will not at the same time perpetuate its dependence. Indeed, the breadth and strength of the enthusiasm over Tanzania's

3. For a clear, and more detailed, statement of this point, see Samir Amin, *L'Afrique de l'Ouest Bloquée. L'Economie Politique de la Colonisation 1880-1970* (Paris: Editions de Minuit, 1971); and *Le Développement du Capitalisme en Côte d'Ivoire* (Paris: Editions de Minuit, 1967). For a similar conclusion, by scholars whose perspective is much closer to that criticized here, see Robert W. Clower et al., *Growth Without Development* (Evanston, Ill.: Northwestern University Press, 1966).

4. See Elliot J. Berg, "Structural Transformation versus Gradualism: Recent Economic Development in Ghana and the Ivory Coast," in *Ghana and the Ivory Coast,* ed. Philip Foster and Aristide R. Zolberg (Chicago: University of Chicago Press, 1971).

5. Ibid., p. 230. For a rejoinder see Reginald Green, "Reflections on Economic Strategy, Structure, Implementation, and Necessity: Ghana and the Ivory Coast, 1957-67," in Foster and Zolberg, *Ghana and the Ivory Coast.*

6. Immanuel Wallerstein, "Dependence in an Interdependent World: The Limited Possibilities of Transformation Within the Capitalist World Economy," paper presented at Conference on Dependence and Development in Africa, Ottawa, 1973. Though described slightly differently, structural transformation and self-reliance refer to the same behaviors by national leadership—fundamental reorganization and reorientation of existing institutions and increased reliance on internal sources of capital and skills. Self-reliance is used here, since it is the term common in Tanzania.

7. See, for example, Amin, *L'Afrique de l'Ouest Bloquée*; Arrighi and Saul, "Socialism and Economic Development in Tropical Africa"; Theresa Hayter, *Aid as Imperialism* (Baltimore: Penguin, 1971); and Pierre Jalée, *The Pillage of the Third World* (New York: Monthly Review Press, 1968); and *The Third World in World Economy* (New York: Monthly Review Press, 1969). The literature on Latin America is much more extensive; a useful introduction is James D. Cockcroft et al., eds., *Dependence and Underdevelopment: Latin American's Political Economy* (Garden City, N.J.: Doubleday/Anchor, 1972).

Self-Reliance

experience ("the Tanzanian experiment") at times threatens to obscure a careful, systematic analysis of policies, programs, and outcomes.[8]

Thus far, the task of outlining the components of a self-reliance development strategy has fallen largely to economists.[9] Few political scientists, perhaps reflecting the predominant concern within the discipline for order and stability, have addressed themselves to the political components of such a strategy.[10]

It seems both timely and essential, therefore, to suggest, from the study of local politics in Moshi, several of the major domestic political components of, and constraints on, such a strategy.[11]

What follows must, of course, remain tentative and perhaps a bit speculative. To facilitate further examination, the argument is developed in skeletal form. And it is intended as much for Africans engaged in the doing as for the scholars primarily concerned with observing.

A Strategy of Development

Development is often conceived by scholars as primarily if not wholly, economic growth. But national economic growth, often expressed in terms of the Gross National Product per capita,[12] is a fundamentally misleading criterion for assessing what is happening in a particular society, on two accounts. First, it does not reflect the distribution of the wealth in the society, nor does economic growth over time indicate changes in the distribution of wealth.

8. A useful caution is that of Ali Mazrui, "Tanzaphilia," *Transition* 31 (1967): 20-26.

9. See, for example, Reginald Green, "Political Independence and the National Economy: An Essay in the Political Economy of Decolonisation," in *African Perspectives,* ed. Christopher Allen and R. W. Johnson (London: Cambridge University Press, 1970).

10. There are, of course, important exceptions. See, among others, Arrighi and Saul, "Socialism and Economic Development in Tropical Africa"; Giovanni Arrighi and John S. Saul, "Nationalism and Revolution in Sub-Saharan Africa," in *The Socialist Register 1969* (London: Merlin Press, 1969); and John S. Saul, "The Nature of Tanzania's Political System," *Journal of Commonwealth Political Studies* 10, no. 2 (July 1972): 113-29; 10, no. 3 (November 1972): 198-221.

11. I retain the term *self-reliance strategy,* rather than substituting *socialist strategy,* since although what is involved is a fundamental reorganization of production, the context remains a world capitalist system. Wallerstein makes this point, "Dependence in an Interdependent World," pp. 2-3, 18. Within Tanzania, self-reliance and socialism are interchangeable.

12. The leaps of faith required to use GNP per capita as an index of development are of heroic proportions. On the one hand, the relevant data readily available for African states are likely to be out of date or accurate only within a wide margin for error or both. On the other hand, even were GNP per capita a good indicator of national economic growth it indicates little about development until the relationship between economic growth and development is specified. Certainly it is of little utility in discriminating among African states. See Ann Seidman, *An Economics Textbook for Africa,* 2d ed. (London: Methuen, 1972), p. 3n.

Second, it does not suggest the nature of the relationship, as it exists and as it changes over time, between Third World states, individually and collectively, and the major industrialized nations. Economic growth may well take place without either reducing the poverty of the majority of the population or developing the structures necessary to permit self-sustaining economic progress.[13]

Strategy of development is employed here, therefore, to mean that set of policies and programs designed to promote economic growth *and* the distribution and redistribution of societal resources to the benefit of the mass of the population *and* the reduction of the dependence on the major industrial states. Phrased somewhat differently, what is involved is an attempt to increase, throughout the society, the capacity to master the environment and to regulate both internal and external relationships.[14]

Green has ably summarized the dependent nature of African economies, and, relying on the Tanzanian experience, has gone on to suggest the economic components of a self-reliance strategy of development. The major economic institutions must be brought under national control and integrated into the overall development strategy. Investments must rely primarily on sectors of the economy directly within state control, and within that, largely on the mobilization of domestic resources. The reorganized public sector becomes the major initiator and manager of increases in production. The outflow of capital must be sharply curtailed. Since foreign investment must continue to provide development capital, its sources must be diversified (to reduce dependence on particular states or firms) and its uses must be integrated into the overall strategy. The widening of the gap between urban and rural incomes must be arrested and even reversed. And all of this must be done while maintaining steady economic growth. Green's conclusion is that Tanzania's efforts in this direction, though not without serious problems, have thus far been quite successful:

> The Tanzanian experience to date is that even in the short term a clearly enunciated and carefully pursued strategy of development including economic independence as a goal can be consistent with an accelerating rate of economic as well as social and political development.[15]

13. This is the thrust of Amin's argument; see, *Le Développement du Capitalism en Côte d'Ivoire* and *L'Afrique de l'Ouest Bloquée.* An abridged and very abbreviated summary in English of Amin's conclusions on the Ivory Coast is in Irving L. Markovitz, ed., *African Politics and Society* (New York: Free Press, 1970), pp. 277-88. See also Arrighi and Saul, "Socialism and Economic Development in Tropical Africa."

14. Since the concern here is with the political implications of such a strategy at the local level, this discussion will deal only indirectly with national dependence—constraints on change in the organization of society imposed by the nature and conduct of external relationships.

15. Green, "Political Independence and the National Economy," especially pp. 288-324. Green's work is especially useful in that he proposes a list of readily quantifiable indicators of dependence (and thus independence). The conclusion cited is from p. 324.

Self-Reliance

In terms of the polity,[16] a self-reliance strategy of development requires that the national leadership simultaneously establish and maintain a new order and use it to facilitate change. In other words, in states where resources have been exploited primarily to benefit the major capitalist powers, where infrastructure has been designed primarily to suit colonial needs, and where little of the periphery has been integrated into a single national unit, the leadership must build both a state and a nation. Those new relationships must be fashioned such that they eliminate, not perpetuate, the dependence.

Let us now turn back to the study of Moshi to explore what that means.

Obstacles to Development

Few authors have written on African politics without commenting on the obstacles to establishing order in African states. Most of those commentaries focus on problems of ethnicity, regionalism, separatism, and irredentism. Indeed, cleavages of that sort do exist within almost every African state. But the problems that flow from lines of division among Africans, and not uncommonly the lines of division themselves, had their origins and flourished in an existing order, and it is that inherited order that is the major political obstacle to development.

One component of the inherited order is the colonial experience and the structures created to suit colonial needs. Kilimanjaro was organized during colonial rule around the production of agricultural crops for export to European markets (primarily coffee, but also sisal). Kilimanjaro was an economic enclave in Tanganyika: the proceeds of coffee sales benefited the rest of the territory little, and even within the district, some areas prospered much more than others.[17] The pervasiveness of that pattern has been reflected throughout this study. Political conflict revolved around the production and profits of coffee. Production requirements largely dictated the location and timing of infrastructural developments. The infrastructure created further exacerbated uneven growth among different sections of the district. That in turn contributed to the creation and organization of ethnicity in the struggle for advantage.

The British administration assisted in the creation and destruction of chiefship in a very short period. In the process, it fostered the entrenchment of particular political elites in the local political system. As those largely educated and employed by the colonial order fought for and gained some control

16. Obviously, the thrust of this argument is that the economic and political components of a self-reliance strategy are not separable in practice. For analytic purposes, it is useful to distinguish them.

17. The export enclave is common throughout Africa (and throughout much of the Third World). It is important however, not to lose sight of the role of the enclave in the extension of the externally oriented market economy into the rural hinterland. For an outline of this phenomenon, see Ann Seidman, *Comparative Development Strategies in East Africa* (Nairobi: EAPH, 1972), especially Chapter 1, Part 2.

over the allocation of resources, they began to alter the basis of political recruitment to ensure their security of tenure. Relying both on appeals to the precolonial culture and on the political leverage that grew out of their interaction with the colonial regime, new elites maneuvered themselves into power locally.

At the same time, all of this nurtured an antagonism between Kilimanjaro and the rest of Tanganyika, an antagonism that meant that even the anticolonial struggle could be spread throughout Kilimanjaro only in the context of a local struggle for control.

The colonial experience, then, fostered an ordering of the economy and the polity in which effective control was located either externally or within a few externally oriented, relatively prosperous areas dominated by European-trained elites and successful entrepreneurs.

The second component of the inherited order, directly related to the first, grew out of the struggle to end colonial rule. When the British (and the Germans before them) came to Tanganyika, they sought allies from among what they took to be the traditional leadership. Indirect rule accorded to chiefs the lowest level of the colonial administration. But in the long run, the colonial administration proved to be an unstable base for African political power: it undermined, as well as supported, those to whom it assigned authority.

The Europeans sought new allies among an elite that was itself a function of the colonial situation. When the chiefship was ended in Kilimanjaro, local authority was represented by an individual educated in colonial schools and drawn from the colonial civil service. As has been noted widely, almost all of the most visible figures in the anticolonial struggle, throughout Africa, were drawn from that same stratum.

The mass support for the anticolonial struggle notwithstanding, its leadership was heavily recruited from that small group of Africans with education and with experience as employees of the colonial administration. That leadership ultimately became the leaders of independent Tanzania, both locally and nationally. Although that leadership has been in power for a very short time throughout Africa, the evidence is already quite clear that it has prospered immensely in power and that it has proved reluctant to yield authority.

This is especially important at the local level, where, as the Kilimanjaro case shows, much of the mass anticolonial involvement was at the same time anticenter. Local elites, profiting and entrenching themselves still surther, become formidable obstacles to the fundamental changes they perceive to threaten their position. In fact, as has been suggested, this tendency is already noticeable in Kilimanjaro, where the local party organization clearly reflects an anticenter orientation. The inherited political order, then, includes a set of structures designed largely to meet the needs of the colonial exploitation of national resources and a set of elites little committed to fundamental social change.

A Political Strategy

The major obstacle to development, then, is the existing order. The principal structure in Tanzania designed and refined to overcome that obstacle is the party. As was noted earlier, although observers generally focus on TANU and change, the party's first priority must be the establishment of a new order, a new order constructed to facilitate, if not initiate, change. In Nyerere's terms, the problem is one of building socialism where much of the leadership is not socialist.[18]

A self-reliance strategy for the creation of a new order thus has two operative elements. One is to prevent the current elite from so monopolizing political power that it is an obstacle to socialist development and so strongly entrenched that its behavior remains effectively unchallenged. The second, following directly from the first, is to restructure the political base of the regime. Institutions must be fashioned to ensure that the leadership is accountable, and thus responsive, to an increasingly greater portion of the citizenry. And a committed socialist leadership must attempt to convert mass involvement in the anticolonial struggle to mass involvement in the construction of socialism.

That these two very difficult political tasks—restructuring both the leadership and the base of the party—are to be accomplished at the same time that significant changes are required in the behavior of ordinary Tanzanians imposes severe constraints on how those changes are managed. Agricultural production is to be substantially increased. At the same time, social relationships are to be reorganized.

Thus far, the national leadership has been quite unwilling, and perhaps unable, to rely heavily on coercion as a mechanism for securing change in behavior. That means that it must rely on economic and identive incentives.

The party must, and does to use immediate, material rewards to encourage desired behavior. That the party is involved in this exchange is clear in Moshi. Party cadres spend a good part of their time securing for individuals and for groups the specific allocations in which they are interested. For some, it is jobs; for others, medical care and education; for still others, licenses and assistance in business. Those material incentives over time seem to have reinforced support for the regime, particularly among the most disadvantaged segments of the Moshi population.

But the economic rewards available to the Tanzanian leadership are sorely limited. The paucity of national resources, the underdevelopment of the colonial period, and the need to reinvest much of the economic surplus produced, all reduce the pool from which such rewards might be drawn.

In addition, most of the existing structures for distributing societal resources reflect their colonial and capitalist origins. Those structures combine with the need to increase exports to allocate greater benefits to successful in-

18. Nyerere, *Freedom and Socialism,* Introduction, especially pp. 26-32.

dividual entrepreneurs than to struggling cooperatives, to those who have
capital available than to those who need it, and to those who hire labor than
to those who offer it.[19]

To supplement that limited economic base, therefore, the party must
simultaneously develop identive resources. It must generate and nurture a
sense of identification with leadership and goals sufficiently strong to secure
changes of behavior in the absence of coercion and economic rewards.[20] To
do that the party, especially since the Arusha Declaration in 1967, has attempted to become increasingly responsive to local interests and demands.
Competitive elections have provided an opportunity to express complaints,
to choose among candidates, and to renew an identification with a national
movement. Political institutions have been reorganized to foster greater
participation by ordinary citizens.[21] In some cases, even parochial demands
apparently inconsistent with national policy have been tolerated and supported.

To summarize briefly: the major obstacle to development is the existing
political order. A self-reliance strategy to overcome the obstacles posed by
that order requires a restructuring of both the leadership and the base of
the party. That reconstruction is to be accomplished while simultaneously
increasing production and reorganizing social relationships. In the absence
of coercion and significant material incentives, the identification of Tanzanians
with the goals and leadership of their country must be mobilized to institutionalize a new order that can facilitate change.

It is necessary now to explore, relying on the Moshi case and the Tanzanian experience, the micropolitical implications of these political components
of a self-reliance strategy of development.

The Micropolitical Implications

A self-reliance strategy of development has three immediate operational
implications. One has to do with the reorganization of leadership and of the
patterns of recruitment to leadership. The second has to do with accountability
to a broad mass, rather than local elite, political base. And, to achieve the first
two, the third has to do with the maintenance of the party as a responsive,
open institution.

Since the middle of the 1960s, there has been a major reorganization of

19. David Feldman elaborates this point in a case study of tobacco growers: "The
Economics of Ideology: Some Problems of Achieving Rural Socialism in Tanzania," in
Leys, *Politics and Change in Developing Countries.*
20. For a discussion of this point, by an observer skeptical of the viability of relying
on identive resources, see John R. Nellis, *A Theory of Ideology: The Tanzanian Example* (Nairobi: Oxford University Press, 1972), especially Chapters 5, 6, and 8.
21. There have been, of course, successes and significant failures in this
regard. The concern here is to outline the core components of the strategy
employed.

national and local leadership in Tanzania. The leadership provisions of the Arusha Declaration began the restructuring of the relationship between leaders and ordinary citizens by attempting to limit the profitability of becoming a leader. Though it was enforced slowly and selectively over the next several years, the intention was clear: no longer was access to leadership to be a means for becoming rich and for passing that wealth on to subsequent generations. The TANU Guidelines of 1971 addressed the political component of the leader-citizen relationship, delineating the responsibilities of leaders and restraints on their behavior. Since their publication, the provisions of the TANU Guidelines have been widely employed as a platform for challenging and criticizing leaders at all levels. The nationalization of housing of substantial value in Tanzania in 1971-72, among its other impacts, closed an important loophole in the leadership provisions of the Arusha Declaration. Profit-making housing, even when acquired and registered in the name of children or other relatives, would no longer be a safe haven for leaders' surplus capital or a channel for increasing income. Almost simultaneously, the responsibility of leaders to the rural populace was reemphasized in a series of steps toward greater decentralization of the direction and administration of the state.

The postcolonial leadership—those who were drawn from the educated and civil service elite of the colonial period and those who were most active in the anticolonial struggle—were challenged. Leadership was not to be a means for becoming rich. And leaders were to be increasingly responsive to the population as a whole.

During this period the turnover in leadership, local as well as national, has been very great. Political appointees have had their commissions revoked. In the parliamentary elections of 1965 and 1970 many incumbents were not returned to office. Outcomes in local and party elections were similar. The implementation of the decentralization decisions also involved major shifts in personnel. In the brief period 1968-69 few leadership positions in Kilimanjaro were unaffected. By election and by appointment, commissioners, MPs, chairmen, and administrators were replaced.

As was suggested earlier, this search for a more committed socialist leadership runs parallel to another set of leadership changes, that involving the interplay between the facilitation and management of change. In particular circumstances, technical and managerial competence were deemed as important as political skills.

The general point seems very clear: radical social change requires politicians to secure support and managers to implement. Each must have some of the skills of the other. And neither must use access to power to accrue wealth. As major changes in the composition of the state, or in the selection of goals, are achieved, the politicians will be replaced by managers. And as new initiatives encounter resistance, managers will be succeeded by politicians.

Intertwined with the reorganization of leadership is the attempt to expand the popular base of the regime. The anticolonial struggle in Tanzania, as in much of Africa, was constructed from disparate local discontents. The Independence government came into power, and through the 1960s remained in power, relying on the support of local elites, largely unchallenged within their localities.[22] The series of changes described above have provided people up-country with leverage for effectively challenging local elites, replacing them, and altering the nature of political recruitment.

Structurally, the reorganization of the political base involves greater mass participation in development planning and implementation, more open recruitment to leadership positions, and the shift of important decision-making, even the decision-makers themselves, from the center to the periphery. The increasing recognition of the village as the major organizational and decision-making unit is another step in this process.

The shift in the power base also requires a very great responsiveness of the government and party to the daily needs and demands of the mass of the population. As Bienen has stressed, the party's responsive capability is severely limited by the lack of resources and skilled personnel.[23] What the Moshi case suggests is that the major structural innovation within the party, the cell leaders, as well as much of the attention of the party at all levels, has been focused less on initiating change than on responding to the daily needs of ordinary citizens.

Cell leaders in Moshi, and throughout Tanzania, are individuals very much like their neighbors.[24] They are heavily involved in dispute settlement. They deal with the myriad little problems that arise in the daily life of their communities. In doing so they develop local level institutions in which there is widespread participation. To the extent that those institutions are responsive to the dislocations of social mobilization, they can legitimize policy and programs and can have substantial integrative potential. Where they are not domi-

22. The dependence of the national leadership on more-or-less autonomous local elites is common throughout Africa. See, among others, Cherry Gertzel's analysis of this relationship in Kenya, *The Politics of Independent Kenya* (Evanston, Ill.: Northwestern University Press, 1970). Several recent studies, in addition to this volume, have focused on local politics in Tanzania. See, among others: Goran Hyden, *Political Development in Rural Tanzania* [West Lake]; Clyde R. Ingle, *From Village to State in Tanzania* [Tanga and Handeni] (Ithaca, N.Y.: Cornell University Press, 1972); J. Gus Liebenow, *Colonial Rule and Political Development in Tanzania: The Case of the Makonde*; G. Andrew Maguire, *Toward "Uruhu" in Tanzania* [Mwanza] (Cambridge: Cambridge University Press, 1969); and P. M. van Hekken and H. U. E. Thoden van Velzen, *Land Scarcity and Rural Inequality in Tanzania* [Rungwe] (The Hague: Mouton, 1972).

23. Bienen, *Tanzania: Party Transformation,* Introduction to the Expanded Edition and Chapter 14. Bienen is self-consciously responding to criticism on the significance of this point, especially to Lionel Cliffe, "Tanzania—Socialist Transformation and Party Development," *The African Review* 1, no. 1 (March 1971): 119-235.

24. The analysis of cell leaders in Moshi, reported in Chapter 8, is substantially supported by studies of cell leaders in other parts of Tanzania. See Proctor, *The Cell System of the Tanganyika African National Union*; and O'Barr and Samoff, *Cell Leaders in Tanzania: Agents of Order and Change.*

nated by district and regional leadership, they can provide effective bases for challenging that leadership.

The Moshi case suggests also that, because local politics has thus far been primarily concerned with local problems, attempts to influence and determine the direction of change are focused on the outputs, rather than the inputs, of the political process. That thus far the most significant form of local participation has been not in the creation, but rather in the implementation, of policies reflects the impact of the inherited political order and at the same time indicates the magnitude of the reordering required.

A self-reliance strategy of development, then, requires an effective challenge to the elite leadership and a broad base for the regime. To accomplish both requires a particular sort of institutional arrangement. In this context, the party must strive simultaneously to provide direction, to generate and support an effective check on decisions taken at the center, to be open to mass participation, and to stimulate support for and involvement in specific programs, all the while permitting and encouraging challenge to its own leadership.

That this is developing is clear from the Moshi case. The local party organization in Kilimanjaro is not monolithic, but is rather a coalition of local factions. It does not exercise clear control over major local decisions. It does not encompass all aspects of an individual's daily life. And there is a tension among party sections, which on the one hand need to be partially autonomous, responsive organizations, and which on the other hand are distrusted as potential alternative, competing power bases.

Within the one-party state, structural interpenetration, diffuse responsibilities and orientations, and alternative channels for participation permit significant local competition. In these circumstances, the party is heavily concerned with communication and mediation. The party is concerned, as well, with reconciling the conflict between participation and directed change (or between the political and economic components of development). As the party is confronted with the dilemma of simultaneously establishing and maintaining a new order and facilitating change, a major task is to manage the alienation of those elements of the society most disadvantaged by change.

It may be useful here to recapitulate the major strands of the argument. The study of Development in the West, rooted in the colonial situation, has paid little attention to the continued process of the underdevelopment of most of the Third World, and, therefore, the prescriptions offered have not, and are not likely to, end the dependent situation of Third World states. More recently, especially within the Third World, there has been a search for alternative strategies of development. One strategy proposed involves fundamental structural transformation and greater reliance on internal sources of capital and skills.

While there has been some attention to the economic components of such a self-reliance strategy, there has been little attention to its political elements. Moshi has been used as a case in point to explore those political components and suggest their practical implications for Tanzania and for Africa in general.

Such a strategy must grapple with the major obstacles to development —an inherited political order dominated by the background of colonial rule and by the values, attitudes, and behavior of the postcolonial leadership. Therefore, such a strategy must be designed to challenge the current leadership and to restructure the political base of the regime. It must mount that challenge while continuing to rely on the technical and administrative skills of that leadership. And it must restructure the base while maintaining and increasing agricultural production. In short, it must envision the construction of a new political order without immediately alienating those whose behavior is critical to economic growth.

Such a strategy has three immediate local-level implications. Leadership and patterns of political recruitment must be fundamentally reorganized. The accountability of the leadership must be substantially broadened to involve an increasingly wider portion of the population. And political institutions must be constructed to balance the needs for order and control with those of change and participation.

Paradox

The political components of a self-reliance development strategy thus involve a reorientation and restructuring of the leadership and a reorganization of the power base of the regime to one of greater mass involvement. Over the past several years, Tanzania has clearly and significantly moved in that direction. The very movement in that direction, however, highlights the paradoxes involved.

Historically, much of politics in Tanzania has been focused at the local level. Since the arrival of the colonial powers in Kilimanjaro, politics there has centered on the control over local development and on the prevention of central intrusion. At different times conflict focused on colonial officers, on chiefs, and local associations, but the concern with local interests has remained primary. The local TANU organization in Kilimanjaro, and similarly throughout Tanzania, had its origins in struggles of this sort. Its anticolonial activity was at the same time anticentral.

There must exist, therefore, some tension between national and local interests. And in the process of restructuring the party and securing support for policies and programs, it is often the case that long-run national goals are better served by acceding to short-run local preferences.

Or, to state the problem as it was outlined above, there is necessarily tension between the economic and political components of a self-reliance strategy of development. Especially where skills are in short supply, there is pressure to locate them at the center. Within local institutions, those who possess what are believed to be the essential skills are likely to dominate deliberations and largely determine decisions.

Yet precisely because central resources are severely limited, the center must rely on effective local leaders. To be effective, local leaders must be responsive to local interests. To be responsive to local interests they must, to some extent, resist central direction. That of course means that each effort to secure support is potentially an obstacle to the change for which the support is sought.

Much of the literature on development suggests that what is involved is the manipulation, by relatively few individuals with the requisite technical expertise, of the relevant elements of the economy. Roads are to be constructed in one district, wells to be drilled in another, a new factory in a third, and exchange transactions are to be controlled. Yet even for economic growth (which may occur in a situation of underdevelopment) the problem is less one of technical expertise than of getting people to change their behavior—politics. For our purpose here that prevalent view is hopelessly inadequate, since each such decision involves a challenge to, or (more often) a reinforcement of, an existing set of political arrangements.

A second paradox, then, is that a self-reliance strategy of development requires a direct challenge to the existing order. That challenge always generates, and always must be pursued, in the context of a struggle. (Though these comments are concerned with the domestic components of such a strategy, it must be stressed that they are intertwined with the extranational elements. A commitment to reduce the reliance on foreign capital may restrict the capital available for internal distribution. Beyond that, such a decision constrains domestic behavior, since it requires that a much larger portion of development capital be generated from internal sources—the very farmers, herders, and urban workers to whom the regime is looking for support.)

The elite being challenged does not acquiesce happily. In Kilimanjaro, charges of strong-arm electoral tactics, clerical support for party candidates, and corruption are visible indicators of the struggle by the current elite to maintain control. The very challenge to the political position and to the economic leverage of local elites has also forged an alliance among opponents to change. As of 1970 the struggle for control of the local party was far from clear. Several of the most important programs in the construction of socialism in Tanzania had yet to be implemented effectively in Kilimanjaro.

As has been suggested throughout this study, not only are these elites struggling to retain power, but political structures created within and just after the colonial situation have supported and protected those elites, as well. The paucity of resources and skills has thus far combined with recruitment patterns that rely almost exclusively on educational attainment to perpetuate their dominant position. Moreover, the challenge to that position must be made without immediately alienating those whose skills are critical to the economy. In short, the evidence thus far suggests that there has been significant success in displacing a leadership not committed to socialist development, but also that there have been significant coalitions, built on strong local bases, of opponents to change.

The struggle continues. The successes and the failures alternate in capturing our attention. The long-run outcomes are unclear. What is very clear, however, is that Tanzania has begun, and has begun to institutionalize, a fundamental transformation of its society. In the crucible of its efforts to do that it has both outlined a strategy of fundamental change relevant to much of the world and has encouraged others to seize the initiative.

Reference Matter

Appendix 1

Moshi Political Leadership Survey

The goal of the survey of Moshi leaders was to be as comprehensive as possible. Rather than attempting to locate a narrow set of individuals who could be described as *the elite* of Moshi, the concern was to identify all those who seemed to fill major community leadership roles and then to talk with them to get their understanding of the local political system, the role of the party, and so on. Accordingly, all holders of key political positions during 1968-69, sixty-nine individuals, were interviewed (see Table A). In addition, people who were observed to be major participants in one or more of the three issue-areas studied, a total of thirty-six individuals, were interviewed. Seven individuals who held significant community leadership positions, but who were not politicians or governmental officers (for example, the two bishops), were interviewed. Each person interviewed was asked to name town influentials. With the exception of one person who had moved from town, all those who had been named as an influential by 10 percent or more of the other leaders, some ten individuals, were interviewed. I attempted to use Town Council and TANU celebration lists (lists of local people to be invited to official parties), but I found that the names appearing on those lists were drawn from lists of major town political positions. Since social status was a derived category, it did not yield additional persons to be interviewed. For the reasons discussed in Chapter 6—that tax records proved to be an inadequate source for determining a primarily economic elite, other than Europeans and Asians not directly involved in the local political process—it was impossible to develop an additional category of economic elite. My observation over the year enabled me, however, to identify several major local entrepreneurs, of whom two were interviewed.

Because of the extensive overlaps of positions, all of these methods of selection yielded a total of seventy-eight political leaders to be interviewed. In addition, a 20 percent sample of town party cell leaders, twenty-nine individuals, was interviewed (see Appendix 2).

The basic thrust of the questions used—to ask local leaders how they conceived the local political system and their roles in it—was developed in English.

Appendix 1

Table A. Political Leadership Interviews: Positions for Which Current Occupants in
1968–69 Were Interviewed

National:[a]	Members of Parliament
	Member, TANU National Executive Committee
Regional:	Regional Commissioner
	Administrative Secretary
	TANU Regional Working Committee
	TANU Regional Executive Committee
	TANU Regional Officers[b]
District:	Area Commissioner (2)[c]
	Area Secretary (2)
	Town Clerk (2)
	District Executive Officer
	TANU District Working Committee, Moshi town
	TANU District Executive Committee, Moshi town
	TANU District Officers[b]
	Moshi Town Councillors
	Moshi Town Council Department Heads
	Moshi Town Headmen
	Finance (Executive) Committee, Kilimanjaro District Council
Branch:	Moshi Town Branch Chairmen
	Moshi Town Branch Secretaries
Cell:	Random sample constituting 20% of Moshi town cell leaders

[a]Because of overlaps, many individuals hold several positions. For example, MPs are
also members of their TANU Regional and District Executive Committees, while the
Regional Commissioner is an ex-officio Member of Parliament.

[b]Officers of TANU auxiliaries—UWT, TYL, NUTA, TAPA, Elders, Cooperatives—
are included in this category. This category (at the district level) includes the officers of
both the urban and rural Kilimanjaro districts.

[c]Numbers in parentheses indicate the number of holders of that position actually
interviewed.

Note: Except for 2 members of the TANU Regional Executive Committee, 1 member
of the TANU District Executive Committee, Moshi urban, and 4 members of the
Kilimanjaro District Council Finance (Executive) Committee, and except where positions were vacant for a long period in 1968-69, holders of all of the positions listed
were interviewed. There is no reason to believe that these omissions produce any
systematic distortions.

With the assistance of Robert Ndunguru, a student at Old Moshi Secondary
School, the questions were drafted in Swahili. Only after that was the final
English version drafted. After several trials on Swahili informants, who were
also low-level leaders unlikely to fall into the net of the leadership survey, the
questionnaire was revised slightly and then administered.

The first three months in the field were spent developing competence in
Swahili, surveying government and party records, and getting to be known and
accepted in the community. The bulk of the seventy-eight interviews, which I
conducted personally, took place during the third through ninth months of

Appendix 1

Table B. Political Leadership Interviews: Duration and Language

	Number	Percent
Duration:		
Less than 30 minutes	12	11
31–60 minutes	23	21
1–2 hours	53	50
2–3 hours	14	13
3–5 hours	3	3
Not noted	2	2
	107	100
Language:		
Primarily English	14	13
English and Swahili, equally	4	4
Primarily Swahili	88	82
Not noted	1	1
	107	100

the field work. By the time I asked local leaders for an appointment, most had already gotten to know me, and everyone knew about me and my research. The leadership interviews ranged from forty-five minutes to five hours in length, where necessary over several sittings, and were primarily in Swahili (see Table B). With one exception, there was no one but the respondent and me present during the interview. The questions were phrased identically each time to ensure comparability, and the respondent was encouraged to engage, essentially, in a directed conversation on local politics. The responses were recorded in longhand during the interview and supplemented from recollection immediately after the interview; they were typed the same day. It was often the case that the more formal interview followed and/or preceded conversations with the respondent about specific local problems, decisions, and the like. In only one case did it prove impossible to secure cooperation from a local leader.

The questionnaire schedule used follows. In addition to the questions listed here, respondents were asked to supply biographical data, ranging from their parents' education and jobs through their children's education and jobs.

Appendix 1 Questionnaire Schedule

(Introduction) Kama ujuavyo, nafanya uchunguzi wa maendeleo kuhusu serikali za mitaa na uendeshaji wake katika Tanzania. Uchunguzi ninaofanya ni wa siri. Yote tutakayoongea yatakuwa ya siri kwa maana serikali kuu imetambua umaana wa kazi hiyo na imetaka mambo hayo yaendeshwe kisiri. Kwa hiyo, tunaweza kuzungumza kirafiki bila ya kuogopa. (As you know, I am studying development, especially concerning local government in Tanzania. The study that I am doing is confidential. All that we discuss will be confidential because the central government has recognized the importance of this work and wishes it to be conducted confidentially. Therefore we can chat as friends without fear.)

1. Wewe, kama mwenye ujuzi wa siasa na mambo ya serikali, kadiri unavyowazo [ya maoni yako] jambo la muhimu zaidi kuliko mambo mengine ni jambo gani? (As a person closely involved in the political activity in Moshi, in your opinion, what is the most important problem you see [must deal with]?)

2. Umesema kwamba jambo la ____ ni la muhimu sana [____ ni shida ya kwanza hapo mjini]. Mpaka hivi sasa, matendo yako katika shida za ____ ni namna gani? (You have said ____ is the most important problem you see. What exactly do *you* do about it?)

3. Umekwishanieleza mambo ya ____. Je, kuna mambo gani ya muhimu yafuatayo? (You have explained ____ to me. What are some of the other important issues in Moshi?)

4. Wenzako wanafikiri shida ya elimu ni ya muhimu sana. Wewe mwenyewe, unafikiriaje? Mpaka hivi sasa, matendo yako katika shida hii ni namna gani? (The difficulty of getting an education is an issue that concerns a great many people. Are you involved in this matter in any way?)

5. Wenzako wanasema kuwa kuna shida ya kazi. Na hasa kuhusu wasichana wafikao hapa mjini kutafuta kazi na hawapati. Wewe mwenyewe, unafikiriaje? Mpaka hivi sasa, matendo yako katika shida hii ni ya namna gani? (Many

244

people say that unemployment is an important issue in town. Perhaps especially of girls who come to town seeking jobs, who don't find jobs, but stay on in town anyway. Are you involved in this matter in any way?)

6. Hivi hivi, ninapendelea kujua njia ambazo serikali ya hapa mjini hutumia katika kuwapa ruhusa au liseni, hasa Waafrika kuliko Wahindi ama wageni, katika mambo ya biashara na usafirshaji. Mambo hayo yanakuhusu? (I am interested in the system of granting licenses for local trade and transport. This is one way in which the governments in some countries make sure that Africans or citizens get the best opportunities. Are you involved in this in any way?)

7. Katika mji wa Moshi, ukitaka kuvutia mambo katika upande wako, utafanyaje? Kuna watu wa pekee ambao lazima uwaone? Au kuna kikundi, chama, ushirika ambacho lazima ukione? (In Moshi town, if you wanted to have some influence on a particular matter, what exactly would you do? Are there any special people you would see? Is there any organization or group you would go to?)

8. Kama ungetaka kuvutia mambo katika upande wako, shauri ambalo limekwishakatwa au litakatwa Dar es Salaam, utafanyaje? (If you wanted to have some influence on some matter in which the decision was made in Dar es Salaam, what exactly would you do?)

9. Miaka miwili imepita tangu Mwalimu Nyerere ametangaza Azimio la Arusha. Watu wengi katika nchi ya Tanzania wanazo njia nyingi za kulitekeleza Azimio hili, na wengine wamefaulu kutekeleza Azimio la Arusha zaidi kuliko wengine. Njia gani maarufu watu wa mji wa Moshi wameifuata katika kutimiza hilo Azimio la Arusha? Mpaka hivi sasa, wewe mwenyewe unafanya kazi gani katika kuunga mkono Azimio la Arusha kwa vitendo? (It has been some time since President Nyerere announced the Arusha Declaration. Many people throughout the country have different ways of putting the principles of the Arusha Declaration into effect, and some have been more successful than others. What is the main way in which the people of Moshi have worked to put the principles of the Arusha Declaration into effect? What is your role in this?)

10. Nimesikia watu wakizungumza kuhusu mambo ya kujenga taifa. Unaelewa nini na neno hilo la kujenga taifa? Mpaka hivi sasa, wewe mwenyewe unafanya kazi gani katika mambo ya kujenga taifa? (I have often heard many people speaking about nation-building. In your view, what is nation-building exactly? What is your role?)

11. Wageni toka ng'ambo hufikiria kuwa ni ngumu, au pengine haiwezekani, kujenga taifa la umoja katika nchi ambayo una madhehebu mengi ya kidini na makabila mengi yanayohitilifiana. Unafikiriaje? (Many foreigners think that there are so many different tribes and religions and local interests in Africa that it will be hard to build a unified nation. What do you think?)

Appendix 1

12. Utokea wakati fulani mtu mmoja mwenye kazi kufuata mila ya kabila lake hugongana na kazi na muhimu wake katika serikali. (Kwa mfano Mmasai mila yake humfanya avae nguo au ngozi za wanyama na kufuata simba kuonyesha uhodari wake. Na papo hapo serikali inamlazimu aache mila hizo mbaya na kuacha kufuata simba.) Je, hutokeaje katika jambo hilo? (Sometimes it does happen that a person's responsibility, let us say, to his tribe, is not entirely in agreement with his responsibility to the government. [For example, a Masai believes that to follow the customs of his tribe he must wear a blanket and kill a lion to show his bravery. But to follow the laws of the government, he must discard those habits.] What is happening in such cases?)

13. Ni mara ngapi watu kutoka katika sehemu yako kufika kukuona au kuandikia barua au ni mara ngapi wanawaomba rafiki zao kuwawakilisha kuhusu shida au matatizo yao? Ni watu wangapi ungesema hukufika au hukuona kila juma? Ni watu wangapi kati yao ambao unawafahamu? (How often do people from your local area come to see you, or write to you, or ask their friends to see you, about their problems? How many people would you say contact you each week? How many of these people who contact you would you say you know personally?)

14. Wakati watu wa sehemu yako wanapofika hukutolea shida ama matatizo gani ambayo yanawahusu? (When people from your local area come to see you, what problems are they mostly concerned about?)

15. Kuna chama ama kikundi cha watu ambacho huja kukuona kwa ajili ya shida zao? (Are there any groups or organizations who come to see you about their problems?)

16. Wakati watu wanapofika kwako kwa ajili ya shida hizo ambazo tumeziongelea wewe kama kiongozi unachukua hatua gani? (When people come to see you about these problems we have been discussing, what exactly do you do about them?)

17. Ningependa kujua ni vikundi gani kati ya hivyo ni vya maana katika mji wa Moshi. Kwa upande wako, chama gani au kikundi gani unakifikiria ni cha kufaa na cha maana? (I am interested in finding out what are the most important groups in Moshi. What groups or societies or organizations do you think are most important?)

18. Je, kuna vyama ambavyo hujishughulisha sana na mambo ya siasa katika mji wa Moshi? au katika siasa ya nchi nzima? (Are there any groups that take a very active role in local political matters? in national political matters?)

19. Kama ujuavyo, nauliza watu wengi katika uchunguzi wangu. Kutokana na ujuzi wako unafikiria ni watu gani maarufu katika mji wa Moshi? Na watu

gani hujishughulisha kwa kiasi kikubwa katika siasa hapa mjini? Na watu gani wanaoweza kutoa maoni yao katika kukata mashauri? (As you know, I am speaking to many people in Moshi during the course of my research. From your experience, who would you say are the most important people in Moshi? the people most involved in political activity? the people most able to influence decisions?)

20. Wageni, hata Waafrika, hushangaa jinsi siasa ya chama kimoja cha kidemokrasi huweza kufanya kazi katika nchi ya Tanzania. Unafikiria TANU ifanye nini kuhusiana na mambo ya mitaa hapa Moshi? (Many people in other countries have wondered exactly how a one-party democracy works. What do you think the role of TANU should be in matters that concern Moshi?)

21. Tume iliyochaguliwa na Rais Nyerere kuchungua namna gani wataweza kuunda nchi yenye chama kimoja cha kidemokrasi walitazama katika uwezekano wa kuunganisha TANU na serikali katika shirika moja. Walikata shauri kuwa hilo halitakuwa wazo zuri kwa sababu TANU na serikali ina kazi ya pekee ya kujenga taifa. Katika sehemu fulani fulani ni ngumu kutambua ipi ni kazi ya TANU na ipi ni kazi ya serikali kwa vile zote mbili hufanya kazi pamoja. Je, hapo Moshi, kuna nini [kuhusiana na jambo hilo]? Ungesema kuna tofauti gani katika kazi zifanywazo na serikali na TANU kuhusu mambo ya hapa Moshi? (The Commission that was appointed by President Nyerere to examine just how to set up a democratic one-party state looked into the possibility of combining TANU and the government into one organization. They decided this would not be a good idea, since the government and TANU each has its own role to play in building the nation. In some places, TANU and the government work so closely together that it is hard to say what is the responsibility of each. What about Moshi? What would you say are the differences between what TANU does and what the government does, when it concerns local matters?)

22. Watu wengi hufikiria kuwa mashauri na matatizo mengi lazima yakatwe na viongozi wa Dar es Salaam, lakini wengine hufikiria kuwa ni nzuri zaidi mashauri yahusikanayo mambo ya miji yenyewe yakatwe katika kila mji. Unafikiriaje? Je, ni mambo mengi yanayohusikana na Moshi hukatwa Dar es Salaam? (Some people think that all decisions should be made by the leaders in Dar es Salaam, while others think that it is better for decisions about local matters to be made in each town. What do you think? Are many of the decisions about matters that concern Moshi made in Dar es Salaam?)

23. Wewe mwenyewe, unafanya kazi gani? Na hiyo kazi, umeipata lini? Je, una kazi nyingine zaidi ya hiyo ambayo umekwishaitaja, labda katika chama cha TANU au serikalini? (What is your exact position? When did you get that position? Do you have any other position, perhaps in TANU or the national government?)

24. (if national) Watu wengine wameniambia kuwa ni ngumu kuwa katika [national] na muda ule ule kuwa [local]. Je, unafikiria hiyo ni hivyo? Katika uchaguzi wa Bunge wa mwaka 1965 mawaziri na wabunge wengine walishindwa katika uchaguzi huo kwa sababu walitumia muda mchache katika sehemu yao. Je, unaona kuwa [national] hukuzuia sana kwenda kwenye wilaya yako? Je, hilo ni tatizo kwako? (Some people have told me that it is difficult to be both a [national] and at the same time a [local]. Do you think this is so? In the Parliamentary Elections in 1965 some Ministers and Members of Parliament were defeated because they spent very little time in their constituencies. Do you find that being a [national] keeps you away from your district very much? Is this a problem for you?)

(if no national) Watu fulani ambao hufanya kazi ya siasa katika sehemu yao hushiriki pia katika mambo yahusuyo taifa. Je, unafikiria kuwa kuna uwezekano mtu kujishughulisha katika mambo ya taifa na bado kuweza kufanya kazi nzuri hapa Moshi? (Some people who play an important role in their local areas also participate in making decisions at the national level. Do you think that a person can be involved in national affairs and still do a good job in Moshi?)

25. Kama ujuavyo, nafanya uchunguzi wa maendeleo, kuhusu serikali za mitaa na uendeshaji wake katika Tanzania. Je, kuna kitu ambacho ungetaka kuongeza kwa hayo niliyokwishayasema? Je, juna kitu ambacho nimekiacha? Je, kuna mambo yanayonifanya nijishughulishe sana nayo? (As you know, I am studying local government, administration, and development in Tanzania. Is there anything that you would like to add to what you have already said? Is there anything that I have left out? Are there some things I should devote more attention to?)

Closing. Nakushukuru sana kwa msaada wako ulionipa katika uchunguzi wangu. Ujue kuwa mambo hayo yote tuliyokwishasema ni ya siri na wala usiyatoe nje. Nataka kuhakikishia kuwa sitayatoa mambo hayo nje. (I want to thank you very much for the help you have given me in my study. Remember that everything we have discussed is confidential, and you should not speak about it with others. And I want to assure you that I will not speak of this to others.)

Appendix 2

Moshi Cell Leader Survey

To supplement the Moshi Political Leadership Survey, which was largely concentrated at the district (town) level, a 20 percent sample of the urban party
cell leaders was interviewed.

The most difficult problem in the Moshi Cell Leader Survey proved to
be the creation of a reliable sampling frame. The party maintained no list, or
map, of cells in town. Nor was it possible to locate, anywhere in town (including party, Town Council, and governmental offices), a complete list of
town cell leaders. A thorough search of party files yielded several incomplete,
outdated, and in several cases overlapping lists of cell leaders by ward. In
consultation with the appropriate branch (coterminous with ward) chairmen
I corrected, updated, and verified the names on those lists, thus producing
lists of current cell leaders by ward. So that the Cell Leader Survey would
tap ordinary cell leaders, those individuals listed as cell leaders who had already
been interviewed as part of the larger leadership survey were removed. From
those amended lists a 20 percent random sample by ward was drawn. Since
the residential patterns and community composition varied by ward, and
since the town population was not evenly dispersed throughout the wards,
it was essential that the samples be of each ward rather than of the town as a
whole. Several other corrections, all to ensure that the final sample would
adequately reflect the regular town inhabitants, were made (in other words,
what resulted was a stratified random sample). A small agricultural community on the edge of town, not at all integrated into the largely upper-class
residential ward of which it was formally a part, was treated separately: the
20 percent sample was drawn of all of the rest of the ward and of that community. In the small central business ward, where the Asian chairman claimed
to represent an all-Asian ward even though the ward boundaries included,
among other Africans, a new settlement of employees of the coffee curing
factory (in the process of constituting itself as a separate TANU branch),
it was impossible to determine if there were any African cell leaders. Party
files suggested there were, but the branch chairman claimed there were not.
In the event, only the Asian cell leaders were included in the survey, since

otherwise Asians might have been excluded entirely. For the purposes of this study that does not produce significant problems. Although the Asians are relatively overrepresented in regard to the town population as a whole, that overrepresentation permits greater confidence in the comments about the political behavior of the Asian community. Finally, the police barracks and the police training academy, both of which had highly transient and largely nonlocal populations that were in the process of forming party branches of their own, were not included in the Moshi Cell Leader Survey.

Once the 20 percent sample had been drawn, Rachel Samoff, who developed and administered the Cell Leader Survey, approached the appropriate branch chairmen to make initial contacts with the cell leaders. She and the branch chairman walked around the branch, locating the cell leaders and their homes. She made appointments for the interviews and subsequently returned to administer the questionnaire. Relying so heavily on the branch chairmen had both advantages and disadvantages. On the one hand, in general the branch chairman was in the best position to know who the cell leaders were, where they could be located, and to provide a positive introduction for the interview. In the one branch where the chairman was both newly elected and disliked by many branch residents, other leaders were used as intermediaries. On the other hand, branch chairmen could be expected to feel that the branch as a whole was being evaluated and that the responses of their cell leaders would be compared with the responses from other branches. In fact in at least one case, after the first several interviews, the succeeding cell leaders seemed to have been forewarned of several questions. In Moshi in 1969, however, it would have been impossible to secure reasonable lists and positive receptions without working through the branch chairmen; the probes of the interview were designed to discover and work around responses that were not the respondent's own.

The questionnaire schedule used for the Moshi Political Leadership Survey was adapted for cell leader use. Rachel Samoff conducted the interviews at the respondents' homes in Swahili. The responses were recorded in longhand during the interviews, which lasted about one hour. Immediately after the interviews the recorded responses were supplemented by recollection. Only one cell leader proved unwilling to cooperate, and the next cell leader on the randomized list for that ward was interviewed instead. It might be noted that the branch chairman was irate when he discovered the case of noncooperation and subsequently dismissed the cell leader for failing to live up to his charge to serve the public.

What follows is the complete set of questions asked of cell leader respondents. The questions were drafted in Swahili (adapted from the Moshi Political Leadership Survey); an approximate English translation follows.

Appendix 2 Questionnaire Schedule

(First Meeting) Namsaidia mume wangu katika uchunguzi wa maendeleo hasa
kuhusu serikali za mitaa na uendashaji wake katika Tanzania. (Labda
umekwishamwona katika mkutano fulani—mwenye ndevu, anayependa kuvaa
shati ya kitenge.) Tunatoka kwa Chuo Kikuu cha Dar es Salaam na uchunguzi
tunaofanya unafanyika chini ya mamlaka ya Ofisi ya Makamu wa Pili wa Rais.
Tunakuomba kutusaidia kupata maelezo kidogo juu ya shida za hapa Moshi na
za nyumba kumi zako na kadhalika. Utakuwa na nafasi siku gani. . . . (I am
helping my husband in his study of development, especially concerning local
government and its conduct in Tanzania. [Perhaps you have already seen him
at some meeting or other—he has a beard and likes to wear kitenge shirts.]
We come from University College, Dar es Salaam, and the study we are doing
is being done under the authority of the Office of the Second Vice-President.
We seek your help in gaining some understanding of the problems of Moshi
and of your ten houses and so on. When do you think you will have time. . . .)

(Introduction) Kama ujuavyo, nafanya uchunguzi wa maendeleo, hasa
kuhusu serikali za mitaa na uendeshaji wake katika Tanzania. Uchunguzi
ninaofanya ni wa siri. Yote tutakayoongea yatakuwa ya siri kwa maana
serikali kuu imetambua umaana wa kazi hiyo na imetaka mambo hayo
yaendeshwe kisiri. Kwa hiyo, tunaweza kuzungumza kirafiki bila ya kuogopa.
(As you know, I am studying development, especially concerning local government in Tanzania. The study I am doing is confidential. All that we discuss
will be confidential because the central government has recognized the importance of this work and wishes it to be conducted confidentially. Therefore,
we can chat as friends without fear.)

1. Wewe ukiwa kama balozi, kadiri unavyowazo jambo [shida] la muhimu
sana kuliko mambo mengine kuhusu nyumba kumi zako ni hasa jambo gani?
(As a cell leader, in your opinion what is the most important matter [problem]
in your cell?)

2. Umenieleza kwa kirefu kidogo jambo la ____. Katika jambo hilo
matendo yako ni namna gani, au labda huwezi kufanya kitu cho chote? (You

251

have explained to me the problem of ____. What exactly do you do about that problem, or perhaps you are unable to do anything at all?)

3. Miaka miwili imepita sasa tangu Mwalimu Nyerere ametangaza Azimio la Arusha. Wananchi wa Tanzania wana njia mbali mbali za kutekeleza hilo Azimio la Arusha. Na kusema kweli, wengine wamefaulu kuliko wengine katika kutimiza hilo Azimio la Arusha. Kwenu kuna nini? Hawa jamaa wa nyumba kumi zako wamefuata hasa njia gani katika kutimiza Azimio la Arusha? Au labda unaona ya kuwa Azimio hilo haliwahusu wakaaji wa mji? (Two years have passed since President Nyerere announced the Arusha Declaration. Tanzanians have many different ways of implementing the Arusha Declaration. But, to tell the truth, some have been more successful than others in implementing the Arusha Declaration. How is it where you live? These neighbors of your ten houses—what have they done to put into practice the Arusha Declaration? Or perhaps you think that this Declaration does not concern people who live in town?)

___ leadership code	___ self-reliance (individual)
___ cooperative work	___ do your own job well; general hard work
___ work for good of the community, incl self-help projects	___ social ownership of production/ stores/etc.
___ no change, but greater emphasis on previous policy	___ no impact, change at all
___ other:	___ other:

4. Unaelewaje kazi yako, kazi ya ubalozi? (How do you understand your job, the job of cell leader?)

    ___ reconciliation, arbitration, adjudication
    ___ receive complaints and pass them upwards
    ___ receive complaints and direct people to proper place
    ___ explain policies of TANU, Tanzania
    ___ lead, exhort, encourage, enthuse the people in my cell
    ___ choose the leaders of TANU, Tanzania
    ___ generalized assistance to the people of my cell
    ___ other:
    ___ other:

5. Bila shaka [kama ulivyosema sasa hivi] mara kwa mara wananchi hufika kwako kukulete ashida ama matatizo yao. Ungesema ni wangapi wanaofika kwako kwa juma moja kwa wastani? (Doubtless [as you have just said] from time to time people come to you to bring their problems. How many people would you say come to see you in a week on the average?)

Appendix 2

6. Mtu wa mwisho aliyeleta shida yake kwako alifika lini? (The last person who brought you his problem came when?)

___ today   ___ within week   ___ longer than month
___ yesterday   ___ between week &   ___ none at all
                   month

7. Sipendi kujua jina lake, lakini yeye alileta shida gani? (I am not interested in his name, but what problem did he bring?)

8. Ulifanyaje? (What did you do about it?)

9. Kuna mtu aliyeleta tatizo lingine kwako, wewe ukiwa kama balozi? Alifika lini? (Is there someone else who brought his problem to you as his cell leader? When did he come?)

___ today   ___ within week   ___ longer than month
___ yesterday   ___ between week & month   ___ none at all

10. Vile vile, sipendi kujua jina lake. Alikuletea shida gani? (Again, I am not interested in his name. What problem did he bring you?)

11. Ukafanyaje? (What did you do about it?)

12. Na kuna shida nyingine ambazo huletwa kwako, wewe ukiwa kama balozi? Shida za namna gani? (And are there other problems that have been brought to you as a cell leader? What sorts of problems?)

13. Wewe, uwezaje? (And you, what could you do about them?)

14. Mara kwa mara inatokea kwamba huwezi ama unashindwa kutoa msaada katika shida fulani. Unaposhindwa, unaomba msaada kwa mtu mwingine. Huyo ni nani? (Sometimes it happens that you are unable to help in some problems. When you are unable to help, you seek aid from someone else. Who is that?)

15. Kabla ya kuwa na mabalozi, mlikuwa mnapeleka shida zenu wapi? [Kwa mfano, aliyepokea shida hizi alikuwa ni nani?] (Before there were cell leaders, where did you take your problems? [For example, who was it who received these problems?])

16. Bado mnaendelea [anaendelea] kufanya hivi? (Do you still continue [does he still continue] to do this?)

17. Kama wewe mwenyewe [binafsi] ukiwa na shida, unakwenda kwa nani? (When you yourself have a [your own] problem, whom do you go to see?)

18. Kama ungetaka msaada katika kazi yako ya ubalozi, ungekwenda kuonana ama kuzungumza na nani? (If you wanted some help in your work as a cell leader, whom would you go to see, or whom would you talk to?)

19. Mara kwa mara, inatokea kwamba wewe unakwenda kuonana ama kuzungumza na: ____. Safari yako ya mwisho ya kuonana naye ilikuwa lini?

Appendix 2

(Sometimes it happens that you go to see or speak with: ____. When was your last visit to see him?)

your branch chairman	a TANU officer (who?)
a member of your branch council	the Area Commissioner
the chairman of the Elders	a regional officer (who?)
the chairman of Moshi town	a Member of Parliament (who?)

20. Mara kwa mara unafanya mkutano na wananchi wa nyumba kumi zako? (Do you occasionally have meetings with the residents of your cell?)

yes/no/formerly did, but no more/just moved into the cell

21. Mkutano wa mwisho ulifanyika lini? Kusudi lake nini? (When did the last meeting take place? What did it concern?)

22. (if election meeting) Kabla ya mkutano huo wa uchaguzi, palikuwa na mkutano mwingine? Mkutano huu ulifanyika lini? Kusudi lake nini? (Before that election meeting, was there another meeting? When was that held? What did it concern?)

23. Kazi ya ubalozi ni ngumu? Kwa nini? (Is the job of a cell leader difficult? In what way?)

24. Kati ya vitu vyote unavyofanya wewe ukiwa kama balozi unaona ni kitu gani ambacho ni cha maana sana [kuliko vitu vingine]? (Among all the things that you do as a cell leader, what do you think is the most important?)

25. Umenieleza kwa kirefu kazi ya ubalozi. Lakini unajua mara kwa mara wageni toka ng'ambo wanashindwa kuelewa kazi ya chama katika nchi yenye Chama Kimoja Cha Kidemokrasi. Maana yake, labda wanaweza kuelewa kazi ya bunge, na hata kazi ya makao makuu ya chama, lakini kazi ya tawi hawaielewi. Katika maoni yako, kazi ya tawi la TANU ni hasa kazi gani? (You have explained to me in detail the work of a cell leader. But sometimes foreigners have difficulty understanding the job of the party in a country with a single democratic party. That is, they can understand the job of the parliament, and even the job of the party headquarters, but they do not understand the job of the branch. In your opinion, what is the job of a TANU branch?)

___ receive complaints from the people	___ govern
___ explain national policy	___ set policy
___ get development for Tanzania	___ carry out policy
___ oversee, check government	___ encourage, exhort
local ___ security ___ justice	___ discipline
___ has no job at all	___ other:
___ other:	

26. Watu wengi hufikiri ya kuwa ni lazima mashauri ama matatizo yakatwe

Appendix 2

Dar es Salaam. Lakini wengine wanaona kwamba matatizo yanayohusu mji
wa Moshi inafaa zaidi yakatwe hapa hapa. Uonaje? Imekwishatokea kwamba
kukata jambo fulani Dar es Salaam kumeleta taabu kidogo? [Unaweza kunipa
mfano, kunieleza kidogo?] (Many people think that all decisions should be
made in Dar es Salaam. But others feel that problems that concern the town
of Moshi are better dealt with right here. What do you think? Has it already
happened that some decision in Dar es Salaam has created some problems
here? [Can you give me an example, explain a little?])

27. Sasa, nimemaliza yale maswali ya uchunguzi wangu. Kama nilivyoeleza,
nafanya uchunguzi wa maendeleo, kuhusu serikali za mitaa na uendeshaji wake
katika Tanzania. Je, kuna kitu ambacho nimekiacha? Au, labda kuna kitu
ambacho ungetaka kuongeza kwa hayo niliyokwishasema? (Now, I have
finished the questions of my study. As I explained, I am studying development,
especially concerning local government and its conduct in Tanzania. Is there
something I have left out? Or, perhaps there is something you would like to
add to what I have said?)

Selected Bibliography

Besides works bearing directly on this study, the bibliography includes related materials that serve to set the study of local politics in Moshi in its broader historical, economic, and methodological contexts.

Abernethy, David B. "Nigeria." In David G. Scanlon, ed., *Church, State, and Education in Africa*. New York: Teachers College Press, 1966.

Abrahams, R. G. *The Political Organization of Unyamwezi*. Cambridge: Cambridge University Press, 1967.

Achebe, Chinua. *A Man of the People*. London: Heinemann, 1966.

"African Elites." *International Social Science Bulletin* 8, 3 (1956).

Alderfer, Harold F. *Local Government in Developing Countries*. New York: McGraw-Hill, 1964.

Allen, Christopher, and R. W. Johnson, eds. *African Perspectives*. London: Cambridge University Press, 1970.

Almond, Gabriel A., and Sidney Verba. *The Civic Culture*. Boston: Little, Brown, abridged ed., 1965.

Almond, Gabriel A., and G. Bingham Powell, Jr. *Comparative Politics: A Developmental Approach*. Boston: Little, Brown, 1966.

Amin, Samir. *L'Afrique de l'Ouest Bloquée. L'Economie Politique de la Colonisation 1880-1970*. Paris: Les Editions de Minuit, 1971.

——. "Capitalism and Development in the Ivory Coast." In Irving Leonard Markovitz, ed., *African Politics and Society*. New York: Free Press, 1970. Pp. 277-88. An abridged translation by I. L. Markovitz of pp. 265-81 of Samir Amin, *Le Développement du Capitalisme en Côte d'Ivoire*.

——. *Le Développement du Capitalisme en Côte d'Ivoire*. Paris: Les Editions de Minuit, 1967.

Anderson, Charles W., Fred R. von der Mehden, and Crawford Young. *Issues of Political Development*. Englewood Cliffs, N.J.: Prentice-Hall, 1967.

Arrighi, Giovanni, and John S. Saul. *Essays on the Political Economy of Africa*. New York: Monthly Review Press, 1973.

——. "Nationalism and Revolution in Sub-Saharan Africa." *Socialist Register 1969*. London: Merlin Press, 1969.

——. "Socialism and Economic Development in Tropical Africa." *Journal of Modern African Studies* 6, 2 (August 1968): 141-69.

Austen, Ralph A. *Northwest Tanzania Under German and British Rule*. New Haven: Yale University Press, 1968.

———. "Notes on the Pre-History of TANU." *Makerere Journal* 9 (1964): 1-6.

Bachrach, Peter, and Morton S. Baratz. "Decisions and Nondecisions: An Analytical Framework." *American Political Science Review* 57 (September 1963): 632-42.

———. *Power and Poverty: Theory and Practice.* New York: Oxford University Press, 1970.

———. "Two Faces of Power." *APSR* 56, 4 (December 1962): 947-52.

Bailey, F. G. *Stratagems and Spoils: A Social Anthropology of Politics.* New York: Schocken, 1969.

Banton, M. "Adaptation and Integration in the Social System of Temne Immigrants in Freetown." *Africa* 26, 4 (1956): 354-67.

———, ed. *Political Systems and the Distribution of Power.* London: Tavistock Publications, 1965.

———. *West African City: A Study of Tribal Life in Freetown.* London: Oxford University Press for the International African Institute, 1957.

Barnekov, Timothy K. *Demand-Stress Regulation: The Merger of Party and State in Tanzania.* Program of Eastern African Studies, Occasional Paper no. 35. Syracuse: Syracuse University, 1967.

Barongo, E. B. M. *Mkiki Mkiki wa Siasa Tanganyika.* Nairobi: East African Literature Bureau, 1966.

Bates, Margaret. "Tanganyika." In Gwendolen M. Carter, ed., *African One-Party States.* Ithaca: Cornell University Press, 1963.

Bennett, George. "An Outline History of TANU." *Makerere Journal* 7 (1963): 15-32.

Berg, Elliot J. "Structural Transformation versus Gradualism: Recent Economic Development in Ghana and the Ivory Coast." In Philip Foster and Aristide R. Zolberg, eds., *Ghana and the Ivory Coast.* Chicago: University of Chicago Press, 1971.

Berg, Elliott J., and Jeffrey Butler. "Trade Unions." In James S. Coleman and Carl Rosberg, Jr., eds., *Political Parties and National Integration in Tropical Africa.* Berkeley: University of California Press, 1964.

Bienen, Henry. "An Ideology for Africa." *Foreign Affairs* 47, 3 (April 1969): 545-59.

———. "The Ruling Party in the African One-Party State: Tanu in Tanzania." *Journal of Commonwealth Political Studies* 5, 3 (November 1967): 214-30.

———. *Tanzania: Party Transformation and Economic Development.* Princeton: Princeton University Press, rev. ed., 1970.

Blondel, Jean, ed. *Comparative Government.* Garden City, N.Y.: Anchor, 1969.

Brenner, Michael J. "Functional Representation and Interest Group Theory." *Comparative Politics* 2, 1 (October 1969): 111-34.

Burke, Fred G. "Research in African Local Government: Past Trends and an

Bibliography

Emerging Approach." *Canadian Journal of African Studies* 3, 1 (Winter 1969): 73-80.

——. *Tanganyika: Preplanning.* Syracuse: Syracuse University Press, 1965.

Butler, Jeffrey, and A. A. Castagno, eds. *Boston University Papers on Africa. Transition in African Politics.* New York: Praeger, 1967.

Cameron, John. *The Development of Education in East Africa.* New York: Teachers College Press, 1970.

——, and W. A. Dodd. *Society, Schools and Progress in Tanzania.* Oxford: Pergamon Press, 1970.

Chaput, Michael, ed. *Patterns of Elite Formation and Distribution in Kenya, Senegal, Tanzania, and Zambia.* Program of Eastern African Studies, Occasional Paper no. 42. Syracuse: Syracuse University, 1968.

Chidzero, B. T. G. *Tanganyika and International Trusteeship.* London: Oxford University Press, 1961.

Cliffe, Lionel. "Arusha Declaration: Challenge to Tanzanians." *East Africa Journal* 3, 12 (March 1967): 3-9.

——, ed. *One Party Democracy: The 1965 Tanzania General Election.* Nairobi: East African Publishing House, 1967.

——. "Personal or Class Interest: Tanzania's Leadership Conditions." In Lionel Cliffe and John S. Saul, eds., *Socialism in Tanzania.* Vol. 1, *Politics.* Nairobi: East African Publishing House, 1972.

——. "Planning Rural Development." *Development and Change* 3, 3 (1971-72): 77-98.

——. "Tanzania—Socialist Transformation and Party Development." *The African Review* 1, 1 (March 1971): 119-235.

——, and John S. Saul. "The District Development Front in Tanzania." In Lionel Cliffe and John S. Saul, eds., *Socialism in Tanzania.* Vol. 1, *Politics.* Nairobi: East African Publishing House, 1972.

——, and John S. Saul, eds. *Socialism in Tanzania.* Vol. 1, *Politics.* Nairobi: East African Publishing House, 1972.

Clignet, Remi, and Philip Foster. *The Fortunate Few.* Evanston, Ill.: Northwestern University Press, 1966.

Clower, Robert W., George Dalton, Mitchell Harwitz, and A. A. Walters. *Growth Without Development.* Evanston, Ill.: Northwestern University Press, 1966.

Cockcroft, James D., et al., eds. *Dependence and Underdevelopment: Latin America's Political Economy.* Garden City, N.J.: Doubleday/Anchor, 1972.

Cohen, Abner. *Customs and Politics in Urban Africa.* Berkeley: University of California Press, 1969.

Coleman, James S., ed. *Education and Political Development.* Princeton: Princeton University Press, 1965.

Bibliography

——, and Carl Rosberg, Jr., eds. *Political Parties and National Integration in Tropical Africa.* Berkeley: University of California Press, 1964.

Collins, Paul D. "A Preliminary Evaluation of the Working of the Regional Development Fund." Rural Development Research Committee, Rural Development Paper no. 1. Mimeographed. Dar es Salaam: University of Dar es Salaam, 1969.

Conference on African Local Institutions and Rural Transformation, 1967. Chester, Pa.: Lincoln University, 1967.

Conference on The Government of African Cities, 1968. Chester, Pa.: Lincoln University, 1968.

Cowan, L. Gray. *The Cost of Learning: The Politics of Primary Education in Kenya.* New York: Teachers College Press, 1970.

——, James O'Connell, and David G. Scanlon, eds. *Education and Nation-Building in Africa.* New York: Praeger, 1965.

Cunningham, G. L. "Peasants, Rural Development, and the Dependence Relationship in Tanzania." Conference Paper, Conference on Dependence and Development in Africa, Ottawa, 1973.

Dahl, Robert A. *Who Governs?* New Haven: Yale University Press, 1961.

Davies, Ioan. *African Trade Unions.* Baltimore: Penguin, 1966.

Decalo, Samuel. *Tanzania: An Introductory Bibliography.* Occasional Papers in Political Science, no. 4. Kingston: University of Rhode Island, 1968.

Diamond, Stanley, and Fred G. Burke, eds. *The Transformation of East Africa.* New York: Basic Books, 1966.

Dodd, William A. *"Education for Self-Reliance" in Tanzania: A Study of Its Vocational Aspects.* New York: Teachers College Press, 1969.

Dryden, Stanley. *Local Administration in Tanzania.* Nairobi: East African Publishing House, 1968.

Dumont, René. *False Start in Africa.* Translated from the French (*L'Afrique Noire est Mal Partie*) by Phyllis Nauts Ott. London: Deutsch, 1966.

Dundas, Charles. *Kilimanjaro and Its People.* 1924; reprint ed., London: Frank Cass, 1968.

East Africa High Commission. East Africa Statistical Department. *Tanganyika Population Census 1957. Analysis of Total Population.* Nairobi, 1958.

——. *Tanganyika Population Census 1957. General African Census, August 1957. Tribal Analysis, Part 1.* Nairobi, 1958.

Feldman, David. "The Economics of Ideology. Some Problems of Achieving Rural Socialism in Tanzania." In Colin Leys, ed., *Politics and Change in Developing Countries.* Cambridge: Cambridge University Press, 1969.

Foster, Philip, and Aristide R. Zolberg, eds. *Ghana and the Ivory Coast.* Chicago: University of Chicago Press, 1971.

Bibliography

Frederick, S. W. "The Life of Joseph Kimalando, as told to S. W. Frederick." *Tanzania Notes and Records* 70 (July 1969): 21-28.

Friedland, William H. "Co-operation, Conflict, and Conscription: TANU-TFL Relations, 1955-1964." In Jeffrey Butler and A. A. Castagno, eds., *Boston University Papers on Africa. Transition in African Politics.* New York: Praeger, 1967.

——. *Vuta Kamba: The Development of Trade Unions in Tanganyika.* Stanford, California: Hoover Institution Press, 1969.

Fuad, Khuri. "Influential Men and the Exercise of Influence in Magburaka, Sierra Leone." Ph.D. dissertation, University of Oregon, 1964.

Fuggles-Couchman, N. R. *Agricultural Change in Tanganyika: 1945-1960.* Stanford, California: Food Research Institute, Stanford University, 1964.

Galtung, Johann. "Structural Theory of Imperialism." *The African Review* 1, 4 (April 1972): 93-138.

Gardner, Brian. *On to Kilimanjaro.* Philadelphia: Macrae Smith Company, 1963.

Geertz, Clifford. *Old Societies and New States: The Quest for Modernity in Asia and Africa.* Glencoe, Ill.: Free Press, 1963.

Gertzel, Cherry. *The Politics of Independent Kenya.* Evanston, Ill.: Northwestern University Press, 1970.

Gillman, C. "A Bibliography of Kilimanjaro, 1944." *Tanganyika Notes and Records* 18 (December 1944): 60-68.

Gitlin, Todd. "Local Pluralism as Theory and Ideology." *Studies on the Left* 5, 3 (1965): 21-45.

Glickman, Harvey. "One-Party System in Tanganyika." *The Annals of the American Academy of Political and Social Science* 358 (March 1965): 136-49.

——. *Some Observations on The Army and Political Unrest in Tanganyika.* Pittsburgh: Duquesne University Press, 1964.

Gouldner, Alvin W. *The Coming Crisis of Western Sociology.* New York: Avon, 1970.

Great Britain, Colonial Office. *Development of African Local Government in Tanganyika.* Colonial no. 277. London: H.M.S.O., 1951.

Green, Reginald H. "Four African Development Plans: Ghana, Kenya, Nigeria, and Tanzania." *Journal of Modern African Studies* 3, 2 (August 1965): 249-79.

——. "Political Independence and the National Economy: An Essay in the Political Economy of Decolonisation." In Christopher Allen and R. W. Johnson, eds., *African Perspectives.* London: Cambridge University Press, 1970.

——. "Reflections on Economic Strategy, Structure, Implementation, and Necessity: Ghana and the Ivory Coast, 1957-67." In Philip Foster and Aristide

R. Zolberg, eds. *Ghana and the Ivory Coast*. Chicago: University of Chicago Press, 1971.

Griner, Madeline. "Problems of Administration in Tanganyika Territory in the Development of Self-Government." Ph.D. dissertation, New York University, 1956.

Gulliver, P. H., ed. *Tradition and Transition in East Africa*. Berkeley: University of California Press, 1969.

Gutmann, Bruno. *Das Recht der Dschagga*. From the Arbeiten zur Entwicklungspsychologie, no. 7, pp. 1-733. Translated for Human Relations Area Files by A. M. Nagler. Munich: C. H. Beck, 1926.

——. *Die Stammeslehren der Dschagga*. From the Arbeiten zur Entwicklungspsychologie, no. 12. Translated for Human Relations Area Files by Ward Goodenough and Dorothy Crawford. Munich: C. H. Beck'sche Verlagsbuchhandlung, 1932.

Halpern, Manfred. *The Politics of Social Change in the Middle East and North Africa*. Princeton, N.J.: Princeton University Press, 1963.

Hanna, William John. "Influence and Influentials in Two Urban-Centered African Communities." *Comparative Politics* 2, 1 (October 1969): 17-40.

——. "Methodology, Technology, and the Study of African Elites." *African Studies Review* 13, 1 (April 1970): 95-103.

——, and Judith Lynne Hanna. "The Political Structure of Urban-Centered African Communities." In Horace Miner, ed., *The City in Modern Africa*. New York: Praeger, 1967.

——, and Judith Lynne Hanna. *Urban Dynamics in Black Africa*. Chicago: Aldine, 1970.

Hayter, Theresa. *Aid as Imperialism*. Baltimore: Penguin, 1971.

Heidenheimer, Arnold J., ed. *Political Corruption*. New York: Holt, Rinehart and Winston, 1970.

Helleiner, G. K. "Tanzania's Second Plan" Socialism and Self-Reliance." *East Africa Journal* 5, 12 (December 1968): 41-50.

——. "Trade and Aid in Tanzania." *East Africa Journal* 4, 1 (April 1967): 7-17.

Herrick, Allison Butler, et al. *Area Handbook for Tanzania*. Washington: Government Printing Office, 1968.

Hopkins, Raymond F. *Political Roles in a New State: Tanzania's First Decade*. New Haven: Yale University Press, 1971.

Hutchinson, J. A. "The Meaning of Kilimanjaro." *Tanganyika Notes and Records* 64 (March 1965): 65-66.

Hyden, Goran. "Local Government Reform in Kenya." *East Africa Journal* 7, 4 (April 1970): 19-24.

——. "Planning in Tanzania: Lessons of Experience." *East Africa Journal* 6, 10 (October 1969): 13-17.

Bibliography

——. *Political Development in Rural Tanzania. TANU Yajenga Nchi.* Reprint of 1968 Swedish edition. Nairobi: East African Publishing House, 1969.
——. "Political Penetration in a Rural Area." *East African Institute of Social Research,* Conference Papers, January 1966, no. 356.

Ifill, Max B. "Perspectives for Regional Economic Planning in Kilimanjaro Region." Mimeographed. Dar es Salaam, 1969.
Iliffe, John. "The Age of Improvement and Differentiation (1907-45)." In I. N. Kimambo and A. Temu, eds., *A History of Tanzania.* Nairobi: East African Publishing House, 1969.
——. *Tanganyika Under German Rule 1905-1912.* Cambridge: Cambridge University Press, 1969.
Ingle, Clyde R. "Compulsion and Rural Development in Tanzania." *Canadian Journal of African Studies* 4, 1 (1970): 77-100.
——. *From Village to State in Tanzania: The Politics of Rural Development.* Ithaca, N.Y.: Cornell University Press, 1972.
——. "The Ten-House Cell System in Tanzania: A Consideration of an Emerging Village Institution." *Journal of Developing Areas* 6, 2 (January 1972): 211-26.

Jalée, Pierre. *The Pillage of the Third World.* Translated from the French by Mary Klopper. New York: Monthly Review Press, 1968.
——. *The Third World in World Economy.* Translated from the French by Mary Klopper. New York: Monthly Review Press, 1969.
Jensen, S. *Regional Economic Atlas Mainland Tanzania.* Bureau of Resource Assessment and Land Use Planning, Research Paper no. 1. Mimeographed. Dar es Salaam: University College, 1968.
Johnston, H. H. *The Kilima-Njaro Expedition.* London: Kegan Paul, 1886.
Johnston, P. H. "Chagga Constitutional Development." *Journal of African Administration* 5, 3 (July 1953): 134-40.
——. "Some Notes on Land Tenure on Kilimanjaro and the Vihamba of the Wachagga." *Tanganyika Notes and Records* 21 (June 1946): 1-20.

Kadio, K. R. *Arusha Region: Development and Problems.* Mimeographed. Moshi: Regional Administration, 1969.
Kautsky, John H. "Revolutionary and Managerial Elites in Modernizing Regimes." *Comparative Politics* 1, 4 (July 1969): 441-67.
Keegan, Warren J. "Tanganyika's Five-Year Plan: Sober Realism or Buoyant Optimism?" In Tom J. Farer, ed., *Financing African Development.* Cambridge, Mass.: M.I.T. Press, 1965.
Kieran, J. "The Origins of Commercial Arabica Coffee Production in East Africa." *African Historical Studies* 2, 1 (1969): 51-67.
"Kilimanjaro." *Tanganyika Notes and Records* 64 (March 1965).

Bibliography

Kilimanjaro Country. The Guidebook to Northern Tanzania. Nairobi: University Press of Africa, 1968(?).

Kilimanjaro District Council. *Taarifa ya 1967.* Mimeographed. Moshi, 1968.

——. *Taarifa ya 1968.* Mimeographed. Moshi, 1969.

Kilimanjaro Native Cooperative Union. *Thirty-First Annual Report 1962-1963.* Moshi: KNCU, 1966.

Kimambo, I. N., compiler. *Agriculture and Politics in Kilimanjaro.* Mimeographed. Dar es Salaam, 1969.

——. *A Political History of the Pare of Tanzania.* Nairobi: East African Publishing House, 1969.

——, and A. J. Temu, eds. *A History of Tanzania.* Nairobi: East African Publishing House, 1969.

Klerruu, Wilbert. "Whys and Wherefores of the TANU Cell System." *The Nationalist,* 20 September 1965, p. 6.

Koff, David, and George von der Muhll. "Political Socialization in Kenya and Tanzania—A Comparative Analysis." *Journal of Modern African Studies* 5, 1 (May 1967): 13-51.

LaPalombara, Joseph, ed. *Bureaucracy and Political Development.* Princeton, N.J.: Princeton University Press, 1967.

Lee, Eugene C. *Local Taxation in Tanzania.* Dar es Salaam: Oxford University Press, 1965.

Lehmann, F. Rudolf. "Some Field-Notes on the Chaga of Kilimanjaro." *Bantu Studies* 15 (1941): 385-96.

Lema, Alex O. J. "The Role of the Machame Chiefdom in the Politics of the Wachagga since 1930's." Senior dissertation, Department of Political Science, University of Dar es Salaam, 1969.

Lema, Anza Amen. "The Lutheran Church's Contribution to Education in Kilimanjaro." *Tanzania Notes and Records* 68 (February 1968): 87-94.

Le Roy, Alexandre. *Au Kilima-Ndjaro.* Paris: Sanard et Derangeon, 1893(?).

Leubuscher, Charlotte. *Tanganyika Territory: A Study of Economic Policy Under Mandate.* London: Oxford University Press, 1944.

Levine, Katherine. "The TANU Ten-House Cell Cystem." In Lionel Cliffe and John S. Saul, eds., *Socialism in Tanzania.* Vol. 1, *Politics.* Nairobi: East African Publishing House, 1972.

LeVine, Victor T. *Political Leadership in Africa.* Stanford: Hoover Institution, 1967.

Leys, Colin. *Politicians and Policies.* Nairobi: East African Publishing House, 1967.

——, ed. *Politics and Change in Developing Countries.* Cambridge: Cambridge University Press, 1969.

Liebenow, J. Gus. *Colonial Rule and Political Development in Tanzania: The Case of the Makonde.* Evanston, Ill.: Northwestern University Press, 1971.

Bibliography

——. "Some Problems in Introducing Local Government Reform in Tanganyika." *Journal of African Administration* 8, 3 (July 1956): 132-39.

——. "Tribalism, Traditionalism, and Modernism in Chagga Local Government." *Journal of African Administration* 10, 2 (April 1958): 71-82.

Listowel, Judith. *The Making of Tanganyika.* London: Chatto and Windus,
1966.

Little, Kenneth. *West African Urbanization.* Cambridge: Cambridge University
Press, 1966.

Lloyd, P. C. *Africa in Social Change.* Baltimore: Penguin, 1967.

——, ed. *The New Elites of Tropical Africa.* New York: Oxford University
Press, 1966.

Magid, Alvin. "District Councillorship in an African Society: A Study in Role
and Conflict Resolution." Ph.D. dissertation, Michigan State University,
1965.

——. "Methodological Considerations in the Study of African Political and
Administrative Behavior: The Case of Role Conflict Analysis." *African
Studies Review* 13, 1 (April 1970): 75-94.

Maguire, G. Andrew. *Toward "Uhuru" in Tanzania.* Cambridge: Cambridge
University Press, 1969.

Makundi, J. E. S. "Precolonial Forces Against the Creation of One Chagga
Nation." Senior dissertation, Political Science Department, University of
Dar es Salaam, 1969.

Mandelbaum, Seymour J. *Boss Tweed's New York.* New York: Wiley, 1965.

Marealle, P. *The Life of a Mchagga on Earth and After Death.* Nairobi: English
Press Ltd., 1947.

——. "Notes on Chagga Customs." *Tanganyika Notes and Records* 60 (March
1963): 67-90.

Markovitz, Irving Leonard, ed. *African Politics and Society.* New York: Free
Press, 1970.

Maruma, Oliver J. "Chagga Politics: 1930-1952." Senior dissertation, Political
Science Department, University of Dar es Salaam, 1969.

Mazrui, Ali. "Tanzaphilia." *Transition* 31 (1967): 20-26.

Meillassoux, Claude. *The Urbanization of an African Community: Voluntary
Associations in Bamako.* Seattle: University of Washington Press, 1968.

Meister, Albert. *East Africa: The Past in Chains, the Future in Pawn.* Translated from the French (*l'Afrique Peut-elle Partir?*) by Phyllis Nauts Ott.
New York: Walker, 1968.

Merelman, Richard M. "On the Neo-Elitist Critique of Community Power."
American Political Science Review 62, 2 (June 1968): 451-60.

Meyer, Hans. *Across East African Glaciers: An Account of the First Ascent
of Kilimanjaro.* Translated from the German by E. H. S. Calder. London:
George Philip, 1891.

Bibliography

Miller, Norman N. "The Political Survival of Traditional Leadership." *Journal of Modern African Studies* 6, 2 (August 1968): 183-201.

——. "The Rural African Party: Political Participation in Tanzania." *American Political Science Review* 64, 2 (June 1970): 548-71.

——. "Village Leadership and Modernization in Tanzania: Rural Politics Among the Nyamwezi People of Tabora Region." Ph.D. dissertation, Indiana University, 1967.

Miner, Horace, ed. *The City in Modern Africa.* New York: Praeger, 1967.

Moffett, J. P., ed. *Handbook of Tanganyika.* Dar es Salaam: Government Printer, 2d ed., 1958.

——, and J. F. R. Hill. *Tanganyika: A Review of Its Resources and Their Development.* Dar es Salaam: Government Printer, 1955.

Mohiddin, Ahmed. "Revolution by Resolution." *Mawazo* 1, 4 (December 1968): 78-92.

Moshi Town Council. *Standing Orders.* Mimeographed. Moshi, n.d.

Mosley, Leonard. *Duel for Kilimanjaro.* London: Weidenfeld and Nicolson, 1963.

Mramba, Basil P. "Kilimanjaro: Chagga Readjustment to Nationalism." *East African Institute of Social Research,* Conference Papers, Part E, no. 355, 1966.

——. "Kilimanjaro: Localism and Nationalism." Chapter 5 in Lionel Cliffe, ed., *One Party Democracy: The 1965 Tanzania General Election.* Nairobi: East African Publishing House, 1967.

——. "Some Notes on the Political Development of the Chagga of Kilimanjaro." Unpublished Paper. Makerere University College, Kampala, 1967.

Mustafa, Sophia. *The Tanganyika Way.* Dar es Salaam: The East African Literature Bureau, 1961.

Nellis, John R. *A Theory of Ideology: The Tanzanian Example.* Nairobi: Oxford University Press, 1972.

Nsekela, A. J. *Minara Ya Historia Ya Tanganyika.* Arusha, Tanzania: Longmans, 1965.

Ntiro, S. J. *Desturi za Wachagga.* Nairobi: The Eagle Press, 1953.

Nyerere, Julius K. *Decentralisation.* Dar es Salaam: Government Printer, 1972.

——. *Freedom and Socialism/Uhuru na Ujamaa.* Dar es Salaam: Oxford University Press, 1968.

——. *Freedom and Unity/Uhuru na Umoja.* Dar es Salaam: Oxford University Press, 1967.

——. *Kupanga ni Kuchagua.* Dar es Salaam: Government Printer, 1969.

——. "Tanzania Ten Years After Independence." *The African Review* 2, 1 (June 1972): 1-54.

——. *Ujamaa—Essays on Socialism.* Dar es Salaam: Oxford University Press, 1968.

Bibliography

O'Barr, Jean F. "The Role of the Ten-House Cell Leader in Rural Tanzania." *Geneve-Afrique* 10, 2 (1971): 1-16.

——, and Joel Samoff, eds. *Cell Leaders in Tanzania: Agents of Order and Change.* Nairobi: East African Publishing House, 1974.

Oculi, Okello. "Applied Literature and Social Imagination in Africa." *East Africa Journal* 7, 8 (August 1970): 7-20.

Ogot, B. A., and J. A. Kieran, eds. *Zamani: A Survey of East African History.* Nairobi: East African Publishing House, 1968.

Ola, Opeyemi. "The Study of West African Local Government." *Journal of Modern African Studies* 6, 2 (August 1968): 233-48.

Ostheimer, John M. "The Achievement Motive Among the Chagga of Tanzania." Ph.D. dissertation, Yale University, 1967.

Parkin, David. *Neighbors and Nationals in an African City Ward.* Berkeley: University of California Press, 1969.

Parry, Geraint. *Political Elites.* London: Allen and Unwin, 1969.

Polsby, Nelson W. *Community Power and Political Theory.* New Haven: Yale University Press, 1963.

——. "How to Study Community Power: The Pluralist Alternative." *Journal of Politics* 22, 3 (August 1960): 474-84.

Powell, John Duncan. "Peasant Society and Clientelistic Politics." *American Political Science Review* 64, 2 (June 1970): 411-25.

Pratt, R. Cranford. "The Administration of Economic Planning in a Newly Independent State: The Tanzanian Experience, 1963-1966." *Journal of Commonwealth Political Studies* 5, 1 (March 1967): 38-59.

——. "'Multi-Racialism' and Local Government in Tanganyika." *Race* 2, 1 (November 1960): 33-49.

Proctor, J. H., ed. *Building Ujamaa Villages in Tanzania.* University of Dar es Salaam Studies in Political Science, no. 2. Dar es Salaam: Tanzania Publishing House, 1971.

——, ed. *The Cell System of the Tanganyika African National Union.* University of Dar es Salaam Studies in Political Science, no. 1. Dar es Salaam: Tanzania Publishing House, 1970.

Raum, O. M. *Chagga Childhood.* London: Oxford University Press, 1940.

Ray, Robert S. "Labour Force Survey of Tanzania." Mimeographed. Dar es Salaam, 1966.

"Recommendations for Development of Local Government in Tanganyika (A Digest by the African Studies Branch of: The Proposals for Local Government Development. In the Report of the Committee of Constitutional Development in Tanganyika (Dar es Salaam: Government Printer, 1951)." *Journal of African Administration* 4, 1 (January 1952): 29-32.

Reporter (East Africa) 5, 155 (25 March 1966): 11-12.

Bibliography

Resnick Idrian N., ed. *Tanzania: Revolution by Education.* Arusha, Tanzania: Longmans, 1968.

Resnick, Jane, and Idrian N. Resnick. "Tanzania Educates for a New Society." *Africa Report* 16, 1 (January 1971): 26-29.

Rhodes, Robert I., ed. *Imperialism and Underdevelopment: A Reader.* New York: Monthly Review Press, 1970.

Roberts, Andrew, ed. *Tanzania Before 1900.* Nairobi: East African Publishing House, 1968.

Rodney, Walter. *How Europe Underdeveloped Africa.* London: Bogle-L'Ouverture Publications, 1972.

Rosenthal, Donald B. "Deurbanization, Elite Displacement, and Political Change in India." *Comparative Politics* 2, 2 (January 1970): 169-201.

Rudebeck, Lars. *Party and People: A Study of Political Change in Tunisia.* Stockholm: Almqvist & Wiksell, 1967.

Runciman, W. G. *Social Science and Political Theory.* Cambridge: Cambridge University Press, 1965.

Ruthenberg, Hans. *Agricultural Development in Tanganyika.* Berlin: Springer-Verlag, 1964.

———, ed. *Smallholder Farming and Smallholder Development in Tanzania: Ten Case Studies.* Munich: IFO-Institut, 1968.

Rutman, Gilbert L. *The Economy of Tanganyika.* New York: Praeger, 1968.

Rweyemamu, A. H. *Government and Politics in Tanzania: A Bibliography.* Nairobi: East African Academy (Information Circular No. 6), 1972.

———, ed. *Nation-Building in Tanzania.* Nairobi: East African Publishing House, 1970.

Samoff, Joel. "Politics, Politicians, and Party: Moshi, Tanzania 1968-69." Ph.D. dissertation, University of Wisconsin, 1972.

Saul, John S. "African Socialism in One Country: Tanzania." In Giovanni Arrighi and John S. Saul, *Essays on the Political Economy of Africa.* New York: Monthly Review Press, 1973.

———. "Class and Penetration in Tanzania." In Lionel Cliffe and John S. Saul, eds., *Socialism in Tanzania.* Vol. 1, *Politics.* Nairobi: East African Publishing House, 1972.

———. "The Nature of Tanzania's Political System: Issues Raised by the 1965 and 1970 Elections." *Journal of Commonwealth Political Studies.* Part 1 in 10, 2 (July 1972): 113-29, and part 2 in 10, 3 (November 1972): 198-221.

———. "Planning for Socialism in Tanzania: The Socio-Political Context." *Development and Change* 3, 3 (1971-72): 3-25.

Scanlon, David G., ed. *Church, State, and Education in Africa.* New York: Teachers College Press, 1966.

Schaffer, B. B. "The Deadlock in Development Administration." In Colin

Bibliography

Leys, ed., *Politics and Change in Developing Countries.* Cambridge: Cambridge University Press, 1969.

Schattschneider, E. E. *The Semisovereign People.* New York: Holt, Rinehart and Winston, 1960.

Scott, James C. "Corruption, Machine Politics, and Political Change." *American Political Science Review* 33, 4 (December 1969): 1142-58.

Seidman, Ann. *Comparative Development Strategies in East Africa.* Nairobi: East African Publishing House, 1972.

——. *An Economics Textbook for Africa.* London: Methuen, 2d ed., 1972.

Shann, G. N. "The Early Development of Education Among the Chagga." *Tanganyika Notes and Records* 45 (December 1956): 21-32.

——. "The Educational Development of the Chagga Tribe." *Oversea Education* 26, 2 (July 1954): 47-65.

Simpson, Dick. "The Political Evolution of Two African Towns." Ph.D. dissertation, Indiana University, 1968.

Smith, Hadley E., ed. *Agricultural Development in Tanzania.* Nairobi: Oxford University Press, 1965.

——. *Readings on Economic Development and Administration in Tanzania.* London: Oxford University Press, 1966.

Smith, William Edgett. *We Must Run While They Walk.* New York: Random House, 1971.

"Spotlight on Moshi." *Reporter* (East Africa) 5, 160 (3 June 1966): 25-33.

Stahl, Kathleen M. "The Chagga." In P. H. Gulliver, ed., *Tradition and Transition in East Africa.* Berkeley: University of California Press, 1969.

——. *History of the Chagga People of Kilimanjaro.* The Hague: Mouton, 1964.

Staniland, Martin. "The Rhetoric of Centre-Periphery Relations." *Journal of Modern African Studies* 8, 4 (1970): 617-36.

Stephens, Hugh W. "Mobilization, Political Relevance, and Protest in an African State." *Comparative Politics* 3, 2 (January 1971): 255-69.

——. *The Political Transformation of Tanganyika: 1920-1967.* New York: Praeger, 1968.

——. "Social Mobilization and Political Development in Tanganyika." Ph.D. dissertation, Yale University, 1965.

Stinchcombe, Arthur L. *Constructing Social Theories.* New York: Harcourt, Brace & World, 1968.

Stuart-Watt, Eva. *Africa's Dome of Mystery.* London: Marshall, Morgan & Scott, 1930.

Sunden, Rolf. "A Survey of Adult Education Needs in Moshi Town." *Mbioni* 5, 5/6 (1969): 35-42.

Swartz, Marc J., ed. *Local-Level Politics.* Chicago: Aldine, 1968.

——, Victor W. Turner, and Arthur Tuden, eds. *Political Anthropology.* Chicago: Aldine, 1966.

Szentes, Tamas. *Causes, Criteria and International Aspects of the So Called Economic Underdevelopment.* Budapest: Center for Afro-Asian Research of the Hungarian Academy of Sciences, 1967. No. 13.

———. *Economic Policy and Implementation: Problems in Tanzania.* Budapest: Center for Afro-Asian Research of the Hungarian Academy of Sciences, 1970. No. 40.

———. *Interpretations of Economic Underdevelopment.* Budapest: Center for Afro-Asian Research of the Hungarian Academy of Sciences, 1968. No. 16.

———. *Political Economy of Underdevelopment.* Chicago: Imported Publications, 1972.

Tanganyika, Central Statistical Bureau. *African Census Report, 1957.* Dar es Salaam: Government Printer, 1963.

Tanganyika African National Union. *Katiba Ya TANU.* Dar es Salaam: Government Printer, 1967.

———. *Majadiliano ya Mkutano Mkuu wa TANU. Taarifa Rasmi. (Mkutano Mkuu Mwanza) Tarehe 16 Oktoba-20 Oktoba, 1967.* Dar es Salaam: Government Printer, 1967.

———. *Minzania ya Mapato na Matumizi ya Ofisi Kuu na Mikoa, Mwaka wa 1966/1967 na 1967/1968.* Dar es Salaam: TANU Headquarters, 1969.

———. *Taarifa ya Ofisi Kuu Kuhusu Hali na Kazi za Chama, Novemba 1967-Aprili 1969.* Dar es Salaam: Printpak Tanzania Limited, 1969.

———. *Taarifa ya Tume maalum iliyokwenda Mkoa wa Ziwa Magharibi kusikiliza Matatizo juu ya Wabunge wa Mkoa huo na Mkuu wa Mkoa huo.* Dar es Salaam: Government Printer, 1968.

———. *TANU's Guidelines to Safeguard, Consolidate and Further the Tanzanian and African Revolution.* Dar es Salaam: 1971.

———. *Utaratibu na Maongozi ya Chama cha TANU.* Dar es Salaam: Mwananchi Publishing Co., 1966(?).

TANU Youth League. *Muhtasari wa Mafundisho Kwa Vijana wa TANU.* Dar es Salaam: Dar es Salaam Printers Ltd., 1969(?).

Tanzania, United Republic of. *Annual Report of the Permanent Commission of Enquiry June 1966-June 1967.* Dar es Salaam: Government Printer, 1968.

———. *Annual Report of the Permanent Commission of Enquiry July, 1967-June, 1968.* Dar es Salaam: Government Printer, 1969.

———. *A Guide to Tanzania Statistics.* Dar es Salaam: Central Statistical Bureau, Ministry of Economic Affairs and Development Planning, 1968.

———. *The Interim Constitution of Tanzania, 1965.* Dar es Salaam: Government Printer, 1965.

———. *Preliminary Results of the Population Census Taken on the Night of 26-27th August, 1967.* Dar es Salaam: Central Statistical Bureau, Ministry of Economic Affairs and Development Planning, 1968.

Bibliography

——. *Proposals of the Tanzania Government on the Recommendations of the Presidential Commission of Enquiry on the National Union of Tanganyika Workers (NUTA)*. Dar es Salaam: Government Printer, 1967.

——. *Proposals of the Tanzania Government on the Recommendation of the Special Presidential Committee of Enquiry into the Co-operative Movement and Marketing Boards*. Dar es Salaam: Government Printer, 1966.

——. *Provisional Estimates of Fertility, Mortality and Population Growth for Tanzania*. Dar es Salaam: Central Statistical Bureau, Ministry of Economic Affairs and Development Planning, 1968.

——. *Recorded Population Changes 1948-1967, Tanzania*. Dar es Salaam: Central Statistical Bureau, Ministry of Economic Affairs and Development Planning, 1968.

——. *Report of the Presidential Commission on the Establishment of a Democratic One Party State*. Dar es Salaam: Government Printer, 1968.

——. *Report of the Presidential Commission on the National Union of Tanganyika Workers*. Dar es Salaam: Government Printer, 1967.

——. *Report of the Presidential Special Committee of Enquiry into the Co-operative Movement and Marketing Boards*. Dar es Salaam: Government Printer, 1966.

——. *Tanzania Second Five-Year Plan for Economic and Social Development, 1st July, 1969-30th June, 1974,* 2 vols. Dar es Salaam: Government Printer, 1969.

——, Ministry of Economic Affairs and Development Planning, Bureau of Statistics. *1967 Population Census*. Vols. 1-4. Dar es Salaam: Government Printer, 1969-71.

——, Ministry of Economic Affairs and Development Planning, Central Statistical Bureau. *Survey of Employment and Earnings 1968*. Dar es Salaam: Government Printer, 1969.

——, Ministry of Economic Affairs and Development Planning and the Ministry of Finance. *Background to the Budget: An Economic Survey 1968-69*. Dar es Salaam: Government Printer, 1968.

——, Ministry of Economic Affairs and Development Planning and the Ministry of Finance. *The Annual Economic Survey 1968 (A Background to the 1969/70 Budget)*. Dar es Salaam: Government Printer, 1969.

——, Ministry of Lands, Housing & Urban Development, Surveys and Mapping Division. *Tanzania Gazetteer*. Dar es Salaam: Government Printer, 1969.

——, Ministry of Lands, Settlement and Water Development, Surveys and Mapping Division. *Atlas of Tanzania*. Dar es Salaam, 1967.

——, Ministry of Lands, Settlement and Water Development, Town Planning Division. *Annual Report*. Dar es Salaam: Government Printer, 1962-68.

——, Second Vice-President's Office, National Archives. *Moshi*/Accession no. 5. *Northern Province Office*/Accession no. 69.

——, Second Vice-President's Office, National Archives, Provincial and District Books. *Kilimanjaro (Moshi) District Book.* Microfilm, Memorial Library, University of Wisconsin.

Taylor, J. Clagett. *The Political Development of Tanganyika.* Stanford, California: Stanford University Press, 1963.

Temu, A. J. "The Rise and Triumph of Nationalism." In I. N. Kimambo and A. J. Temu, eds., *A History of Tanzania.* Nairobi: East African Publishing House, 1969.

——. "Nationalization in Tanzania." *East Africa Journal* 4, 3 (June 1967): 35-41.

Thoden van Velzen, H. U. E., and J. J. Sterkenburg. "The Party Supreme." *Kroniek van Afrika* 1 (1969): 65-88.

Thomas, Ian D. *Population Density in Tanzania, 1967.* Bureau of Resource Assessment and Land Use Planning, Research Notes no. 5b. Dar es Salaam: University College, 1968.

Tordoff, William. *Government and Politics in Tanzania.* Nairobi: East African Publishing House, 1967.

——. "Regional Administration in Tanganyika." *East African Institute of Social Research,* Conference Papers, 1964.

Trimingham, J. Spencer. *Islam in East Africa.* London: Oxford University Press, 1964.

Uchumi Editorial Board, eds. *Towards Socialist Planning.* Dar es Salaam: Tanzania Publishing House, 1972.

United Nations Trusteeship Council. *Official Records,* Twentieth Session, 1957.

United Nations Visiting Mission to Trust Territories in East Africa, 1954. *Report on Tanganyika.* Trusteeship Council, Fifteenth Session. Supplement no. 3.T/1169. April 1955.

United Nations Visiting Mission to Trust Territories in East Africa, 1957. *Report on Tanganyika.* Trusteeship Council, Twenty-First Session. Supplement no. 2.T/1401. New York, 1958.

United Nations Visiting Mission to Trust Territories in East Africa, 1960. *Report on Tanganyika.* Trusteeship Council, Twenty-Sixth Session. Supplement no. 2.T/1550. New York, 1960.

United Republic of Tanganyika and Zanzibar. *Tanganyika. Five-Year Plan for Economic and Social Development. 1st July, 1964-30th June 1969,* 2 vols. Dar es Salaam: Government Printer, 1964.

Van de Laar, Aart. "Arusha: Before and After." *East Africa Journal* 5, 11 (November 1968): 13-28.

Van Hekken, P. M., and H. U. E. Thoden van Velzen. *Land Scarcity and Rural Inequality in Tanzania.* The Hague: Mouton, 1972.

Vente, Rolf E. *Planning Processes: The East African Case.* Munich: Weltforum Verlag, 1970.

Von Clemm, Michael. "The Political and Economic Development of the Chagga." Ph.D. dissertation, Oxford University, 1963.

Wallerstein, Immanuel. "Dependence in an Interdependent World: The Limited Possibilities of Transformation Within the Capitalist World Economy." Conference Paper, Conference on Dependence and Development in Africa, Ottawa, 1973.

——. "Voluntary Associations." In James S. Coleman and Carl Rosberg, Jr., eds., *Political Parties and National Integration in Tropical Africa.* Berkeley: University of California Press, 1964.

Werlin, Herbert Holland. "The Nairobi City Council: The Problems of Co-operation in African Local Politics." Ph.D. dissertation, University of California at Berkeley, 1966.

Whiteley, W.H. "Chagga Languages." *Tanganyika Notes and Records* 64 (March 1965): 66-67.

Whitlamsmith, G. K., compiler. *Recent Trends in Chagga Political Development.* Moshi: KNCU Printing Press, 1955.

Who Controls Industry in Kenya? Nairobi: East African Publishing House, 1968.

Wolpe, Howard. "Port Harcourt: A Community of Strangers." Ph.D. dissertation, Massachusetts Institute of Technology, 1967.

——. "Port Harcourt: A Community of Strangers." *African Urban Notes* 2, 4 (August 1967). Concluding Chapter of Ph.D. dissertation.

——. "Port Harcourt: Ibo Politics in Microcosm." *Journal of Modern African Studies* 7, 3 (1969): 469-93.

Young, Roland, and Henry Fosbrooke. *Smoke in the Hills. Political Tension in the Morogoro District of Tanganyika.* Evanston: Northwestern University Press, 1960.

Zanzibar na Kuundwa kwa Historia ya Waafrika wa Chama cha Afro-Shirazi. Dar es Salaam: Dar es Salaam Printers, 1969.

Zolberg, Aristide R. *Creating Political Order.* Chicago: Rand McNally, 1966.

——. "The Structure of Political Conflict in the New States of Tropical Africa." *American Political Science Review* 62, 1 (March 1968): 70-87.

Index

Index

DESIGNED BY TED SMITH/GRAPHICS
COMPOSED BY HORNE ASSOCIATES, INC., HANOVER, NEW HAMPSHIRE
MANUFACTURED BY MALLOY LITHOGRAPHING, INC., ANN ARBOR, MICHIGAN
TEXT LINES ARE SET IN PRESS ROMAN, DISPLAY LINES IN TIMES ROMAN

Library of Congress Cataloging in Publication Data
Samoff, Joel.
Tanzania; local politics and the structure of power.
Bibliography: pp. 257-273.
1. Local government—Moshi, Tanzania.
2. Tanganyika African National Union.
I. Title.
JS7697.9.M682S24   1974   320.9'678'26   73-2048
ISBN 0-299-06410-7